IMAGES of America

Royalton, Middleport, and Hartland

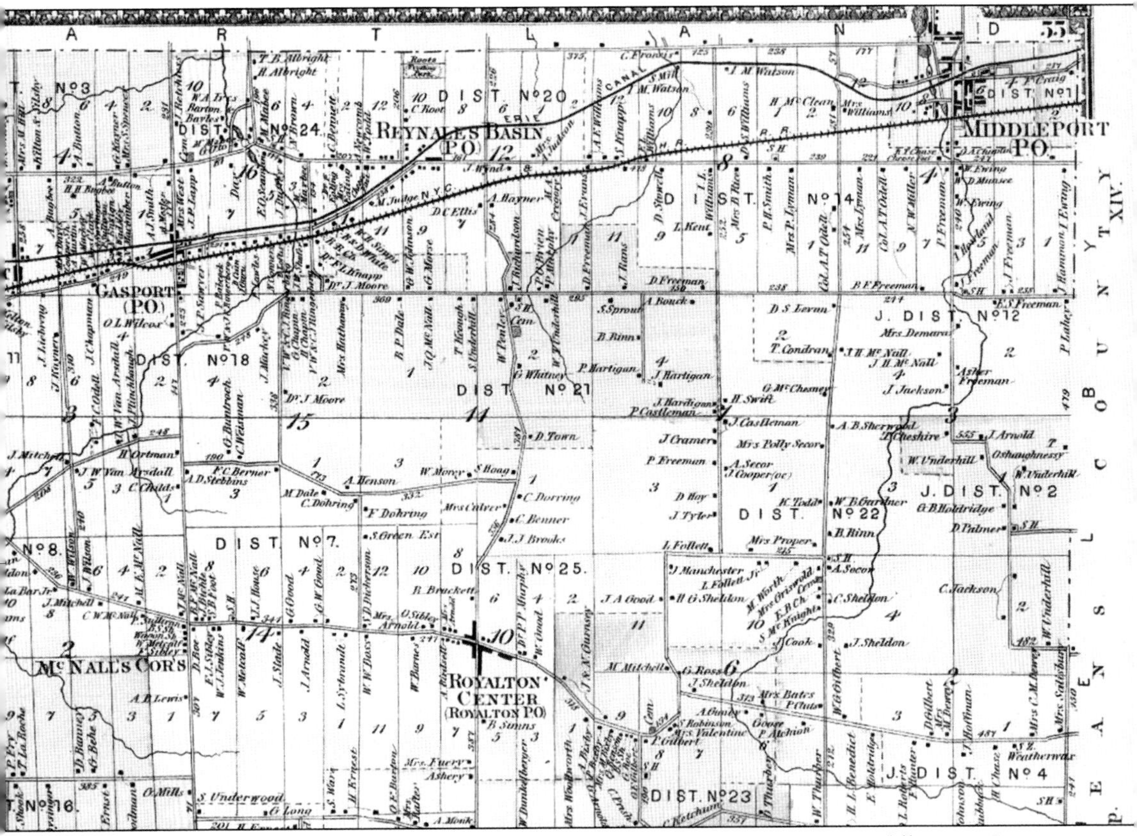

This 1875 map of the town of Royalton shows the population centers. Middleport, Gasport, Reynales Basin, and Royalton Center are clearly identified. The locations were significant settlements in the early development (1820–1880) of Royalton. The New York Central Railroad and the Erie Canal show the east-west configuration of travel during the period with Telegraph Road running alongside. The major north-south axis is Griswold Street and Royalton Center Road, while Chestnut Ridge Road connects near Wolcottsville, through Royalton Center onto Lockport. (Courtesy of the Royalton town historian.)

ON THE COVER: This 1914 photograph shows a downtown Middleport Fourth of July celebration, with all of the citizenry in their absolute best attire. (Courtesy of the Middleport town historian.)

IMAGES
of America

ROYALTON, MIDDLEPORT, AND HARTLAND

Frederick G. Fierch

ARCADIA
PUBLISHING

ISBN 978-0-7385-7238-3

Published by Arcadia Publishing
Charleston SC, Chicago IL, Portsmouth NH, San Francisco CA

Printed in the United States of America

Library of Congress Control Number: 2009933576

For all general information contact Arcadia Publishing at:
Telephone 843-853-2070
Fax 843-853-0044
E-mail sales@arcadiapublishing.com
For customer service and orders:
Toll-Free 1-888-313-2665

Visit us on the Internet at www.arcadiapublishing.com

To my wife, Gloria, and to our wonderful children and grandchildren, and for all of the great people of Royalton and Hartland who make the area a truly unique place to live and grow.

Contents

ACKNOWLEDGMENTS

This book would not have been possible without some very generous and enthusiastic support offered by the historians of the entities involved i.e., Jesse Bieber, town of Royalton historian; Norm LaJoie, town of Hartland historian; and Mrs. Warren Wallace, the village of Middleport historian. Also, I wish to thank Craig Bacon of the Niagara County Historian's Office for his assistance. Most importantly, I also wish to thank Rebecca Schweigurt, clerk of the village of Middleport. She was always eager to assist on any of my requests, regardless of how taxing or trivial. Her stated motivation was to do anything to help promote the area. And for that, she ranks with the mayor of Middleport, Julia Maedl, as the top supporter for showcasing Royalton, Middleport, and Hartland.

I also wish to thank my daughter, Alexandra Peracciny, for doing the very tedious, yet vital task of proofreading the manuscript and offering invaluable advice. And, of course, I wish to thank my family and friends who have been so supportive regarding this book.

The following abbreviations will appear as courtesy lines throughout the book: RTH—Royalton town historian, MVH—Middleport village historian, HTH—Hartland town historian, NCH—Niagara County historian to the village of Middleport. Other citations are not abbreviated.

Foreword

To see these glimpses of the past is to take a step back in time to an era gone but not forgotten. This album of photographs will stir up memories for some, while simply documenting the past for others. I can just hear the comments that the "old-timers" will have when they reminisce about the "good old days," as images of homesteads, villages, and people test their memories. For the current generation, this book serves as a permanent reminder of what once was.

It is amazing to look at the pictures taken decades ago and compare them to what exists today. Take a closer look and you will see that little has changed for some areas, while many images capture in perpetuity buildings and places that no longer exist. Although I have lived in the Royalton-Hartland-Middleport area for more than 40 years, I am still amazed at how much many of the scenes have stayed the same. Yet, I am saddened when a photograph of some of the buildings that were demolished reminds me that the future does not always hold the past in reverence. Times change and buildings are razed for present-day usage, but what a blessing it is that photographs were saved and a selection chosen to represent this area in print. For those who call the towns of Royalton and Hartland and the village of Middleport home, this pictorial book documents the essence of life in a rural community.

Much appreciation goes out to everyone who contributed photographs and articles to this memorable book, with special thanks to Middleport resident Fred Fierch, who served as its coordinator and author. There is no better way of documenting our past than with photographs. Please enjoy this publication, as its sheer existence guarantees that these glimpses of the past will live forever into the future. Enjoy!

—Mayor Julia A. Maedl
Middleport
November 2009

Introduction

The area of southeastern Niagara County in New York State is composed of the towns of Royalton and Hartland, with the former being the southern boundary of the county and the latter adjoining it to the north. Within this area is one incorporated village (Middleport) and a number of hamlets. Some of those sites were prominent in years past but of minor relevance today, such as McNall's Corners, Orangeport, Reynales Basin in Royalton, and North Hartland in the town of Hartland. Others have survived and are vital today as small centers of living—Wolcottsville, Royalton Center, Terry's Corners and Gasport in Royalton, and Johnson Creek and Hartland Corners in the town of Hartland. Each one of these towns has a distinct history and character. One of the goals of this book is to pass the unique character of these towns on to the reader.

There are two main themes which unite the two towns: east-west lines of communication and transportation and an agricultural past containing all of the components one would associate with farming, especially fruit production.

During the 1700s, the main trails in the western New York area passed through Royalton and Hartland. The "Military Trail" entered the area along Tonawanda Creek near Wolcottsville, extended toward the northwest, passing through McNall's Corners, continued along Chestnut Ridge into Lockport and northwest again (along the present Route 93), terminating at Fort Niagara. Originally, it was the only route through the region, the path used by the Neuter Indians and later the Holland Land Company surveyors.

The other major land trail is today's Route 104 or as it is commonly called, Ridge Road. It is entirely in the town of Hartland, passing through both Johnson Creek and Hartland Corners and continuing onto Wright's Corners, where it turns to the west and continues toward Lewiston. In the early days, it too ended at Fort Niagara.

The next east-west link, the Erie Canal, is the most famous and certainly the most important in terms of development of not only this region but also the entire United States. It gave rise to most of the towns and to their names as well: Middleport, Reynales Basin, Slayton, Gasport, and Orangeport. It opened the interior of the United States to New York City, the Atlantic Ocean, and the rest of the world. When the canal originally opened in 1825, it was 40 feet wide and 4 feet deep. It was expanded between 1836 and 1862 to a width of 70 feet and a depth of 7 feet. Finally, between 1906 and 1918 (1910–1911 in Middleport) the final expansion resulted in a canal, which is between 120 to 200 feet wide and 12 to 14 feet deep. These expansions reflect the commercial importance of the Erie Canal as time progressed.

Royalton and Hartland have always played a major role in the agriculture industry of New York. Beyond having incredible and abundant fruit orchards, an entire peripheral set of industries developed in both Gasport and Middleport. Agricultural machinery was invented or innovated in both of those towns. The Friend Manufacturing Company in Gasport produced fruit spraying equipment. Gasport Motor Company produced tractors. In Middleport, Niagara Sprayer also perfected and manufactured spraying equipment. Later Niagara Sprayer was purchased by FMC Corporation and became an agricultural chemical production facility and easily the largest employer in the area.

A critical need arose for a means of storing the fruit, and a trip along the railroad tracks through Royalton will yield the sightings of numerous former cold storage facilities. These held the fruit until it was either moved by barge or rail. This industry was not possible before the canal and later the railroad.

Another facet of the town of Royalton is Belva Lockwood. She was born on Griswold Street south of Middleport in 1830. She trained to become a teacher and later a lawyer. She taught for a while in Gasport. She later became engaged in the struggle for women's rights and eventually became the first woman to run for president of the United States, campaigning in both 1884 and 1888.

Eventually, the transportation and agricultural aspect of the area would wane but would never die. Today the Erie Barge Canal is an important asset for the region, and the fruit farms still produce significant crops.

It is especially rewarding to have this book published at this time, as Niagara County celebrated its bicentennial in 2008, Middleport its sesquicentennial in 2009, the town of Hartland will celebrate its bicentennial in 2012, and the town of Royalton will celebrate its bicentennial in 2017.

One

Royalton

The town of Royalton was originally part of the town of Hartland but was separated in 1817. The original populated areas of the town were Dysinger, Gasport, Middleport, McNall's, Orangeport, Royalton Center, and Wolcottsville.

Joshua Slayton, who was passing through on his way from Vermont, created the first settlement in the town. He paused and decided to develop a farm in the location that is presently Orangeport. Joined a short time later by his brother Thomas, they founded a small area, which became known as Slayton Settlement.

In 1811, Asher Freeman purchased 500 acres of land about one-half mile south of today's Middleport. This led to the development of an area that became known, among other things, as Freeman's Corners and Teapot Hollow. It attracted settlers as it was located astride a main east-west road.

Wolcottsville developed around the Tonawanda Creek and an old Native American trail that passed through Royalton. Severus Swift started a farm in the area around 1818. Later the majority of the area was in the hands of a large farmer named Anson Wolcott. In 1851, Wolcott deeded the entire tract to four trustees (Messers Frederick Moll, Christian Moll, Frederick Weiland, and Carl Martins) who divided it into small lots. By 1873, seventy Prussian families (by way of Bergholz) in the town of Niagara settled the area. These Lutherans constructed the Trinity Complex in the town. Because of the origin of the settlers, the hamlet was commonly called "Prushie," an obvious distortion of Prussia, and the settlers were called "Dutchmen," another distortion, this time of the word Deutschman, or German.

Royalton Center developed because of its location on Niagara Road. It was settled as early as 1808 and had a post office as early as 1824.

Mills were very important to the early development of Royalton. Asher Freeman built a sawmill in Middleport. The first gristmill was located at Mabee's, about a mile northeast of Gasport (its remains are still visible at the corner of South Quaker and Slayton Settlement Roads).

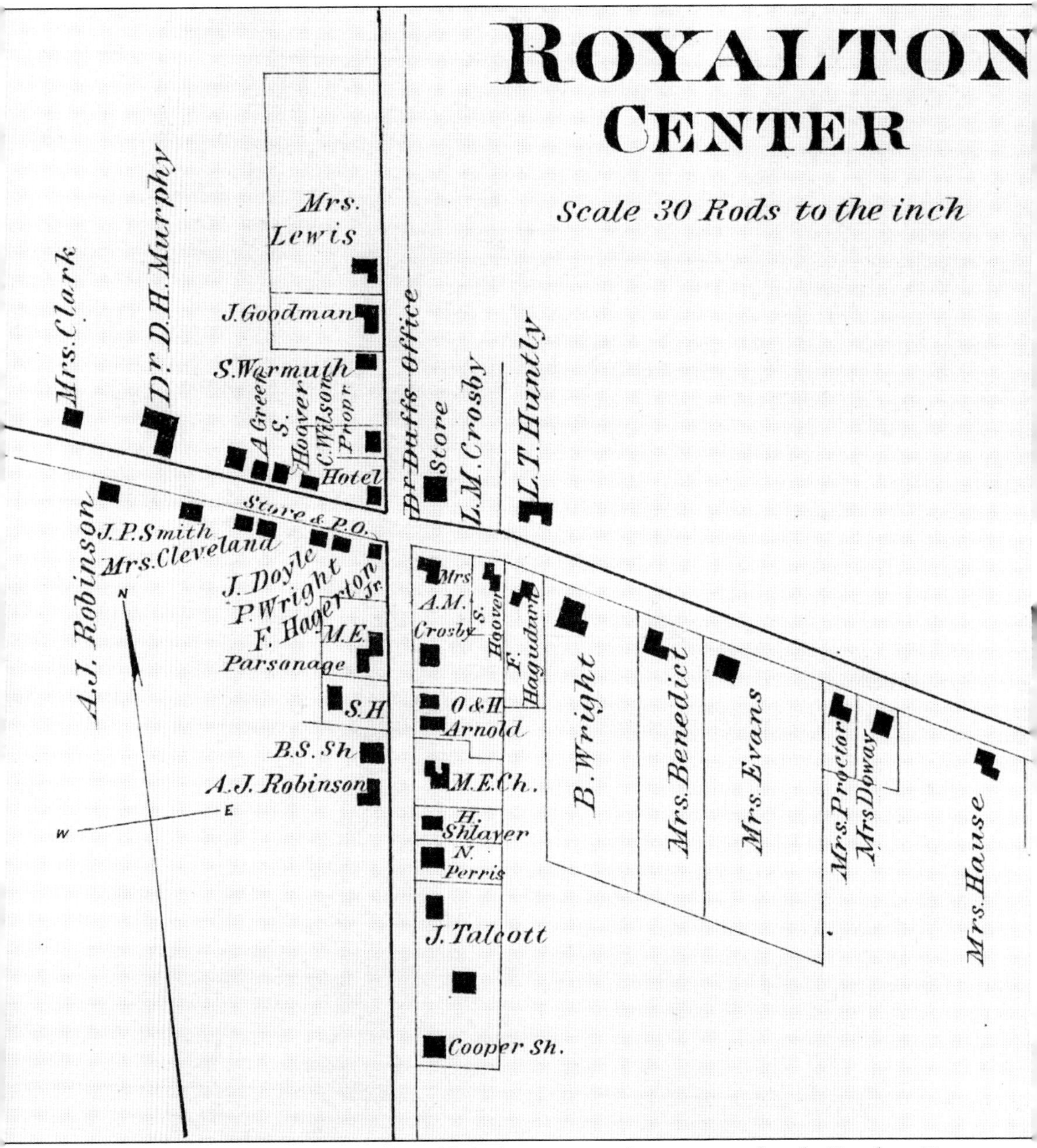

This map, dated 1875, shows a well-established community. It is apparent that the Royalton Center was a self-sustaining community. Interestingly, it shows the post office and store on the southeast corner of the crossroads and a hotel opposite. As late as 1975, a store was on the site (and perhaps) in the same building as the hotel. All of the other structures have disappeared. (RTH.)

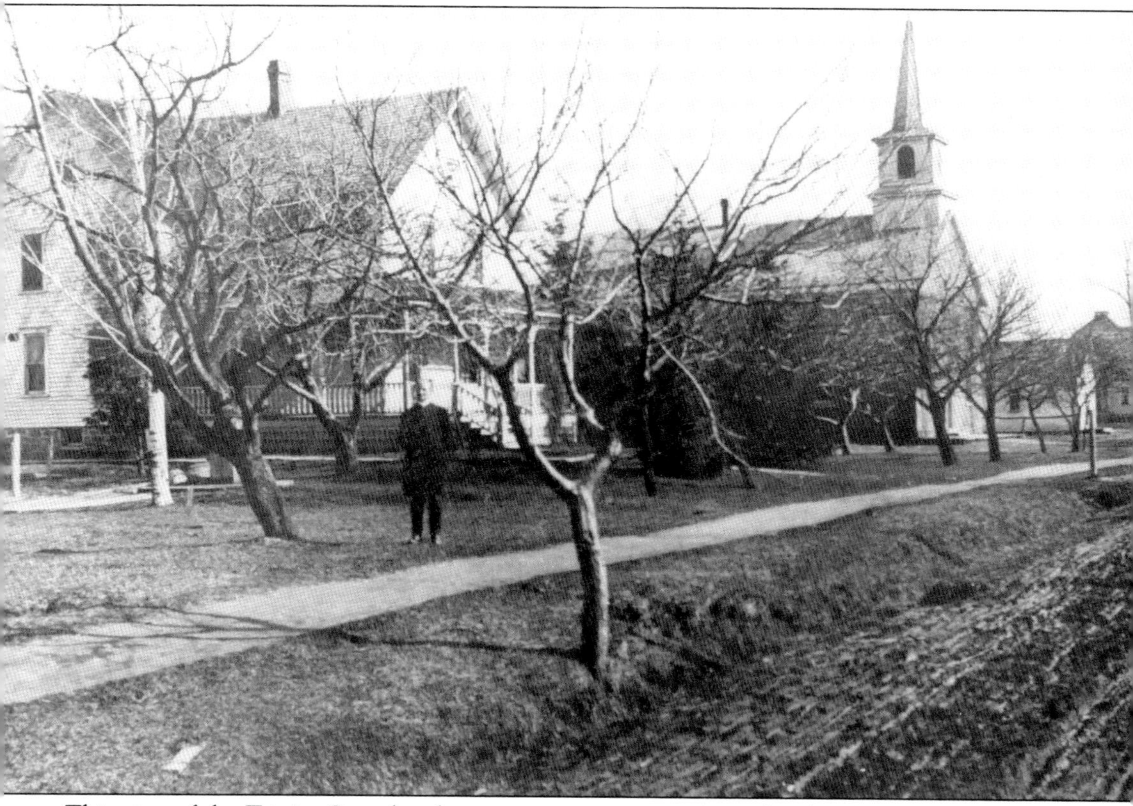

This view of the Trinity Complex shows its appearance in 1912. The church congregation was established on September 9, 1853, by the original 75 Prussian families of Wolcottsville. In 1867, they decided to build a brick church, 35 by 58 feet. The bricks were actually made on the lot where the church was built and naturally the congregation provided all of the labor. When the church was dedicated in 1868, it was completely debt free. In 1878, membership totaled 318 and it was under the Synod of Iowa. The church had grown by the early 1900s, and the exterior of the building underwent cosmetic changes. The basic building was unchanged. (Niagara County Historian's Office.)

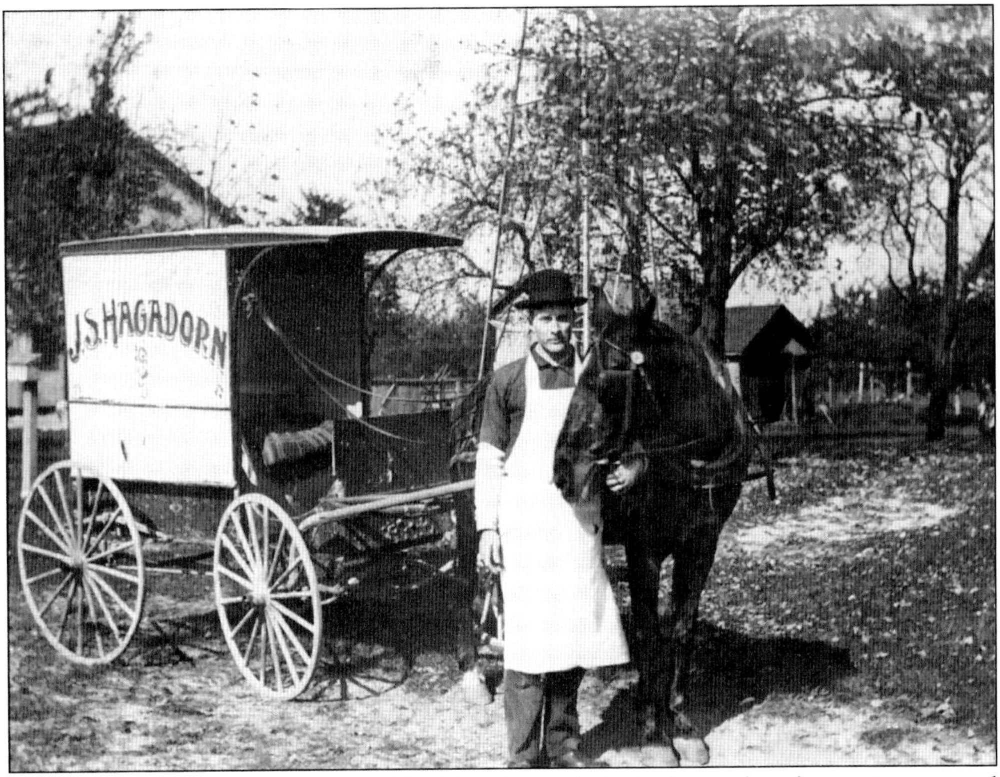

Jake Hagadorn, a dealer in dry goods and groceries, operated a store in Royalton Center. From the photograph, one can see that not only was there a store, but in fact most of the purveyors also dealt with a delivery route. Jake's son Fred was the longest-serving Royalton town clerk and an excellent artist who painted wonderful rural scenes. (RTH.)

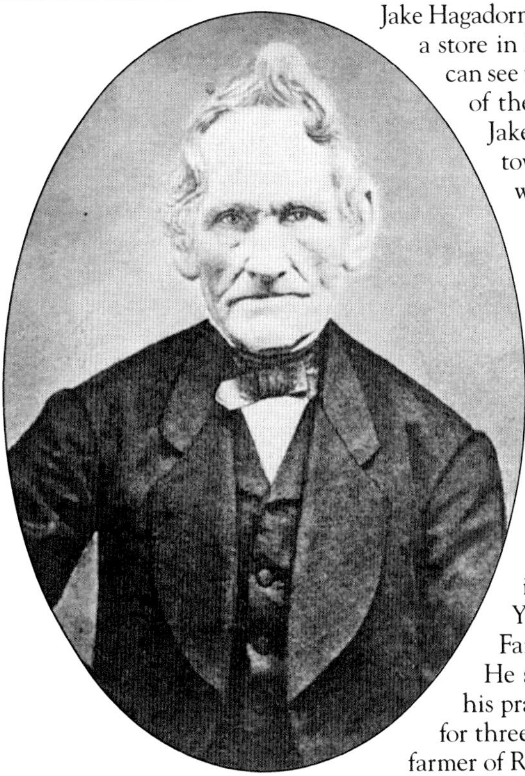

Dr. Samuel Ross of Royalton Center was born in 1802 in Newport, Herkimer County, New York. After attending high school, he enrolled in Fairfield Medical College and graduated in 1823. He soon moved to Royalton Center to establish his practice and also served the town as supervisor for three terms. His son W. W. Ross was a prominent farmer of Royalton Center. (RTH.)

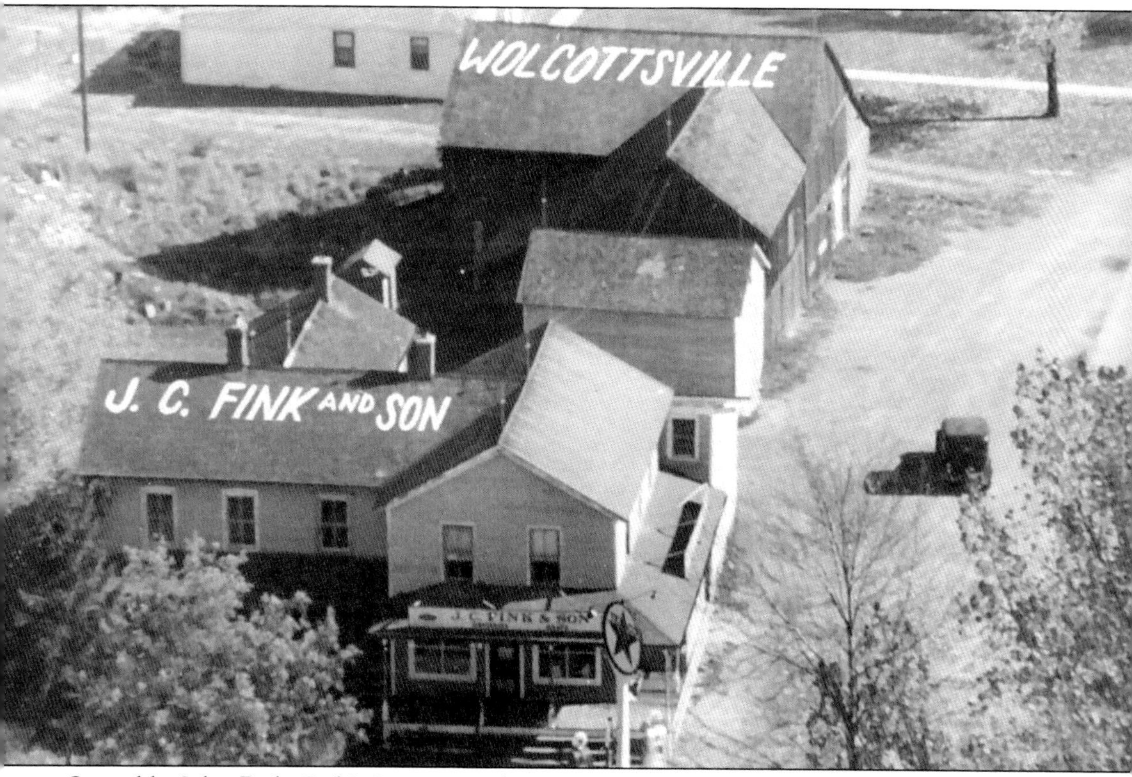

Owned by John Fink, Fink's Store in Wolcottsville was the town store and was quite "typical" in that it was centrally located and served the needs of the area and the surrounding farming community. For a time, it served as the local post office. It was located adjacent to the American Hotel and later was known as Schleef's. Fink wore many hats, as he not only operated the store, but he made the deliveries, sold goods directly from his wagon, handled the mail as keeper of the post for the community, and passed the news from stop to stop. (RTH.)

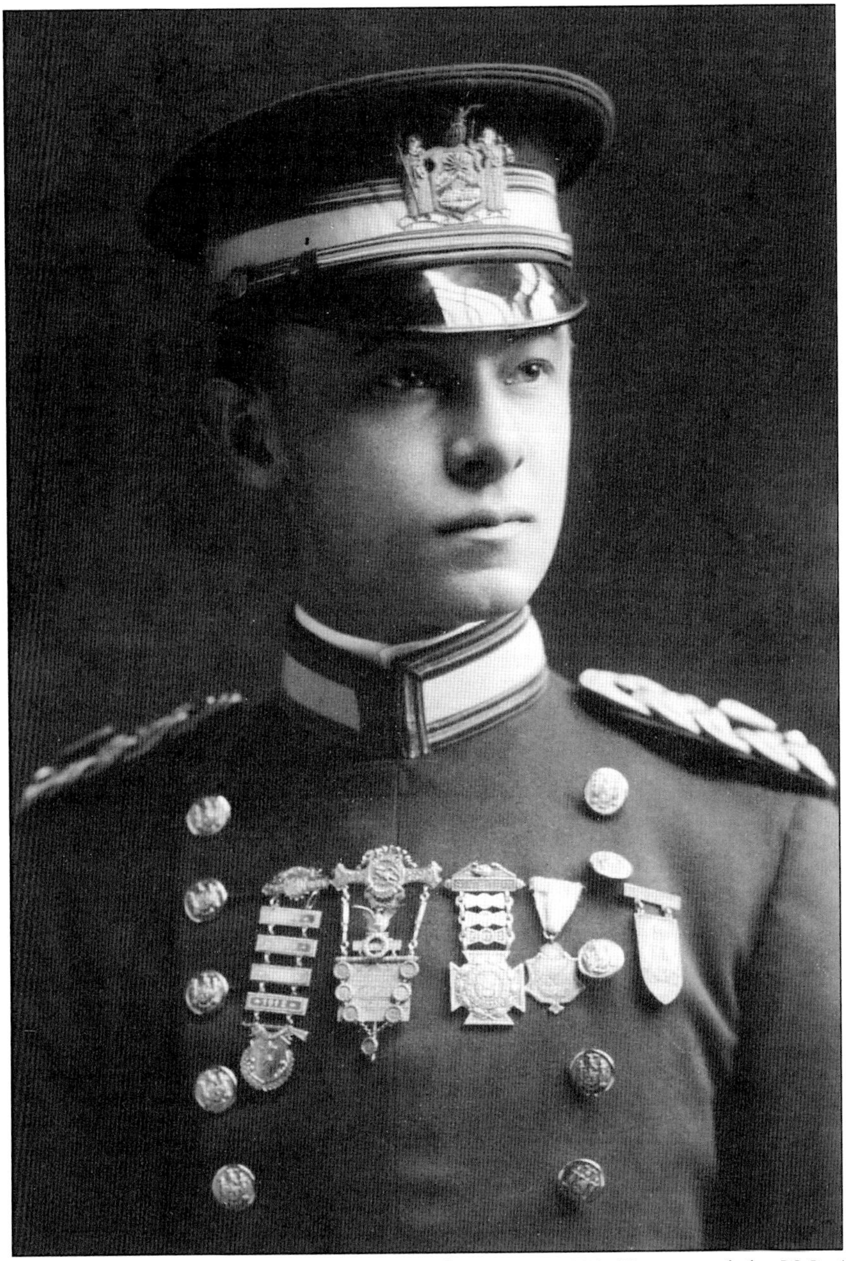

John H. Knuebel was born in Wolcottsville on February 10, 1890. He entered the U.S. Army in 1910 and saw combat along the Mexican border in 1915 under Gen. John Pershing's command. This military expedition was to calm the revolutionary fervor generated by Pancho Villa and Emiliano Zapata. Because of this service, by 1917 he had obtained a commission and was a first lieutenant. What truly distinguished John Kneubel was that he was one of the finest marksmen ever in the U.S. military. He achieved the highest score for the U.S. team during the 1924 PanAm Games in Buenos Aires. He also later captained or coached most of the American rifle teams throughout his military career. His first wife died in 1916 just after the birth of his only child, a daughter named Gretchen Rose. John Kneubel died on June 18, 1957, in the Panama Canal Zone and is buried in Arlington National Cemetery in Section 30. (Author's collection.)

This photograph shows the original Trinity Complex in Wolcottsville. Before the later cosmetic changes occurred, it was a rather plain and ordinary structure, very adequate for its intended usage. Not until the turn of the 20th century were the upgrades made to the edifice, so that it is easily recognizable today. Behind the church is a cemetery, which appears to join with St. Michael's but actually does not. (RTH.)

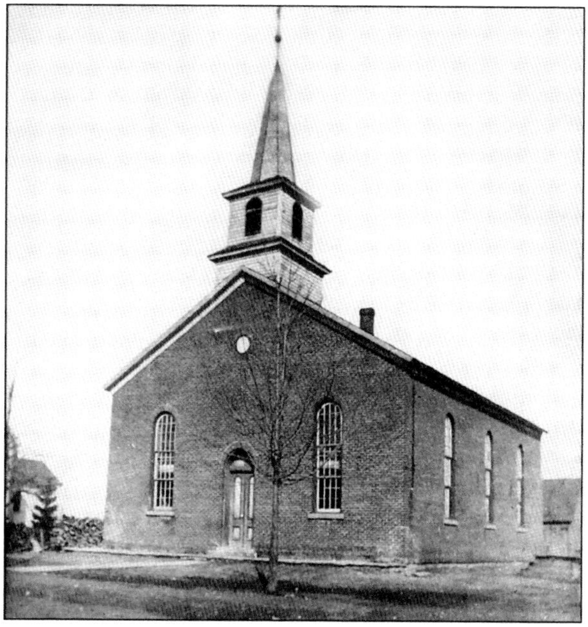

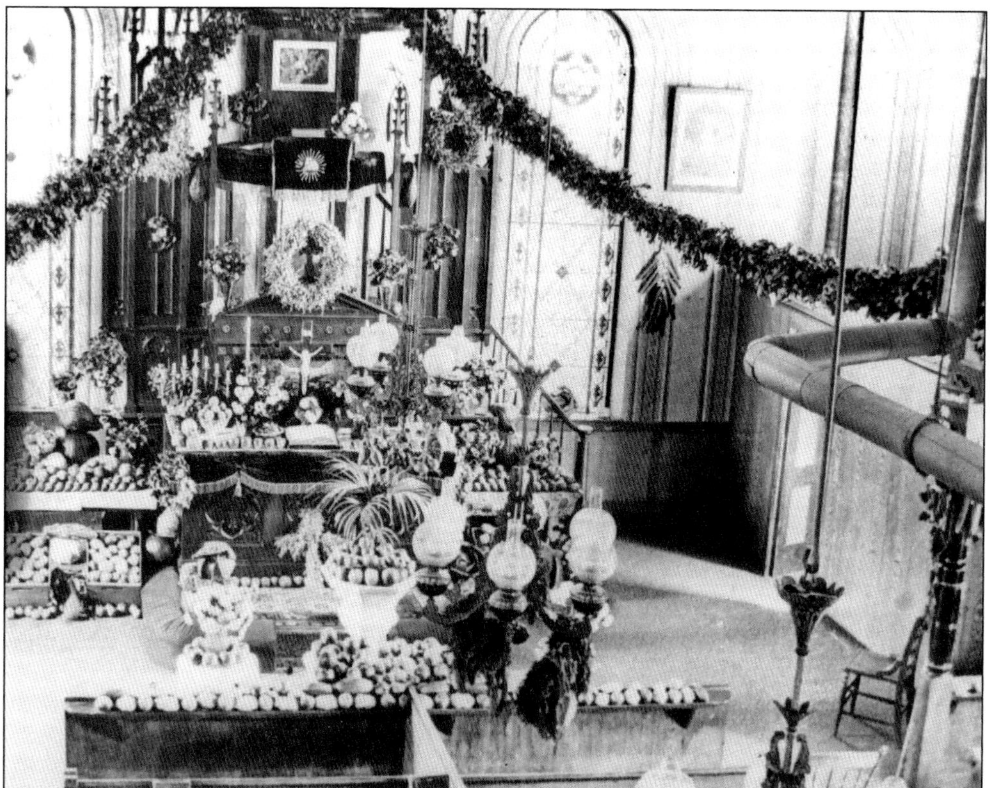

The Trinity Lutheran Church's interior as it appeared in 1912 depicts a rather austere place of worship, which contained all that was required and little more. The congregation at the time was larger than it had ever been previously. It would appear that everyone on the hamlet of Wolcottsville belonged to either Trinity or St. Michael's Lutheran Church. (NCH.)

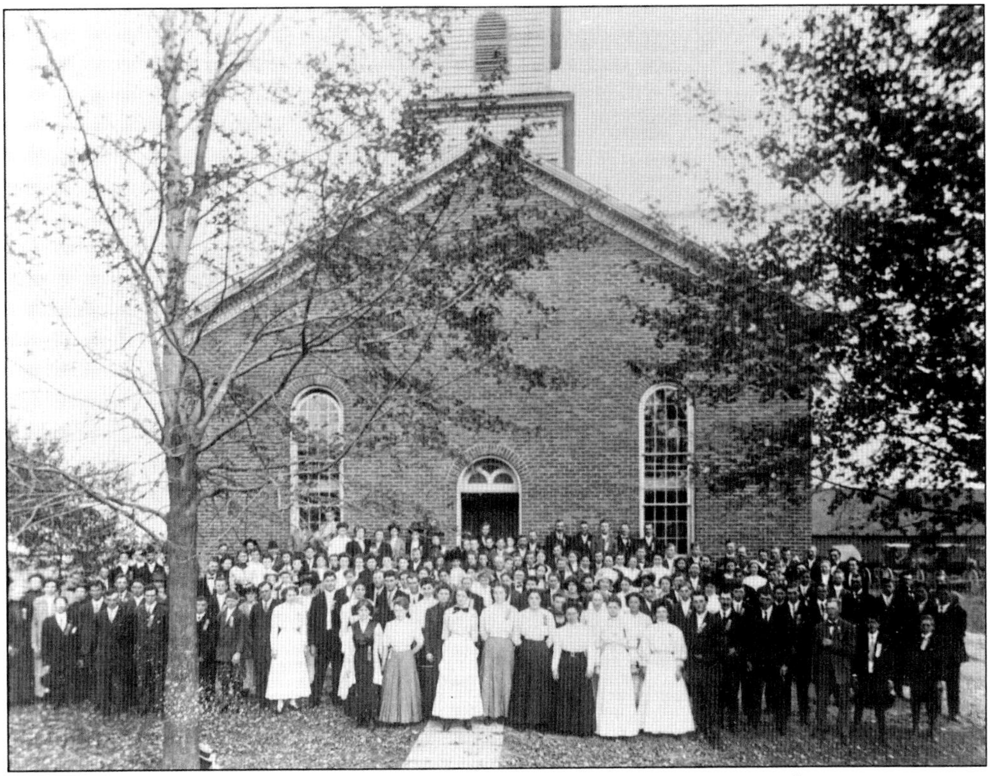

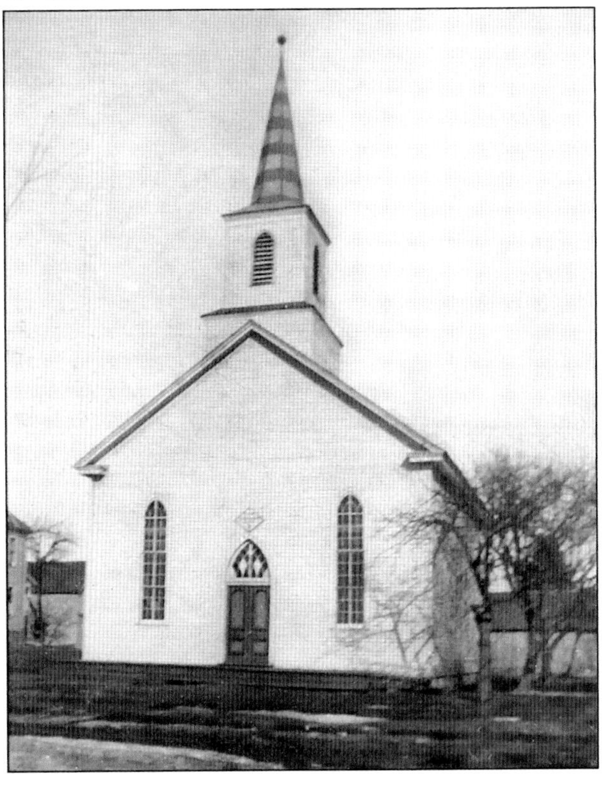

The Trinity Lutheran congregation as it appeared c. 1912. This group photograph probably includes everyone in Wolcottsville who was not affiliated with St. Michael's up the road. As descendants of Germans from Brandenburg and Pomerania, the Lutheran religion was dominant in their lives. (Niagara County Historian's Office.)

Pictured is the St. Michael's Lutheran Church in Wolcottsville, located on the corner of Main Street and Fisk Road. It is a wooden structure built entirely with the congregation's labor and completed in the early 1870s. It is under the Synod of Missouri and was initially founded under the auspices of the Evangelical Association of Royalton, founded in 1858. (RTH.)

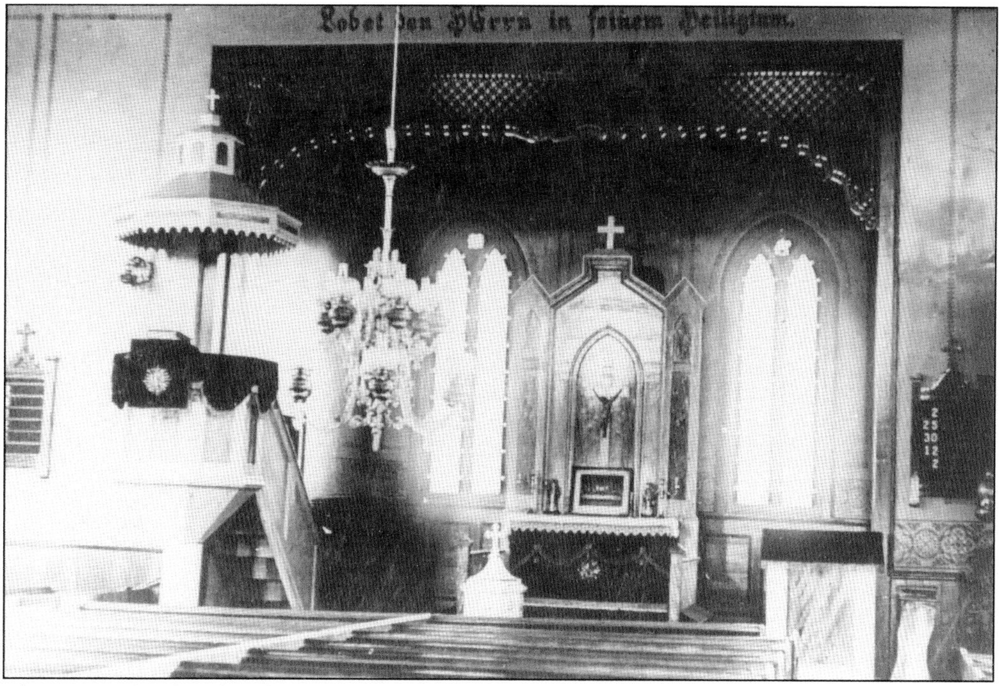

The St. Michael's Church is pictured as it appeared in 1912. Today the edifice is completely changed, as the brick was later added. There is a large cemetery located behind the church on Fisk Road. St. Michael's is still an active and vibrant congregation. The parsonage is located just to the north of the church. (Niagara County Historian's Office.)

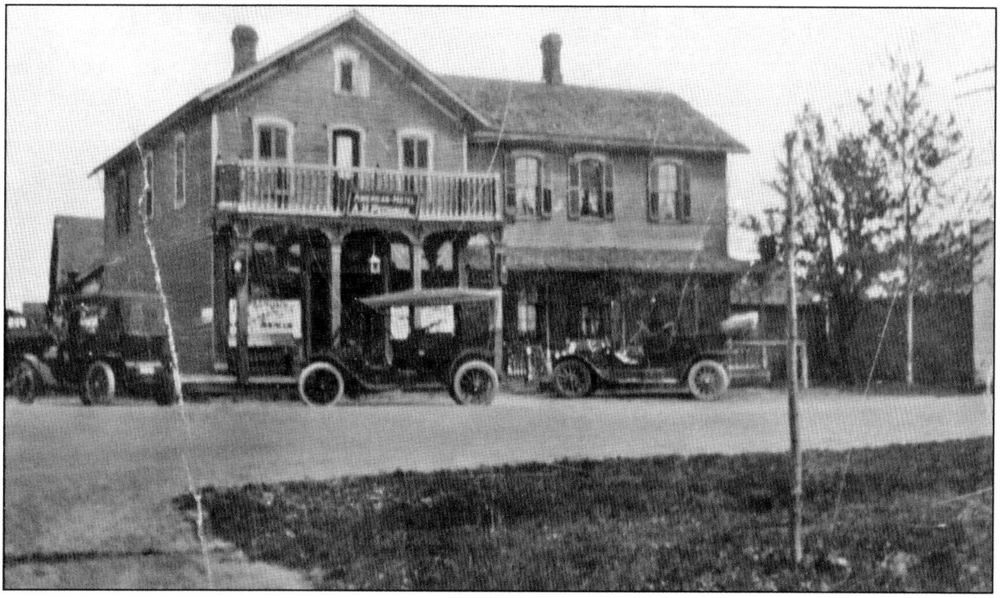

This photograph from the early 1900s shows the Wolcottsville Hotel. This was the original hotel for the hamlet as mentioned in the 1878 official description of the Royalton hamlets. Over the years, the hotel has changed hands several times but still stands, although vacant. The place was famous for its German duck and sauerkraut dinners served through the 1990s. (Niagara County Historian's Office.)

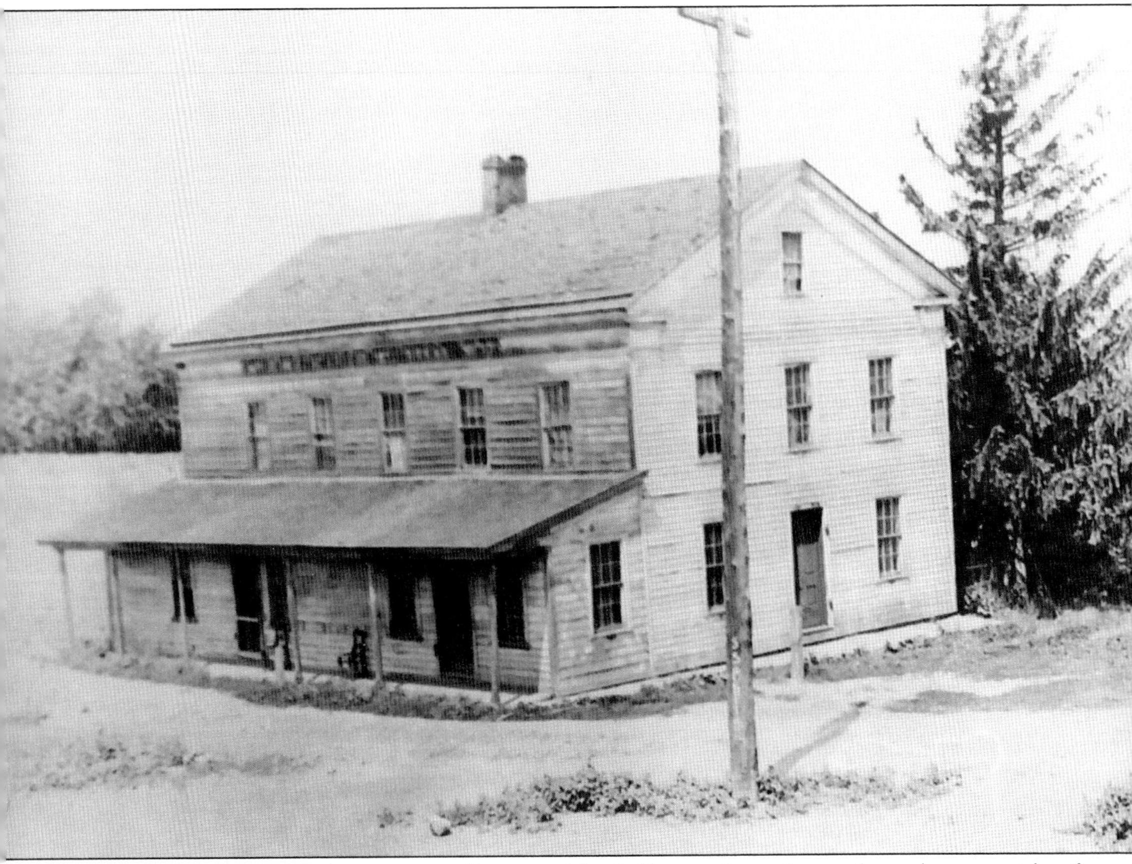

The Orangeport Hotel was originally owned by J. Frey and was located on the west side of Orangeport Road on the Erie Canal. The Orangeport community had a church, a store, a post office (serving both Orangeport and Slayton), a wagon, and a blacksmith shop. There was also a school building. Today very little remains of the former community. This hamlet is located between the New York Central Railroad and Slayton Settlement Road along the Erie Canal. It was the original settlement of the Slayton family, who were the first settlers of Royalton. In 1875, it consisted of about 50 dwellings and 200 inhabitants. Currently, it contains one of the largest cemeteries in the town, a testament to its former size and importance. The land upon which the hamlet stood was all originally owned by the Slaytons. Joshua Slayton was the original founder of Orangeport, and his name should probably have been used for the designation of the place.

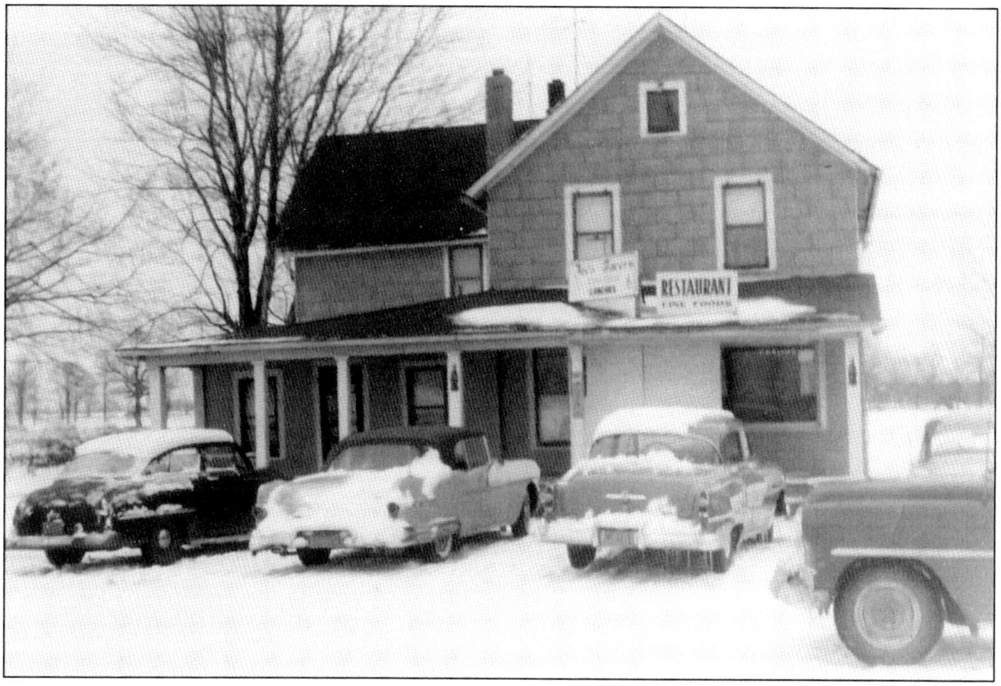

In the southwestern part of the town of Royalton lies a small, populated area known to everyone as Block Church. It would seem obvious that it was named for a religious building at the site, but for the locals of the 20th century, Block Church meant the local tavern, which had many names through the years, probably the best remembered being Campbell's Farmer's Inn. It remains a tavern to this day. (RTH.)

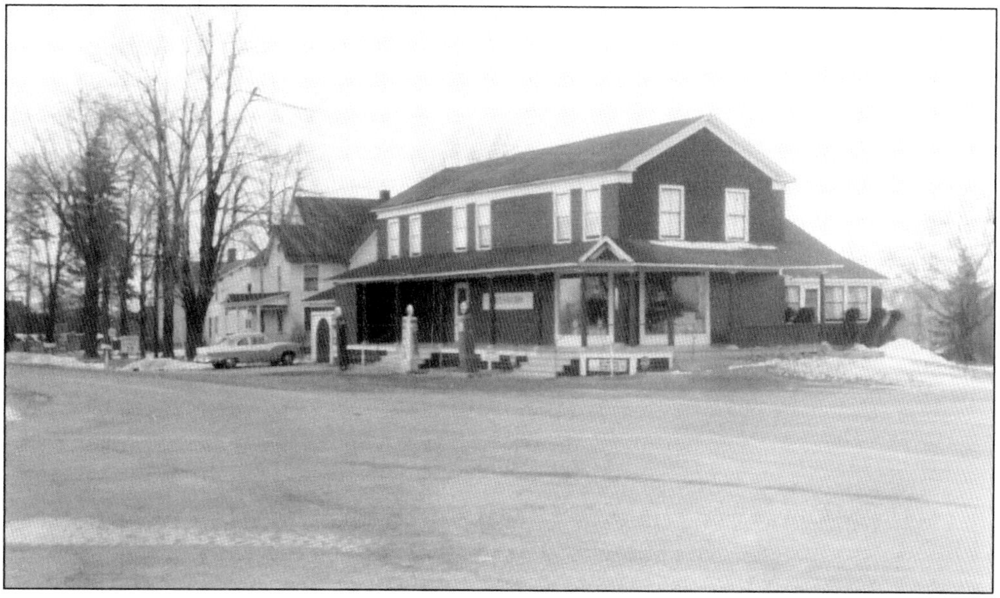

Located at Royalton Center, this photograph shows the country store that was there throughout the latter part of the 20th century. Although the building still stands, it is unoccupied. It once was a gas station as well as a store and was for many years by Winnie and Walt Rosenthal. Its last tenant made it into a diner before closing the doors. (RTH.)

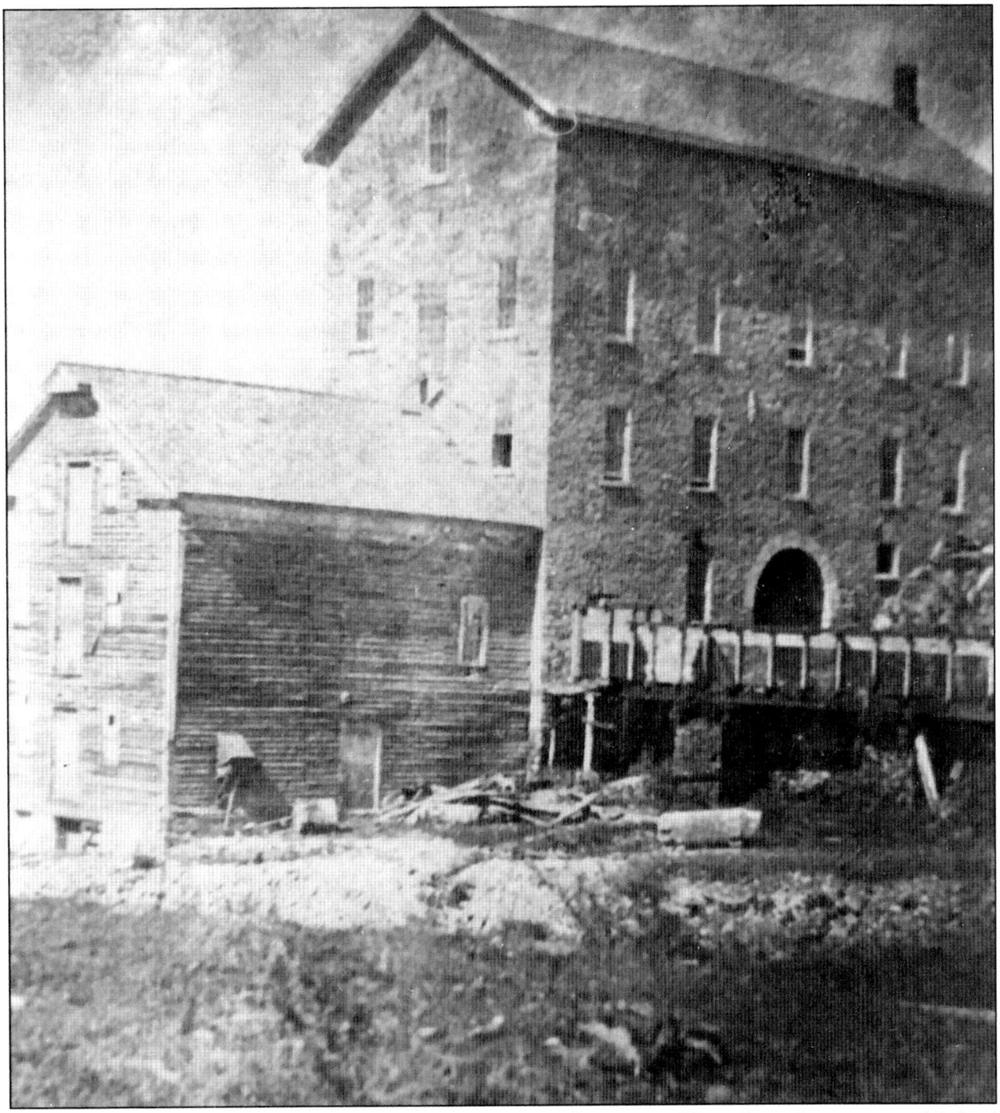

This gristmill, known as Mabee's Mill, was the first in the town of Royalton that was established before 1820. There was also a sawmill located just upstream in the early 1800s. The mill was located on the corner of Slayton Settlement Road and South Quaker Road, where the significant ruins still stand. This was the first of four Mabee mills. Jonathan Mabee built the first mill in the early 1800s. The second was a sawmill erected by Mabee prior to 1820. Jonathan was killed in 1842 and is buried next to the first mill. Jonathan's son Marcus succeeded his father and operated the mills until about 1880. From 1820 to 1880, five mills were located in the area. Two were Mabee gristmills and two were Mabee sawmills. The original mill was sold to John and Ed Ritchie and was known as Ritchie's Mill. The second gristmill is shown in the photograph, and the ruins still sit on the corner noted above. The fifth mill was known as Otto Mill. (RTH.)

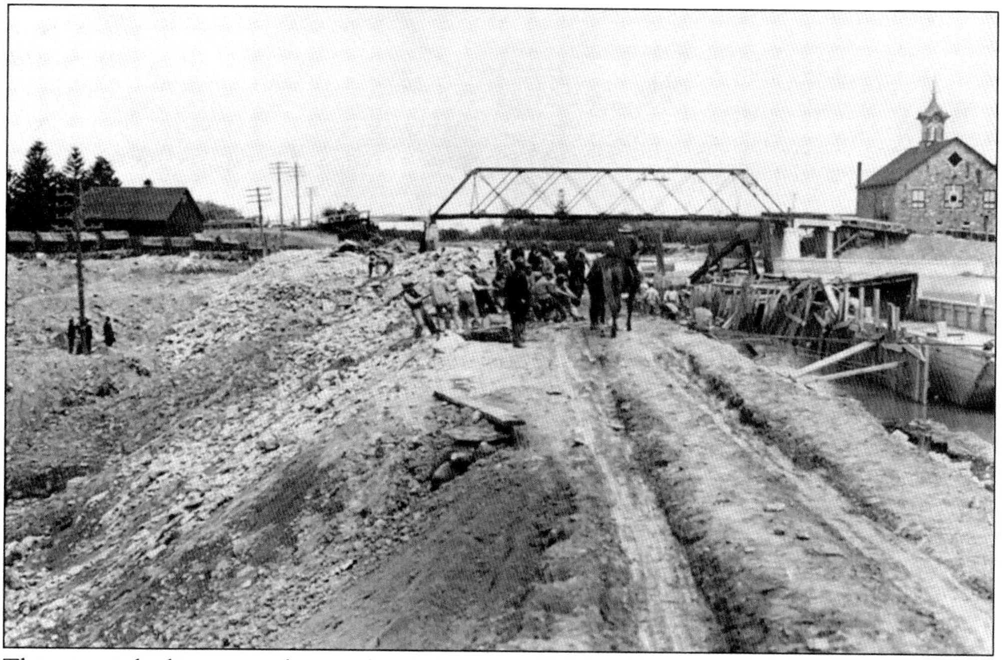

This view is looking east, close to the Mabee sawmill. The Schafer Cold Storage can be seen in the background on the right side of the Bolton Road Bridge. This event was in 1910. Notice as well that the bridge was constructed wide enough to accommodate the extra 100 feet of width of the Erie Canal, which was widened between 1911 and 1914. The barge in the canal is bracing the old canal wall in preparation for the digging of the new width. (RTH.)

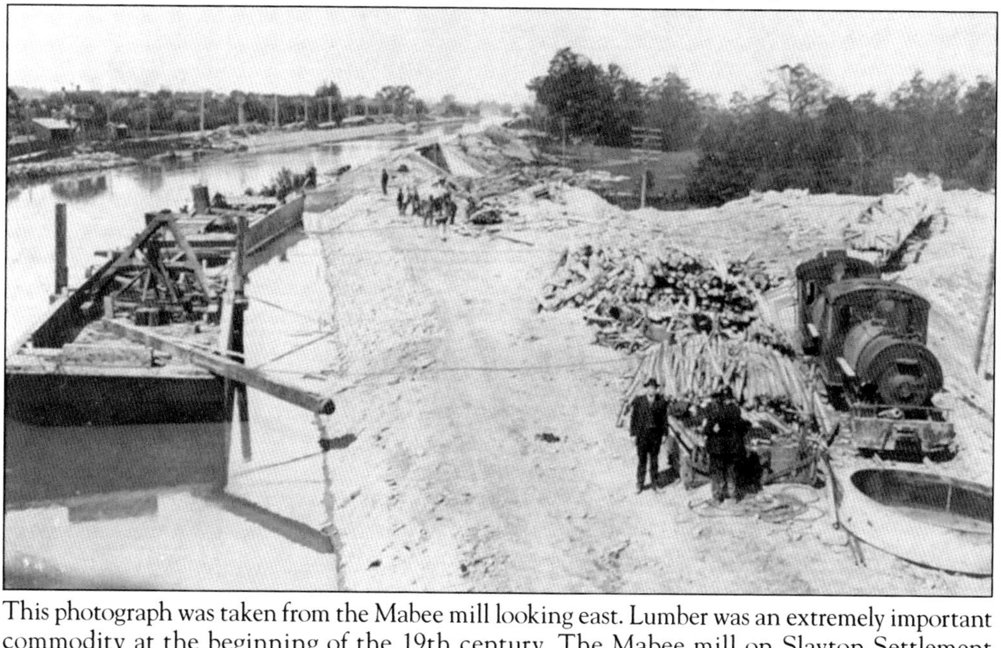

This photograph was taken from the Mabee mill looking east. Lumber was an extremely important commodity at the beginning of the 19th century. The Mabee mill on Slayton Settlement Road provided a valuable service during the Erie Canal expansion in 1910–1914. The lumber was cut into logs at the mill and transported to the canal bank for transshipment to its final destination. (RTH.)

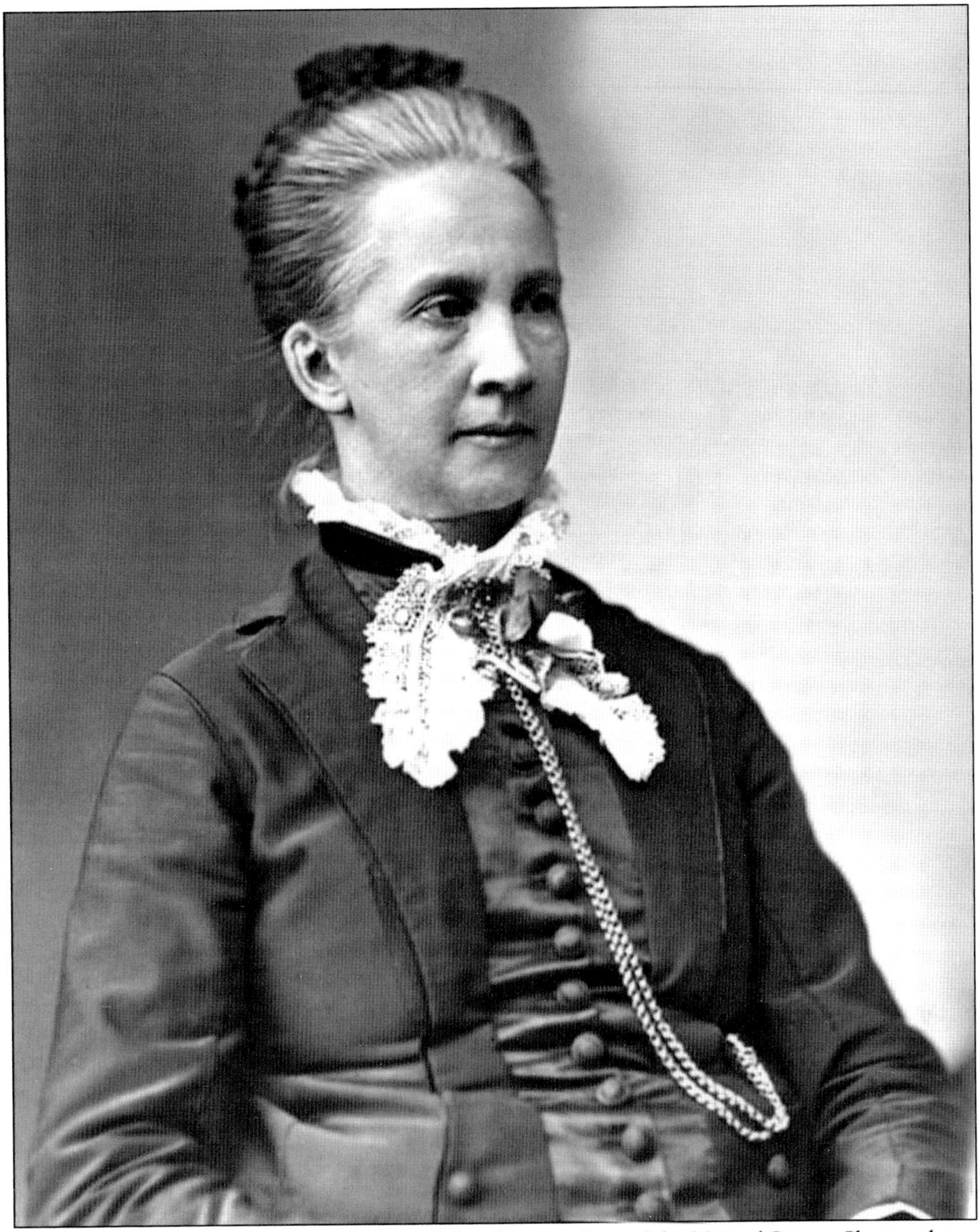

Belva Lockwood was the first woman candidate for president of the United States. She was born Belva Ann Bennett on Griswold Street in the town of Royalton on October 24, 1830. She was very active in working for women's rights, and she was referred to as a suffragist. While working as a teacher early in her career, she advocated equal pay, an idea that did not arrive in the 1850s. She met Susan B. Anthony in 1861 and found that she agreed with Anthony's ideas. It was then that she decided to become a lawyer. She eventually graduated from law school in Washington, D.C., and became one of the first female attorneys in the United States. In 1879, she petitioned Congress to be allowed to practice before the Supreme Court, the first woman to do so. In 1884 and 1888, she ran for president on the ticket of the National Equal Rights Party and was the first woman to appear on official ballots. (RTH.)

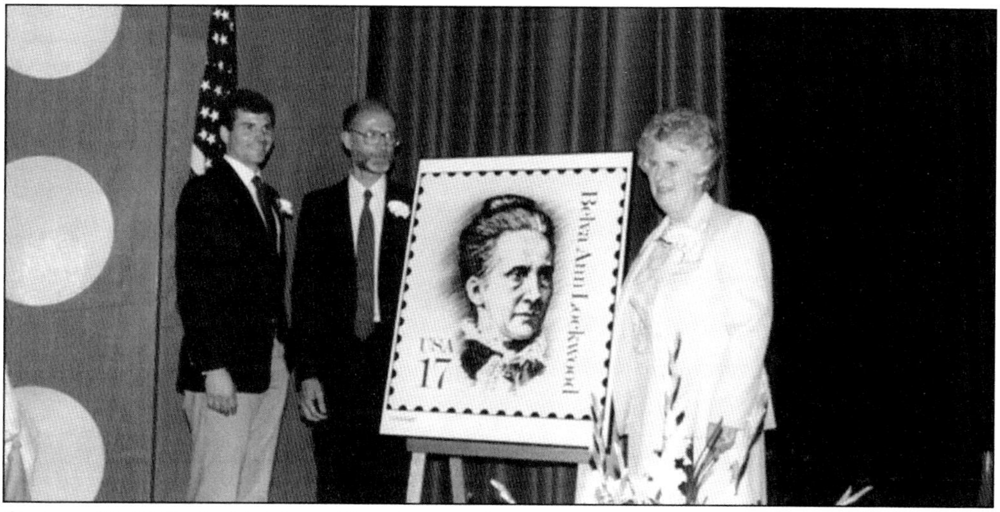

On June 18, 1986, the U.S. Postal Service issued a commemorative postage stamp honoring Belva Lockwood. This first day of issue was celebrated in the auditorium of the Royalton Hartland Central high school. The author was in attendance that day. Pictured above is the unveiling of the stamp, and the second photograph shows the actual postage cancellation. Belva Lockwood's endorsement seems to have been valuable during its time. The endorsement reads: "I have used Fairbank's Fairy Soap and deem it unequaled for bathing purposes, for all sorts of toilet uses, and particularly adapted to the nursery as it is pure and will not injure the skin. Mrs. Belva A. Lockwood, The most prominent, woman lawyer in the world." (Above, MVH; below, RTH.)

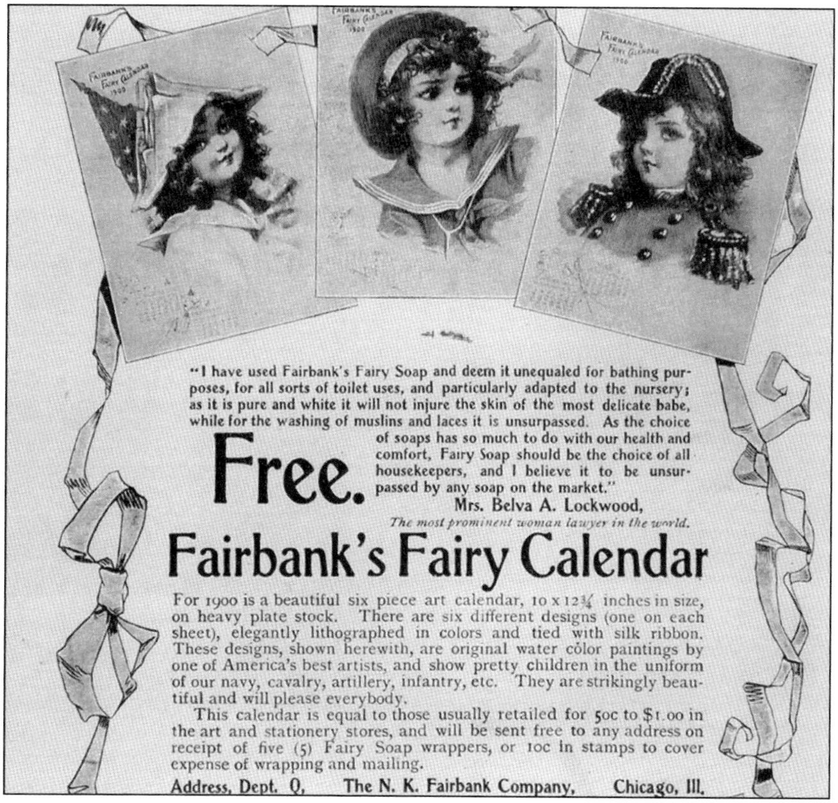

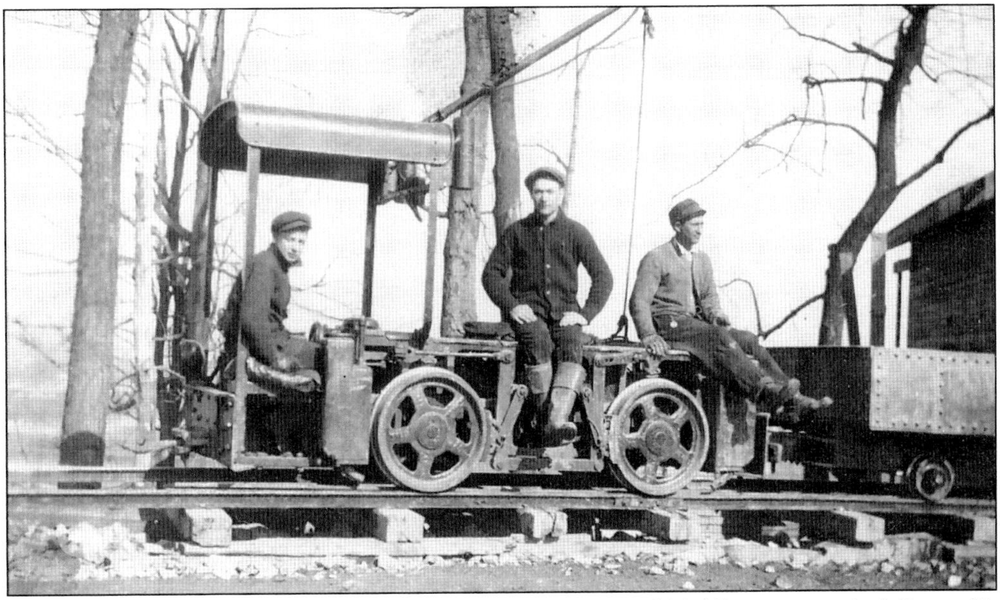

The Wickwire Stone Quarry was located between Gasport and Middleport on today's Route 31. This enterprise was extremely significant in the development of all of the transportation routes in the area. It provided stone for the canal banks, the rail and trolley roadbeds, and stone for the highways constructed in the immediate area. It was still producing material in the 1990s but has since become a waste management site. (RTH.)

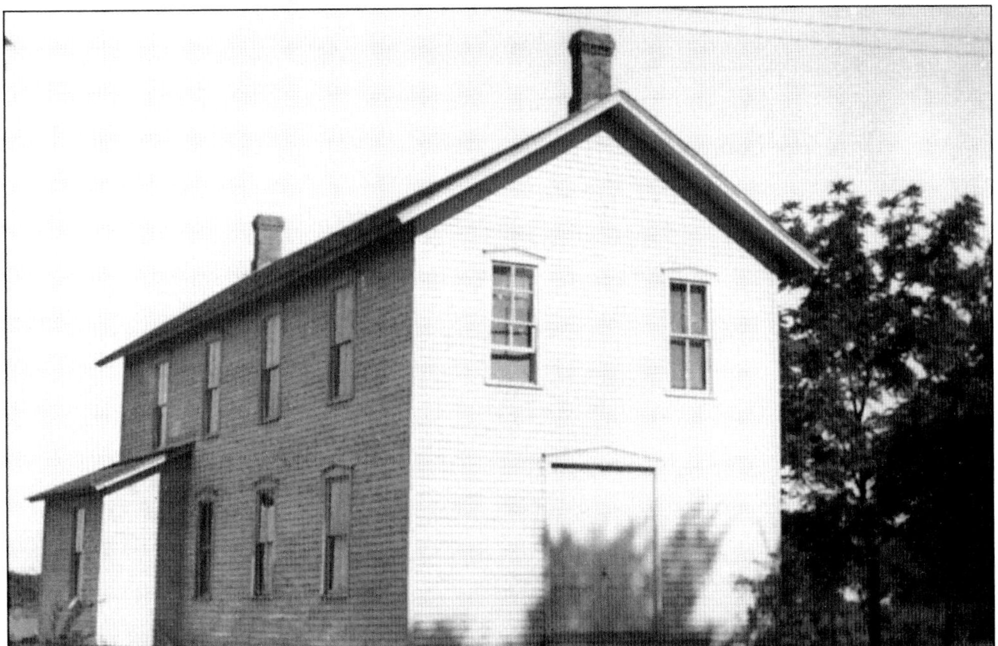

This building was part of the landscape in the town of Royalton during the latter part of the 19th century and was known as Good Templer's Hall. Middleport Council, No. 23, Royal Templars of Temperance was instituted on January 12, 1871. Its first members were Linus Freeman, A. S. Freeman, W. J. Sterritt, John Sage, A. D. Filer, R. B. Oliver, and Henry McClean. (RTH.)

Two

GASPORT

Gasport is a hamlet located on the Erie Canal about 5 miles east of Lockport. The name comes from either one of two sources. The first was because it was a stop on the canal and a port where it received grain and other agricultural produce for transportation to other markets. The second, and more plausible explanation concerns the flowing springs of gas, which were visible to those passing through the area. A scientist from Albany, New York, experimented with the gas to see if it could have a commercial use. In order to do this, he covered a spring with a wooden cask and after a while applied a match. Naturally, the cask exploded, proving indeed that the vapor was natural gas. From that time on, the well was capped, pipes were installed, burners were constructed into the manufacturing buildings, and sufficient gas was available to eventually operate 14 burners. When the canal was widened in 1910, it took the gasworks (which were located on the southern bank of the canal), leaving only the warehouse in its wake.

At the beginning of the 20th century, Gasport had a church, a hotel, a blacksmith and wagon shop, two warehouses, three stores, a steam shingle factory, a vinegar works, a railroad depot, canal station, and a population of about 300 people.

A number of firsts for Gasport are listed in the *History of Niagara County, New York,* published by Sanford and Company in 1878. It states that Samuel Hitchcock built the first house in Gasport in 1824, and it was located on the north side of the canal.

Alfred Colwell had the first warehouse, which was located next to the canal bridge on the south side of the canal. Early settlers to the place are listed as Mr.Woodworth, wagon maker; Mr. Marcy, blacksmith; and Timothy Page, the first physician. It also lists that the first mill was built by Col. John Mabee east of Gasport on Red (Johnson) Creek. That area later became known as Mabee's. Andrew and Amos Brown also built a sawmill south of the village at about the same time. Listed as well is that Sextus Shearer opened the first store in 1823. The railroad station arrived in 1854.

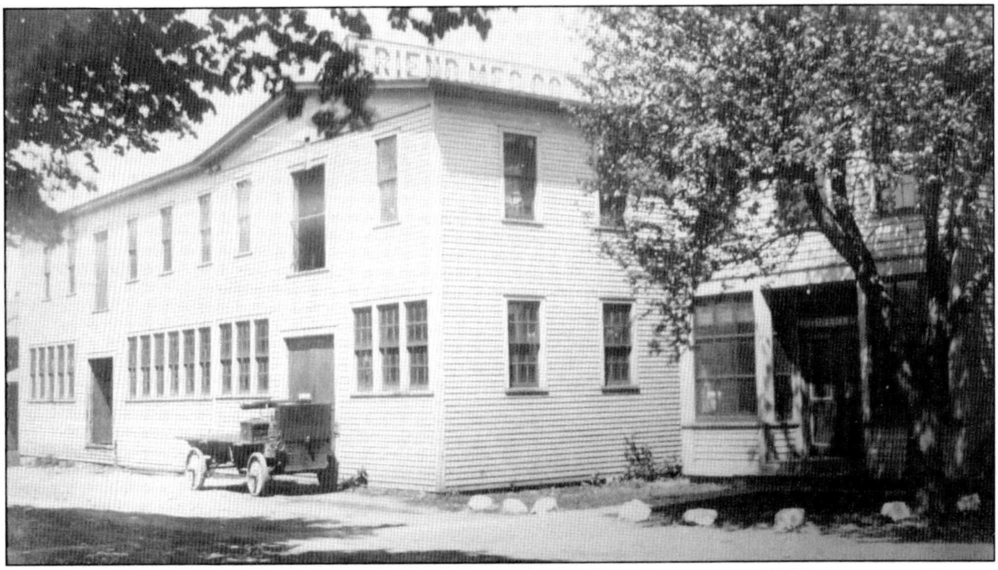

Friend was a manufacturing factory founded and located in Gasport in 1895; it survived until the 1990s. Their primary focus was agricultural equipment, which was the basis for a surprisingly extensive group of companies for such a small town. Friend produced gasoline engines, orchard spray systems, and other crop dressing equipment. For most of its time, it was the largest employer in the village. (RTH.)

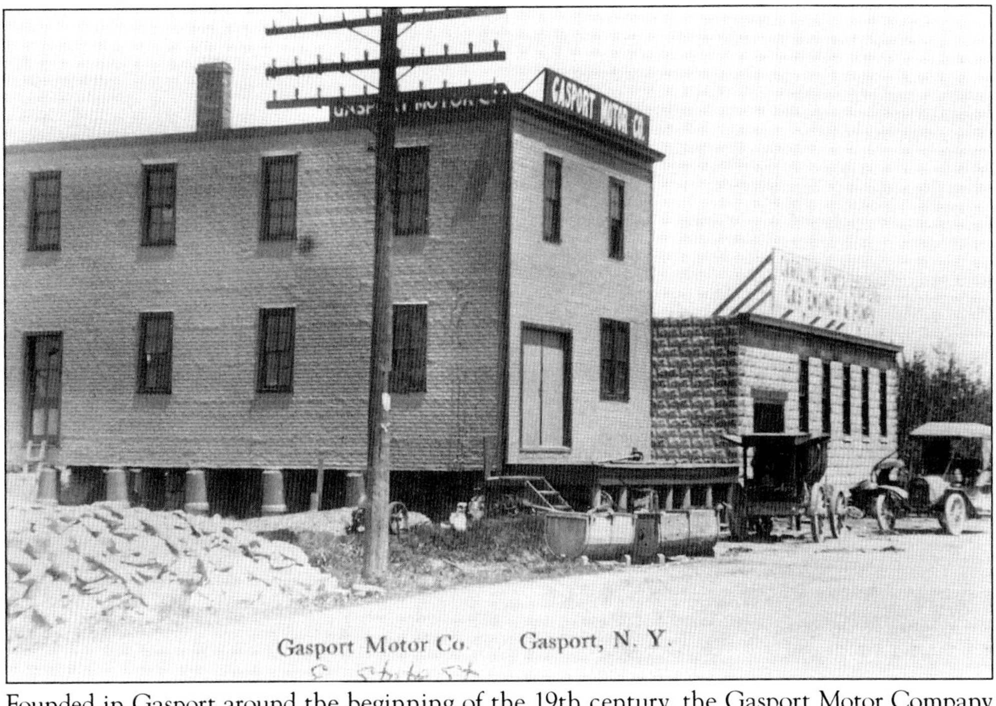

Founded in Gasport around the beginning of the 19th century, the Gasport Motor Company survived until declaring bankruptcy in 1911. Its primary products were gasoline engines and farm tractors. Its manufacturing site was located on the south side of the canal on State Street. After its demise, Friend Manufacturing assumed the equipment and facilities and operations continued as they had under the previous owners. (RTH.)

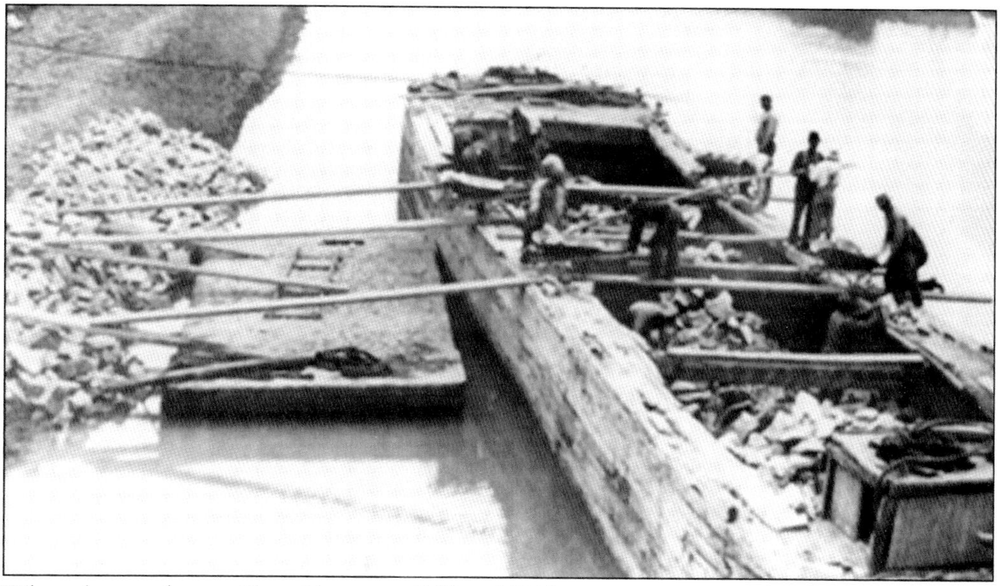

When the canal was widened between 1910 and 1914, crews were required to buttress the banks with rocks to insure that the soil remained firm. This was backbreaking, labor-intensive work. The stone mainly came from the Wickwire in Gasport. It was moved from the pit to the canal where it was loaded on barges and taken to the job site. (RTH.)

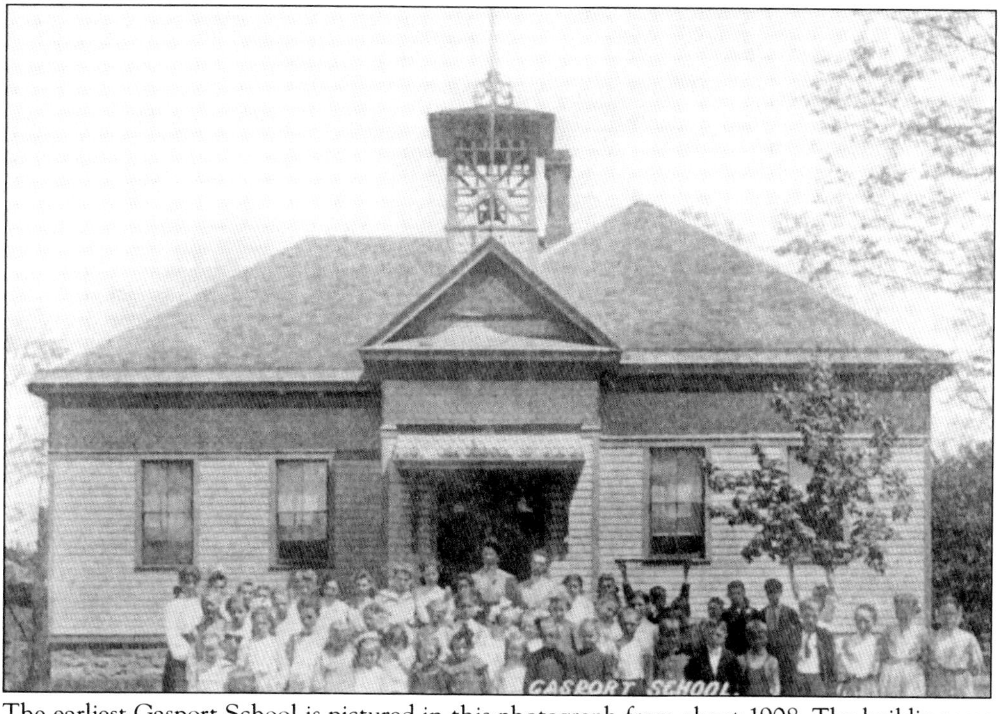

The earliest Gasport School is pictured in this photograph from about 1908. The building was located on Main Street, very close to its junction with West Avenue. It served all grades and was essentially a one-room schoolhouse. It remained in operation until the construction of Gasport High School on the corner of Main Street and Route 31. The population number of Gasport could be estimated at the time by the number of students enrolled in the school. (RTH.)

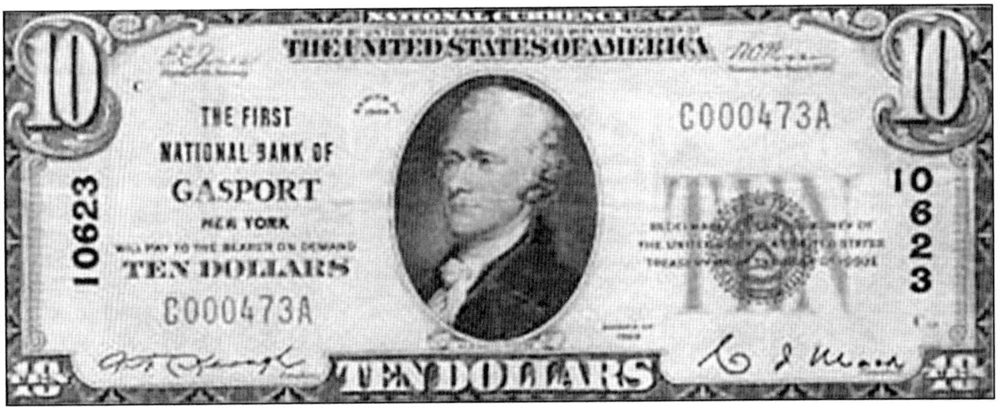

Between 1910 and 1920, most local banks issued cash, which was either stamped with the local designation (such as a Hamilton $10 bill) or were printed with the name of the local bank by the U.S. Mint (such as the second McKinley $10 note). This type of cash was short-lived as the U.S. government standardized the currency and did away with local bank issues, settling instead for district Federal Reserve banks. These banknotes were drawn on the National Bank of Gasport. (RTH.)

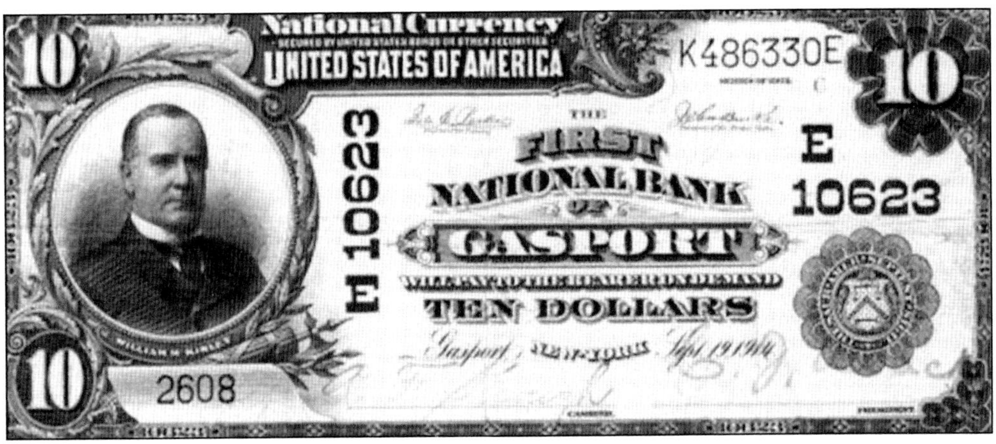

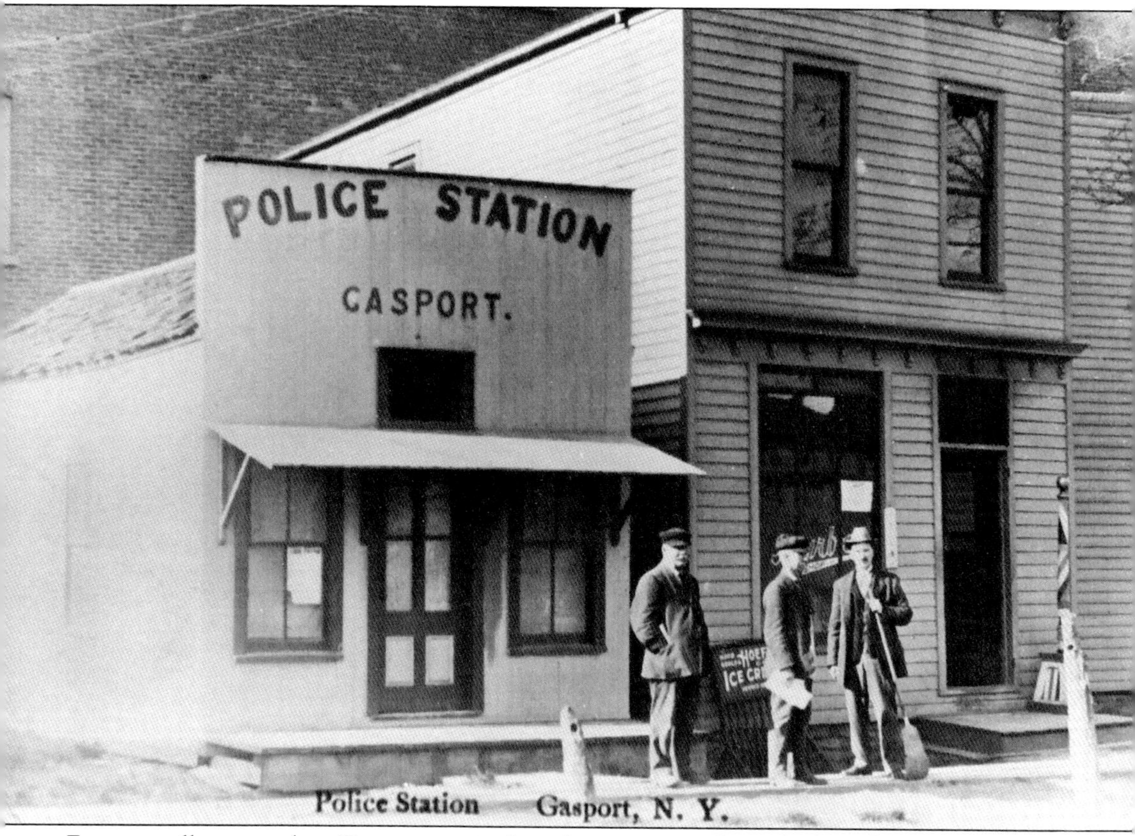

Even a small town such as Gasport required a police station in the early days of the 20th century. The station housed a small jail, which received most of its guests on payday evenings from the local bars. The police station disappeared by 1920 and became an automobile tire store. After that, the building served as a fire station. It has had multiple uses over the years and remains standing on State Street. The picture indicates that Gasport had more than one police officer. The National Bank was located just around the corner from the police station and the local bars were on either side, so the police would seem to have been perfectly located within the town to take care of any problems. (NCH.)

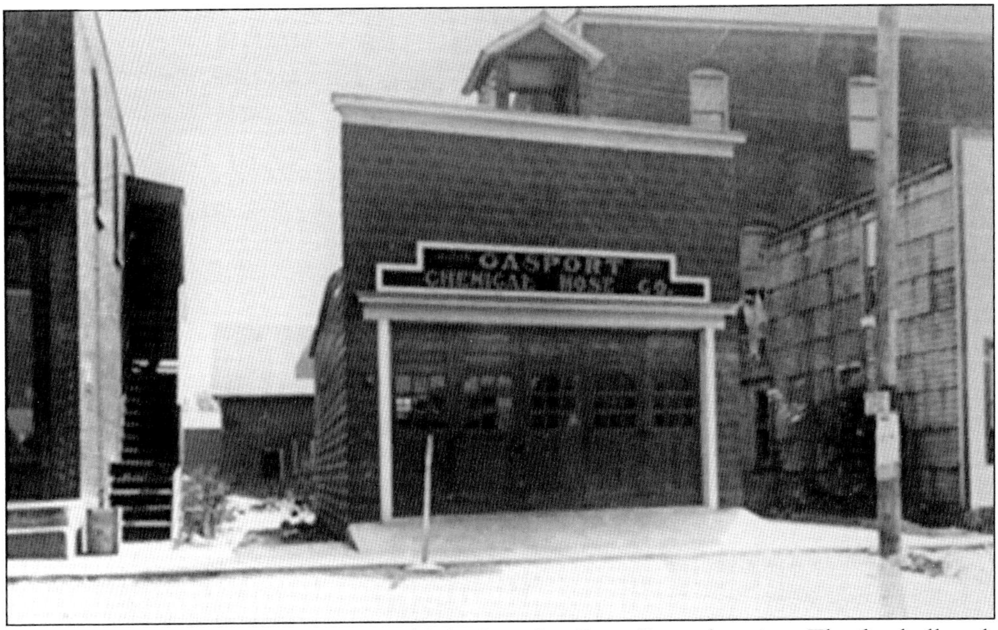

The Gasport Fire Department was established on this State Street location. The fire hall took over the building once occupied by the tire store in the 1920s. It would appear that the town had only one fire truck during this period. The name reads, "Gasport Chemical Hose Co.," which would later become Miller Hose Company and move to its present location further east on State Street. (RTH.)

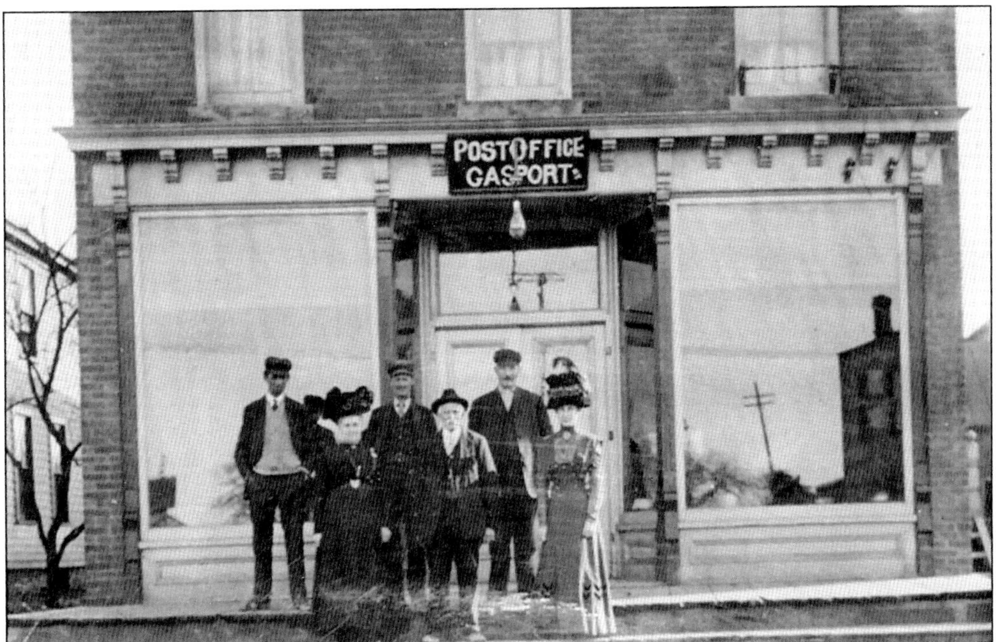

The U.S. Post Office was located in this familiar building. This view is from 1908 and shows the local citizens in their Sunday best. The post office remained in this building until the 1920s, when it was moved to the new location on Main Street. It remained in that location until moving to Route 31 in the 1990s. (RTH.)

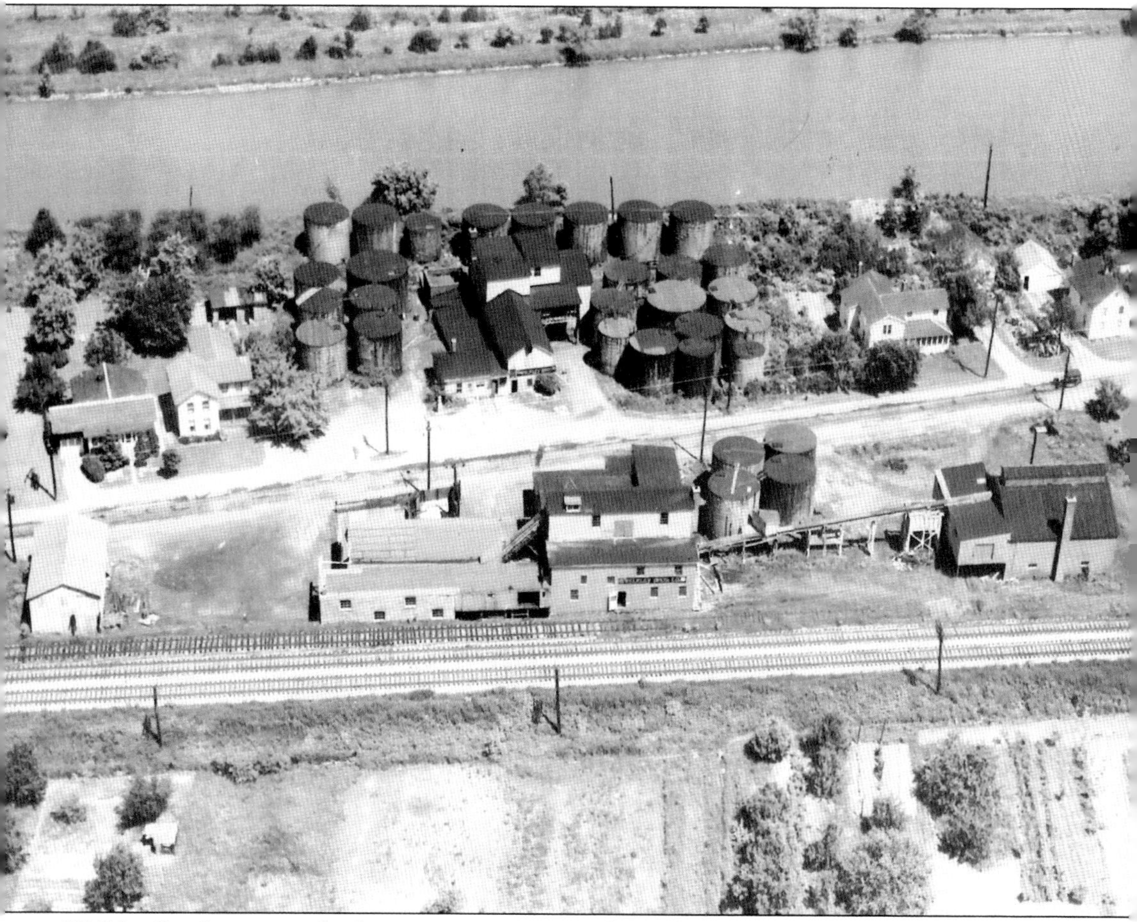

Welkley Brothers was a food-processing enterprise, located on the eastern end of State Street. The picture shows the vast infrastructure that existed in Gasport and allowed the economy to grow. The Erie Canal, Route 31, and the New York Central Railroad are readily recognizable. The large tanks are wooden vats used for cider. Welkley Brothers was a typical fruit enterprise, similar to those found throughout the area surrounding both Gasport and Middleport. This complex had the advantage of being located on the transportation links. Other fruit growers would eventually construct their own cold storage facilities and some would even have processing capabilities. (RTH.)

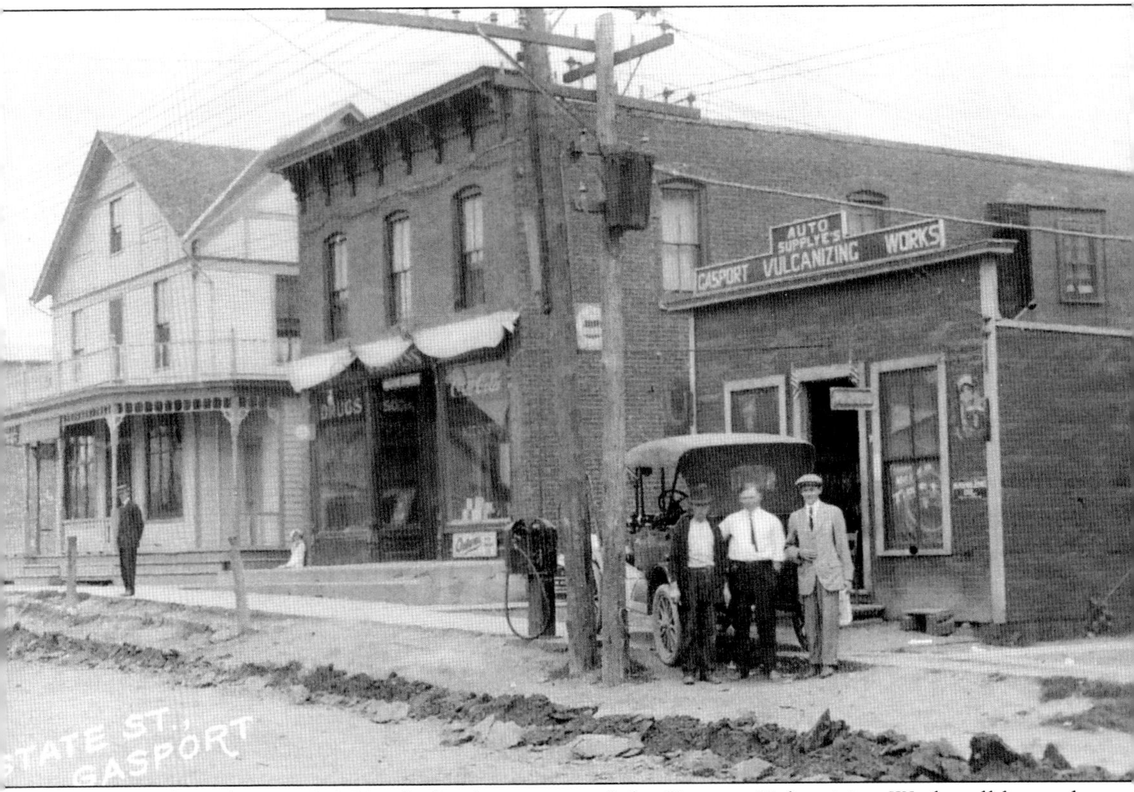

Pictured are the Knight's Hotel, the drugstore, and the Gasport Vulcanizing Works, all located on State Street. At the time of this picture, State Street was unpaved, yet the appearance of the Gasport Vulcanizing Works would indicate that there were enough automobiles and tractors available to make the tire business possible. These same buildings appear often through the years but house different enterprises. (RTH.)

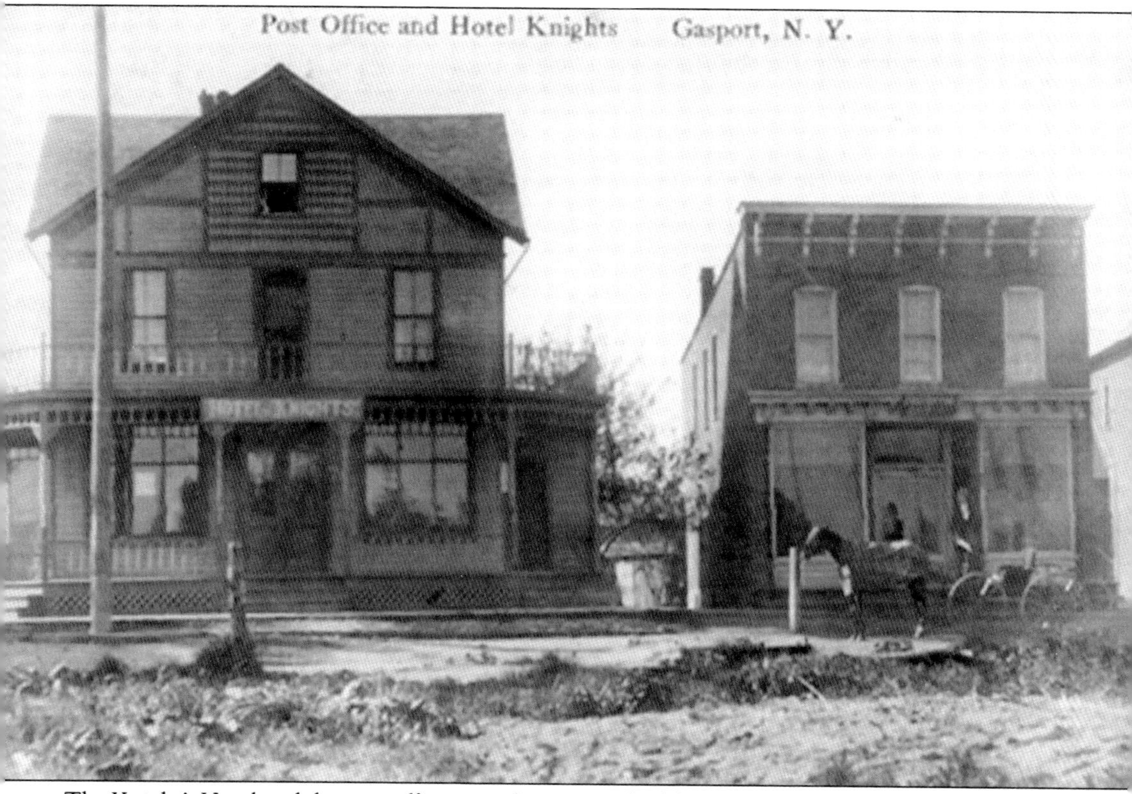

The Knight's Hotel and the post office were the primary buildings at this location. This photograph is from about 1910 and shows the two buildings, which were located on the south side of State Street near the Main Street intersection. Both buildings are pictured later having different uses. Actually, these buildings appear in nearly all pictures of State Street. The hotel served the Gasport community for numerous years and remained a hotel into the 1960s. Later it was demolished and remains a vacant lot today. The post office building remained in this location until it moved around the corner onto Main Street. In the 1990s, it moved again to its present location on the corner of Main Street and Route 31. (RTH.)

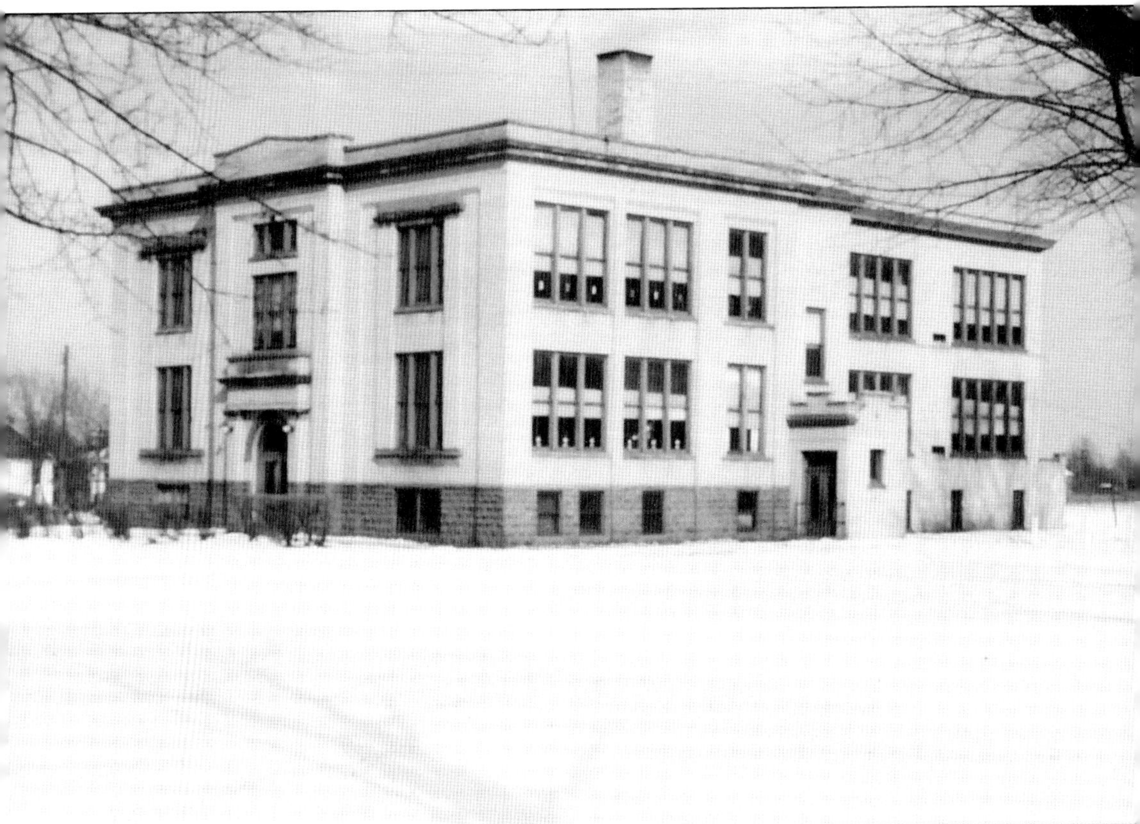

The Gasport School served the hamlet and surrounding area as an independent entity until 1958. Originally, it housed classes from kindergarten through the graduating 12th grade. Basketball and baseball athletic teams represented Gasport High School. The school district also contained rural schools that fed the high school in the student's later years. In 1946, Gasport High School and Middleport High School combined their districts and became the Royalton-Hartland Central School District. Originally, the Gasport building housed the local elementary students from kindergarten through sixth grade. Upon entering seventh grade, the Gasport students were transferred to Middleport for the remainder of their school years. The Gasport building, located on Main Street at the corner of Route 31, continued to serve the community until the present Gasport Elementary School was constructed in 1958. After that, it was demolished. (RTH.)

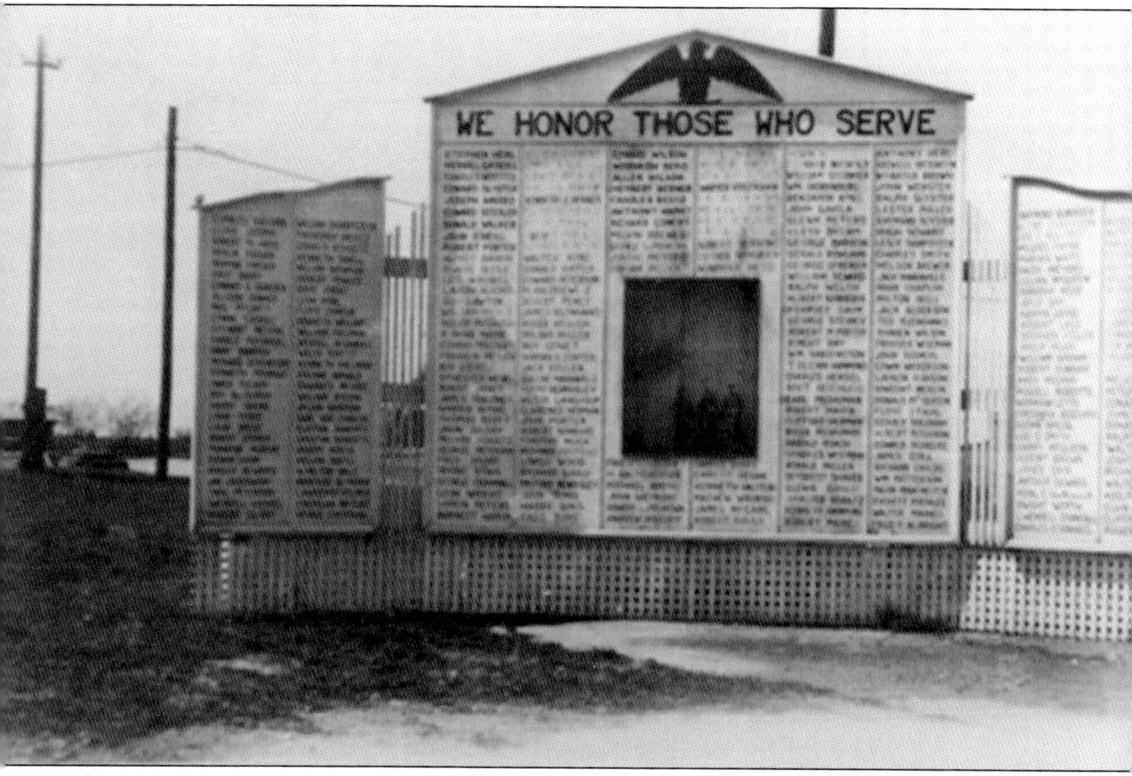

This sign was erected during World War II and listed all of the local residents who were serving in the military. These included not just those from Gasport, but from the entire general area. There was a large group of National Guard soldiers from the area who had trained at Fort Niagara, were activated in 1940, and sent to the Philippine Islands. They were captured, suffered the Bataan Death March, and stayed in prison camps to either die or be liberated. The Wall of Honor was continually updated to include those killed, wounded, or captured. After 1945, the sign was removed, and Gasport eventually constructed its own veteran's monument, as did Middleport. (RTH.)

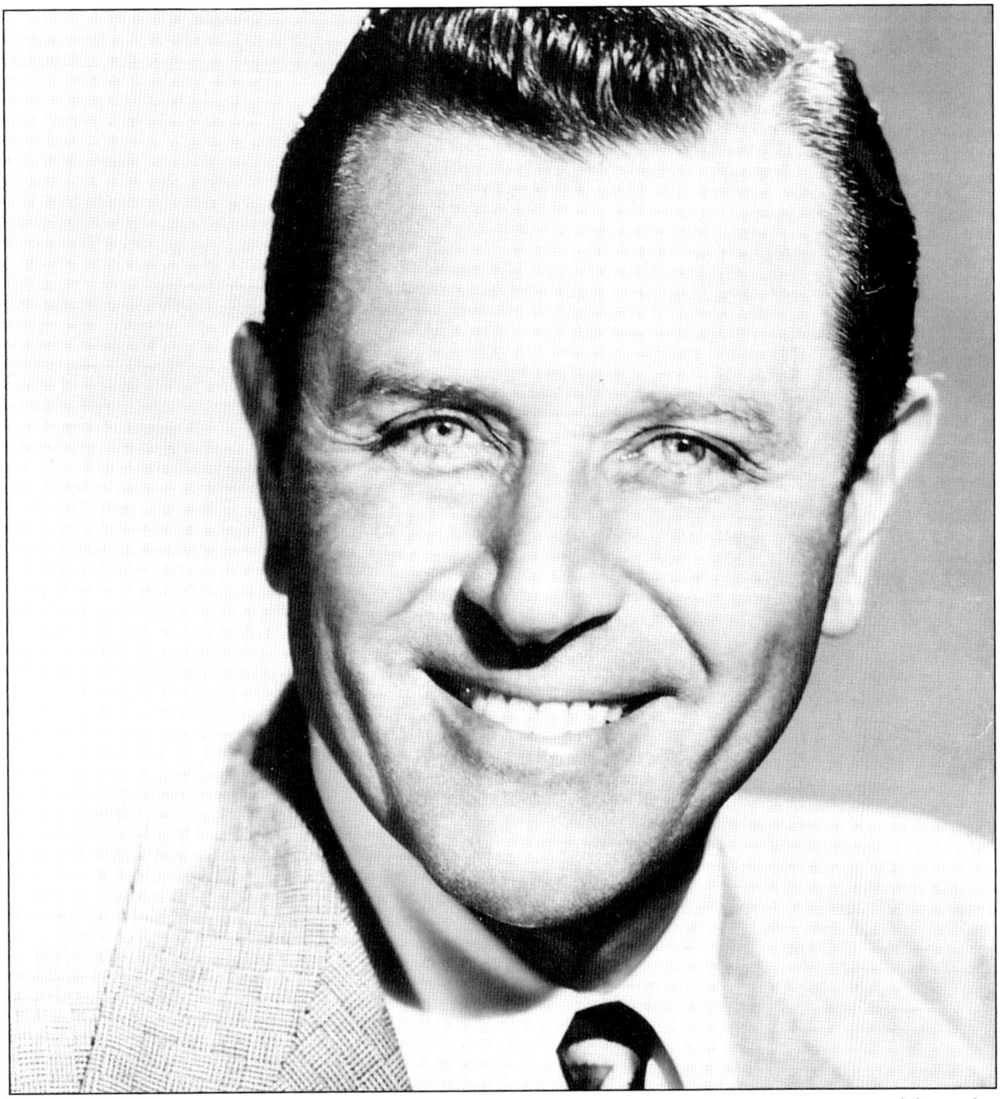

John Warren Hull was a celebrated singer, actor, and television host whose career spanned from the 1920s through the 1960s. He was born in Gasport on January 17, 1903, to John and Laura (Shafer) Hull, who were Quakers. There were two daughters in the family as well. Warren gained his musical interest from his father and his work from the Friend's Church in Gasport. He attended Lockport High School, graduating in 1922. He later attended the Eastman School of Music in Rochester. After a period of time, he made his way to New York City and earned roles in Broadway musicals between 1927 and 1929. He dabbled for a while in radio as both a singer and actor. His talents and looks gained him a film contract with Warner Brothers, where he was slated for "A" movie roles but found himself relegated to "B" parts. All together, he was on the marquee in 15 films. In 1951, he accepted the role as host on the new medium of television for a show entitled *Strike It Rich*. The show lasted six seasons and provided Hull with financial security for the remainder of his life. He was married four times and had a total of four children. He died of heart failure in Waterbury, Connecticut, on September 14, 1974. He has two stars on the Hollywood Walk of Fame, one for radio and the other for television. (RTH.)

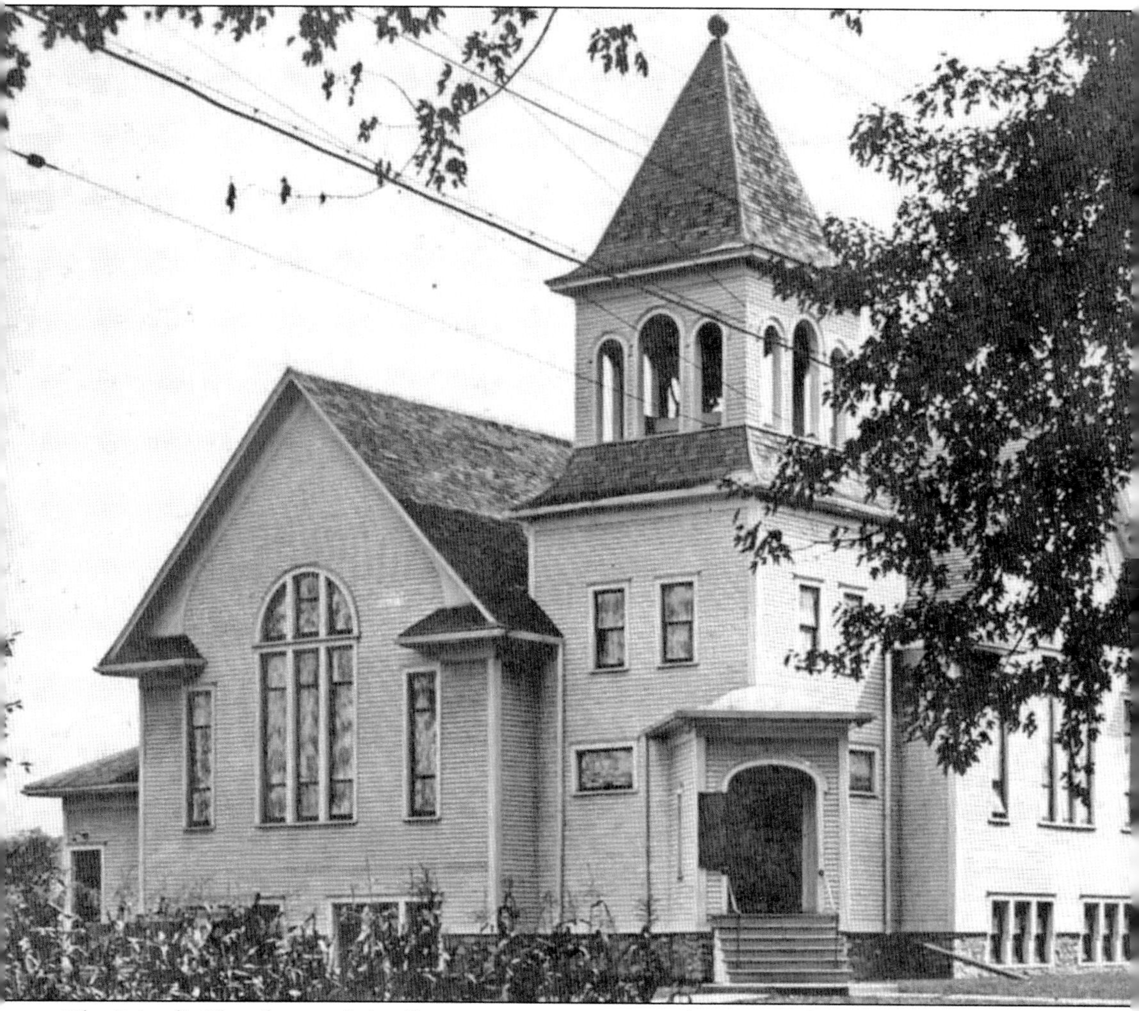

The Friend's Church served the Gasport community as a religious site for more than a century. Originally founded by the Quakers, it served as their house of worship and their meetinghouse. This is a more modern photograph of the building, which has had many uses over the years. Besides a church, it has been a meeting hall and a school. It is one of the most beautiful architectural landmarks in the hamlet. Today it still retains its artistic charm, although it serves as a private dwelling. The original pastor was the Reverend George Hull. Might that have been the father or other relative of Warren Hull that was mentioned on the previous page? (NCH.)

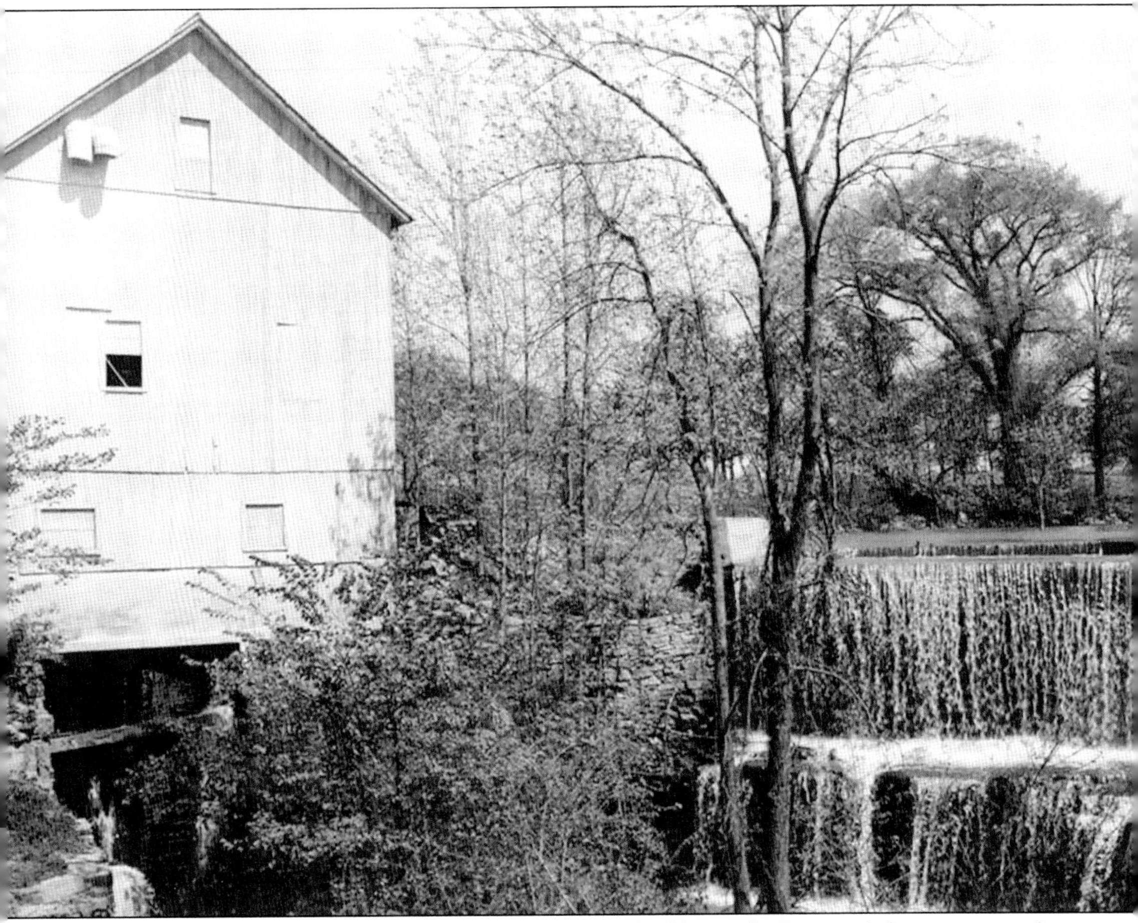

Gottlieb Otto emigrated from Germany and established his mill along with his two sons. Otto Mill was located on South Quaker Road. It was part of the mill complex located along Red (or Johnson) Creek in the early 1800s. It was one of the very few processing mills on the creek that was not owned by the Mabee family. The Otto Mill was a gristmill and is in disrepair, but the dam was reconstructed in the 1990s. The remnants of this operation make a beautiful picture, as seen today from Slayton Settlement Road. (RTH.)

Three

MIDDLEPORT

Middleport essentially began in 1811 when Asher Freeman purchased land there from the Holland Land Company located in Batavia. The size of the tract was 500 acres, which cost him $1,625, and he quickly started selling off pieces of land. He constructed his first house south of the town near what is today the intersection of South Main Street and Telegraph Road. It was not long before the area was referred to as Freeman's Corners. By 1817, Freeman had constructed a sawmill and his permanent home. That house is still located at 106 Telegraph Road.

Bennett, Taylor, Land, and Mather owned the land of the present-day Middleport. As progress on the Erie Canal moved through the area, lots along the canal were sold to businesses and they flourished. After the canal opened in 1825, its benefits were the impetus for the growth of the village along its path. Lumber was the main industry in the beginning, and numerous sawmills were founded. Other industries followed, including Gad Mather's tannery, a carding mill in 1828, John Macker, tailor, in 1830, and Middleport's first blast furnace in 1840.

Regarding education, the first academy was established in 1842. The Middleport Academy, as it was known, educated the community's youth until the Middleport Union School was completed at the corner of Vernon Street and Park Avenue. It was a magnificent building, which tragically burned in 1910. By 1911, another building had been completed at its present location on State Street.

The name Middleport is the product of the Erie Canal. The village is equidistant from Lockport to the west and Albion to the east, about one day's journey in either direction by barge.

The fire department was established in 1884 and consisted of the W. J. Sterritt Engine Company, the L. H. Spalding Hose Company, and the A. D. Rich Hook and Ladder Company. By the outset of the 20th century, Middleport was a thriving, self-sufficient community.

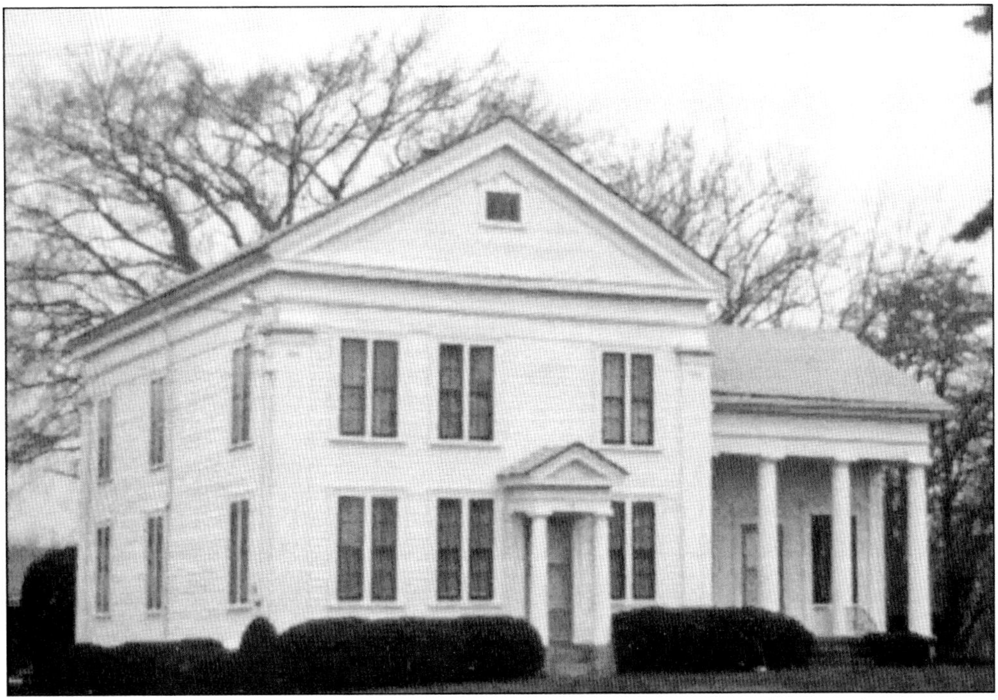

Asher Freeman is generally credited with the founding of Middleport. This is a photograph of his house, which is located on Telegraph Road about a quarter of a mile south of the canal. The intersection where the Freeman House is located was once called Freeman's Corners and Teapot Hollow. The Freeman House was once a "stop" on the Underground Railroad, which assisted slaves in escaping to Canada during the Civil War. (NCH.)

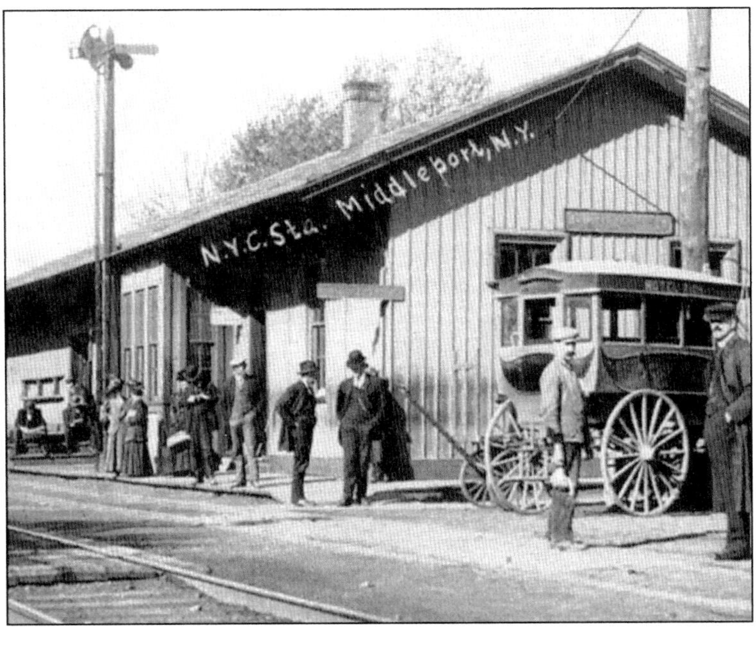

This is a great photograph of the New York Central depot in Middleport around 1910. The station was located on Vernon Street, next to the American Hotel. Both passenger and freight service were available from here until 1955. The sign on the end of the building reads "American Express," and the carriage is from the Rich Hotel. (NCH.)

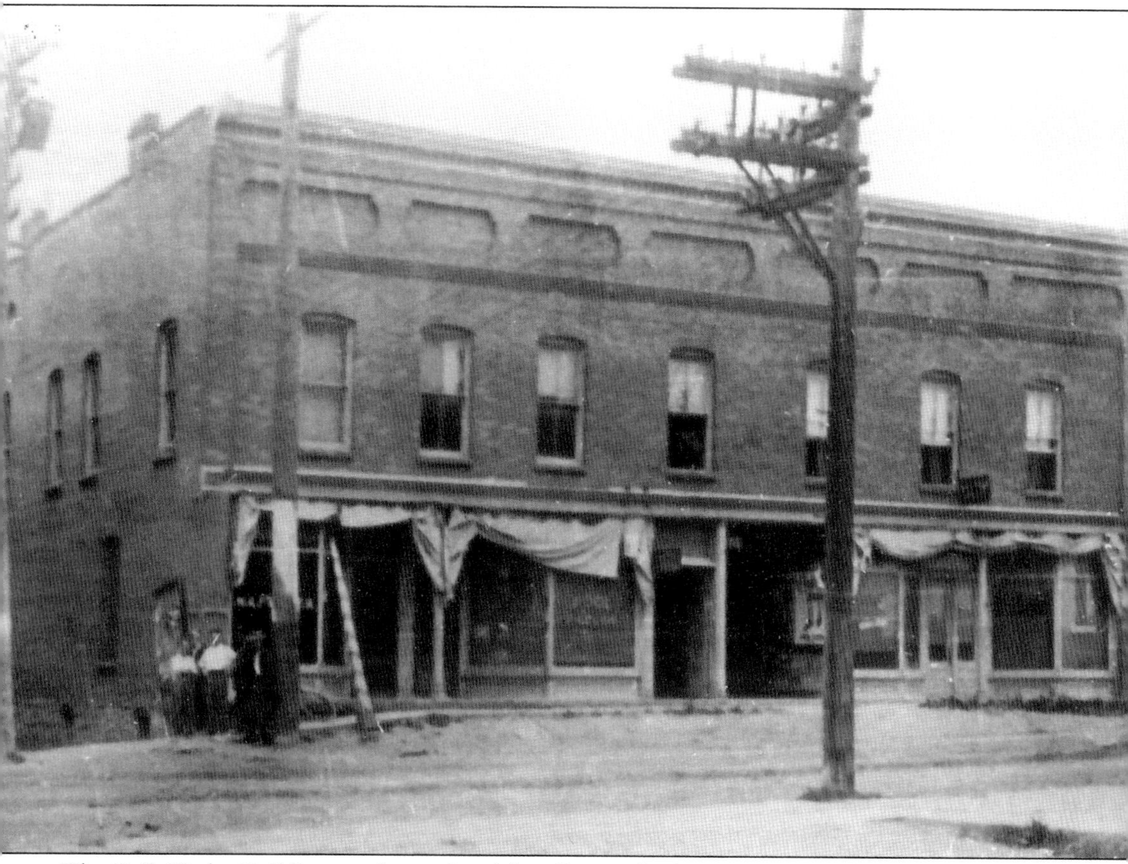

The C. B. Taylor Building was located on Main Street, the last structure on the west side next to the canal. It was demolished when the canal was widened in 1910. Until that time, it had been a significant commercial site with its proximity to the canal. Dr. William McFadden had a dental office on the second floor. Many of today's residents still have Dr. McFadden's dental handiwork. This was an excellent structure that was sacrificed in the name of progress. The alley, which leads off today's Main Street, did not exist at the time of the Taylor Building, but there was an alley to the south. This led down to the Bennett and Compton Building. Although neither structure survived the 1920s, both were critical in the commerce of Middleport. (MVH.)

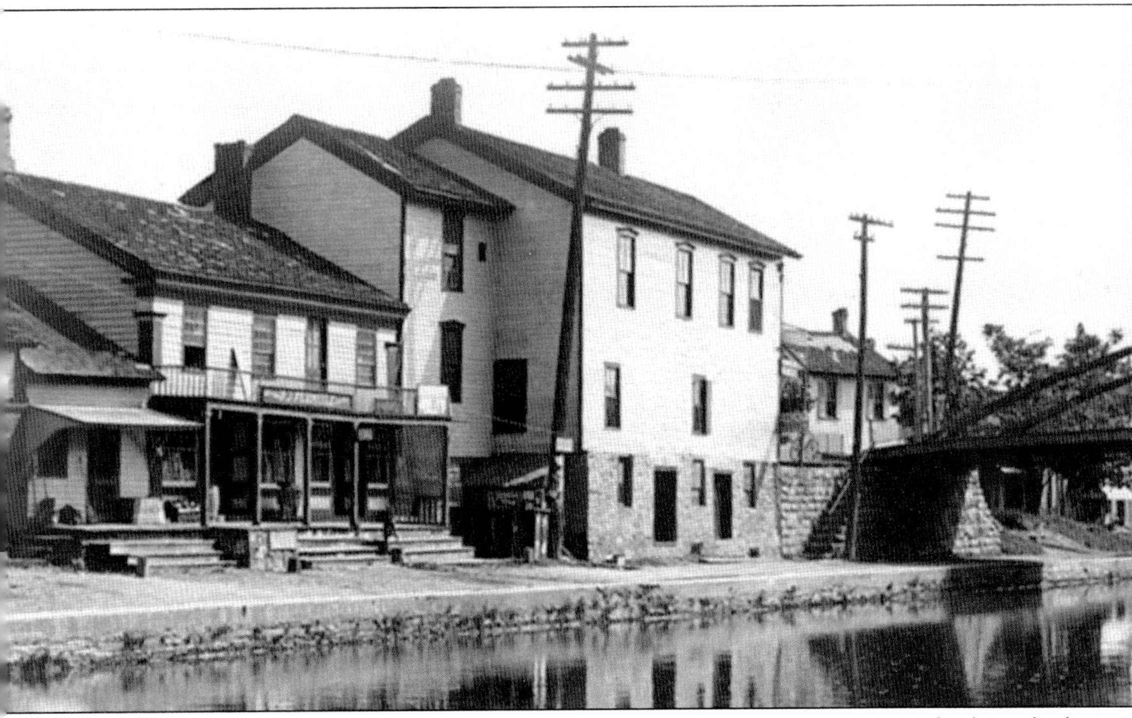

This view of the north side of the Erie Canal shows the old elevated stationary bridge, which connected both sides of Main Street. The store to the right is Fermoile's Provision, which served both the needs of the canal traffic and the residents of the north side of the canal. The primary part of the structure in the center of the picture was once a hotel and later just a bar. The entire building was lost to fire, but the cellar remnants were still there into the 1960s. On the right side of the picture there are buildings, which remain on North Main Street today. The canal frontage, however, looked wonderful in this picture with a picturesque walkway and residential homes. The entire area today looks much different. Front Street, as the area is called, eventually would be the home of Tony Nicolia's bar and restaurant. (MVH.)

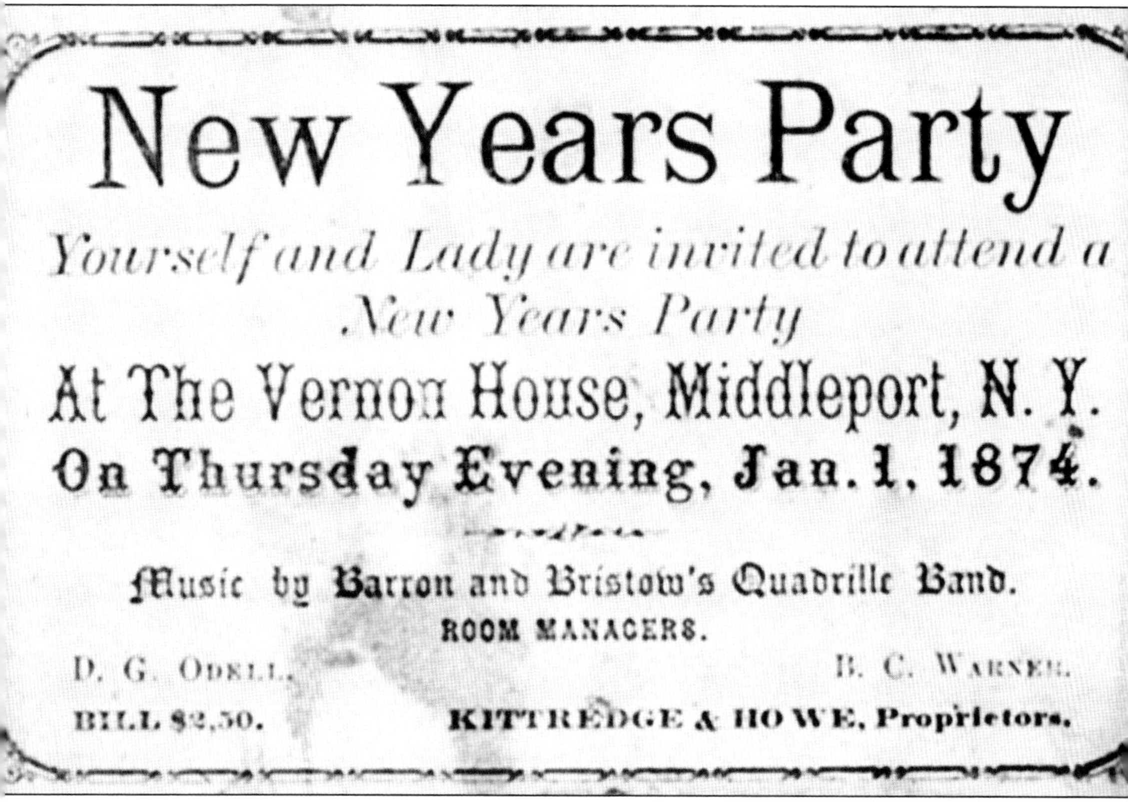

New Years Party

Yourself and Lady are invited to attend a New Years Party

At The Vernon House, Middleport, N. Y.

On Thursday Evening, Jan. 1, 1874.

Music by Barron and Bristow's Quadrille Band.

ROOM MANAGERS.

D. G. Odell, B. C. Warner.

BILL $2,50. KITTREDGE & HOWE, Proprietors.

The large structure next to the depot on Vernon Street was once known as the Vernon House. This 1874 invitation demonstrates the kinds of activities that were held there in the early days. The Vernon House was the second largest hotel in town, surpassed only by the Hotel Rich. The fact that such a small village would have two large hotels should be an indication of the magnitude of both commercial and employment opportunities that the community offered. The Vernon House catered to the needs of Niagara Sprayer, which was located just around the corner on Cemetery Street. It also found a lucrative trade from the New York Central Railroad located next door. It would later become the American Hotel. (NCH.)

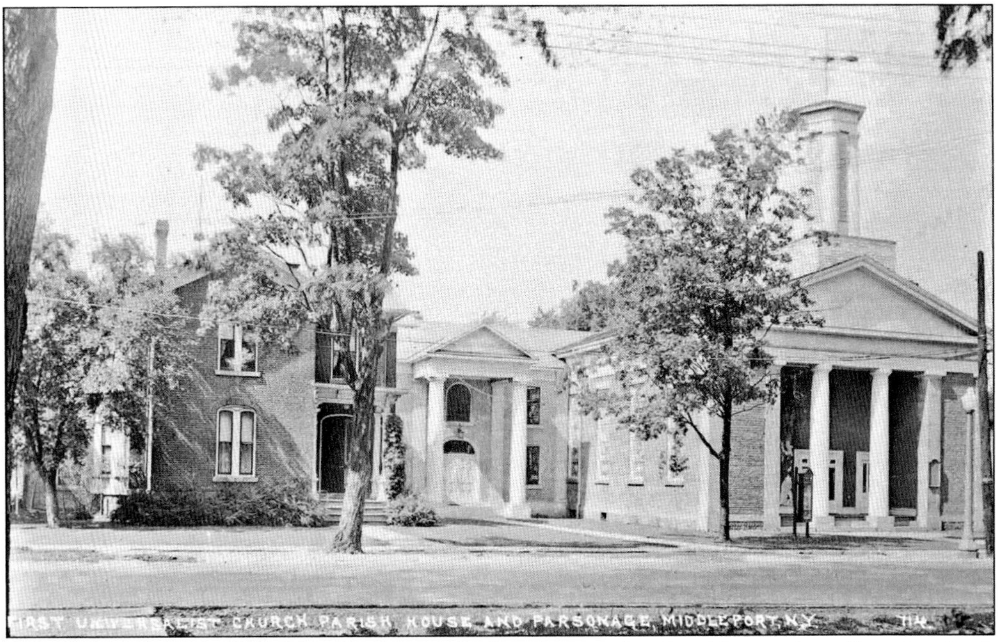

The Universalist Church and parsonage was built in 1841 and is the oldest in the village. It is built in the cobblestone style that is unique to the area and was built for $10,000. In 1878, it was noted that 45 families constituted the congregation and that an active Sunday school was attached to the building. It is still used today. (NCH.)

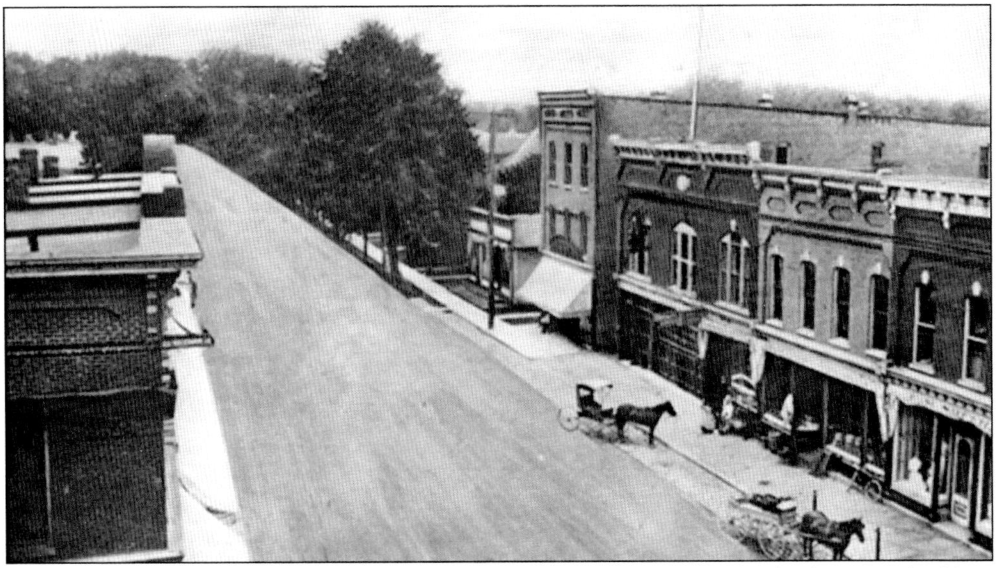

This view of Main Street looks south before the widening of the canal. The fireman's building is in view, so the picture was taken after 1892. The small sign attached to the building at the far left advertises the telegraph. Power lines are evident, but the street itself is unpaved. (NCH.)

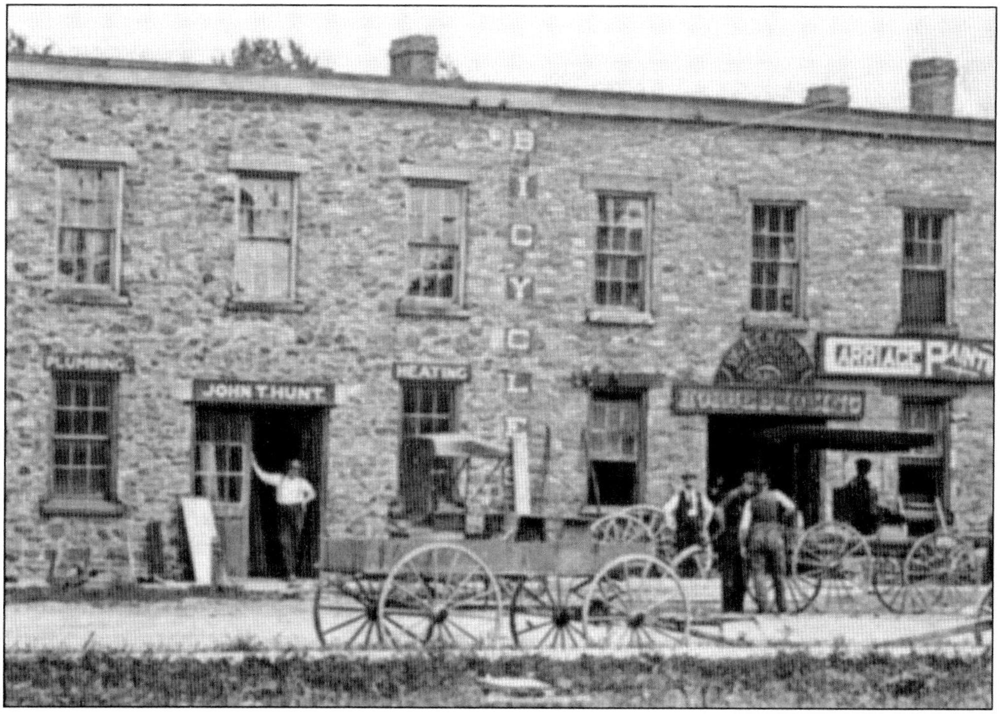

This photograph of the blast furnace shows the building identical to its appearance today. Although the building at the time shown is used as a plumbing, heating, and carriage shop, it was fully utilized as an industrial facility. Because of the angle of the picture, it would seem as though there was no structure across the street on the northwest corner of Vernon Street at the time. (NCH.)

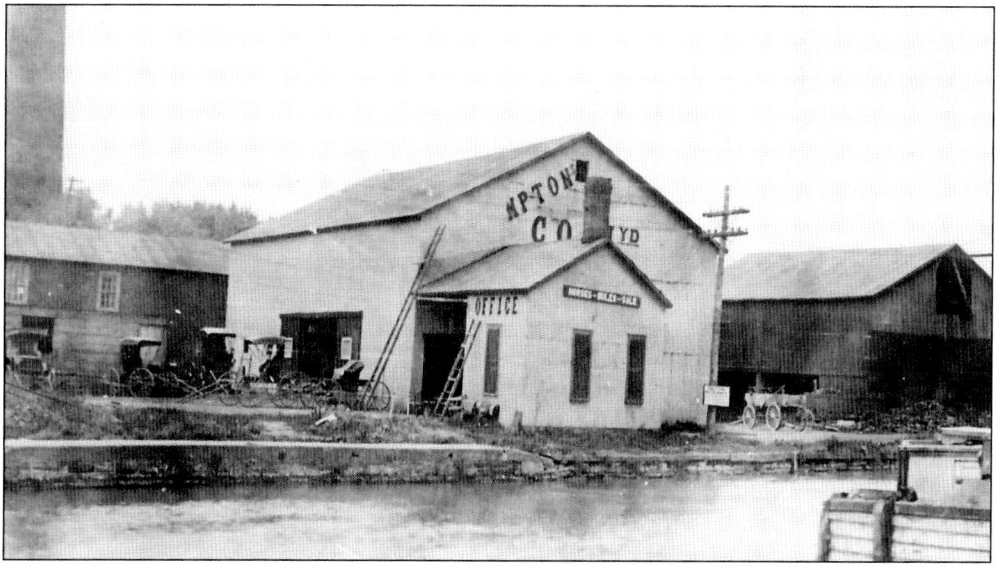

The old Compton and Bennett Works was located on the south canal bank, behind the west side of Main Street. The company made furniture and carriages and sold horses and mules. It also serviced the canal barges and general canal traffic. Later the site was the location of the Niagara Sprayer sulfur shed. (NCH.)

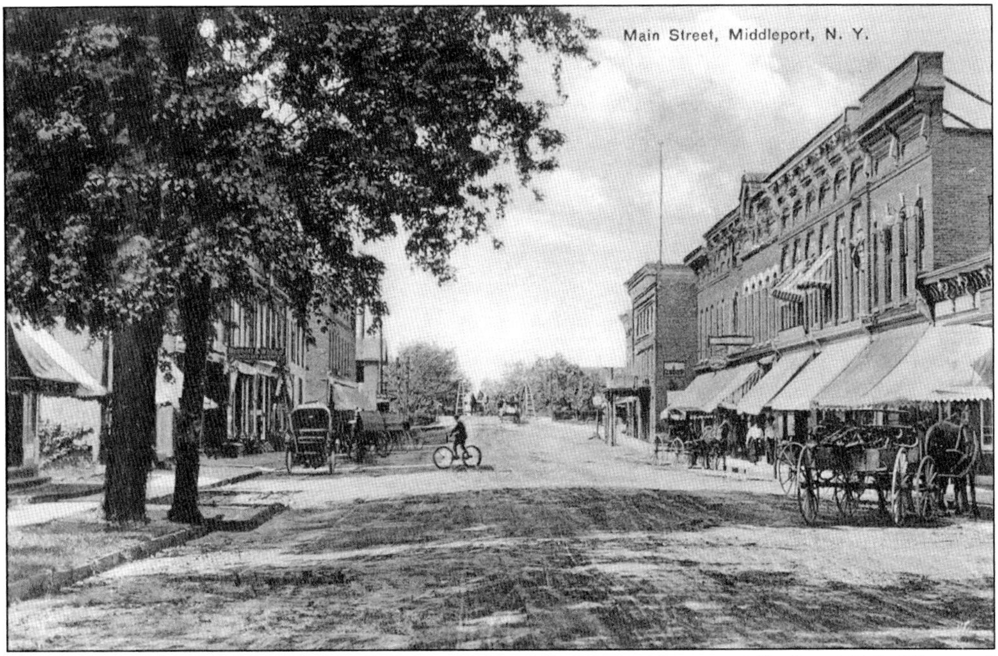

This view of Main Street looks north prior to the widening on the canal (before 1911). The rigid canal bridge is clearly in view as well as the Taylor Building on the left side, just before the canal. There is a great amount of activity in the village on the day this picture was taken. (NCH.)

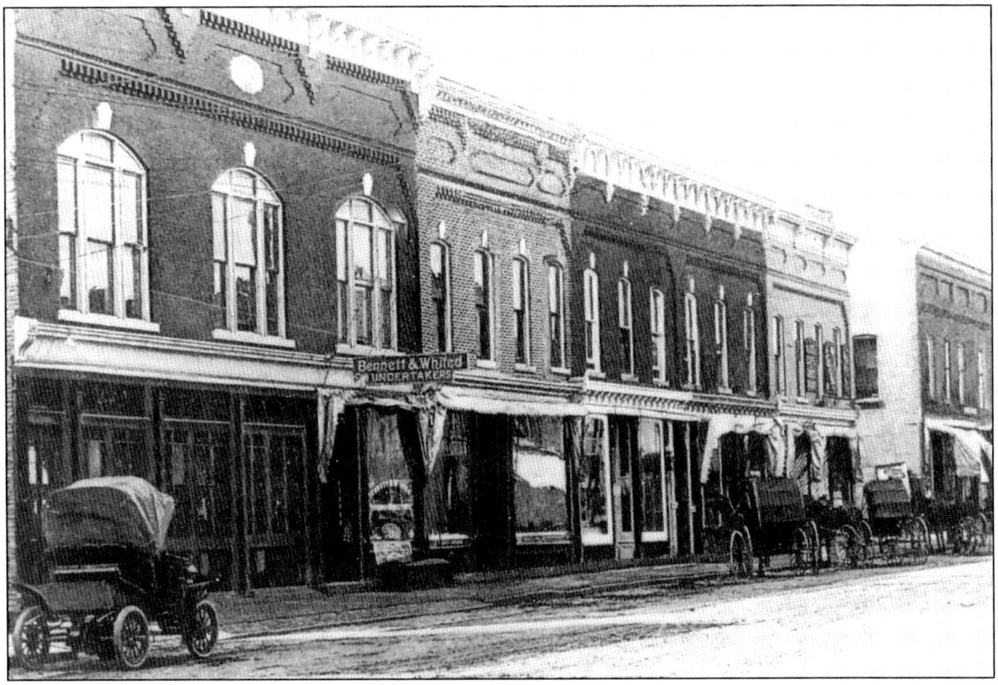

This photograph shows Main Street in 1900 upon the completion of the fireman's building, which was finished in 1892. A portion of that site was rented out to Bennett and Whited, Undertakers. On the far right is the Taylor Building, with the remaining structures the same as they are today. (MVH.)

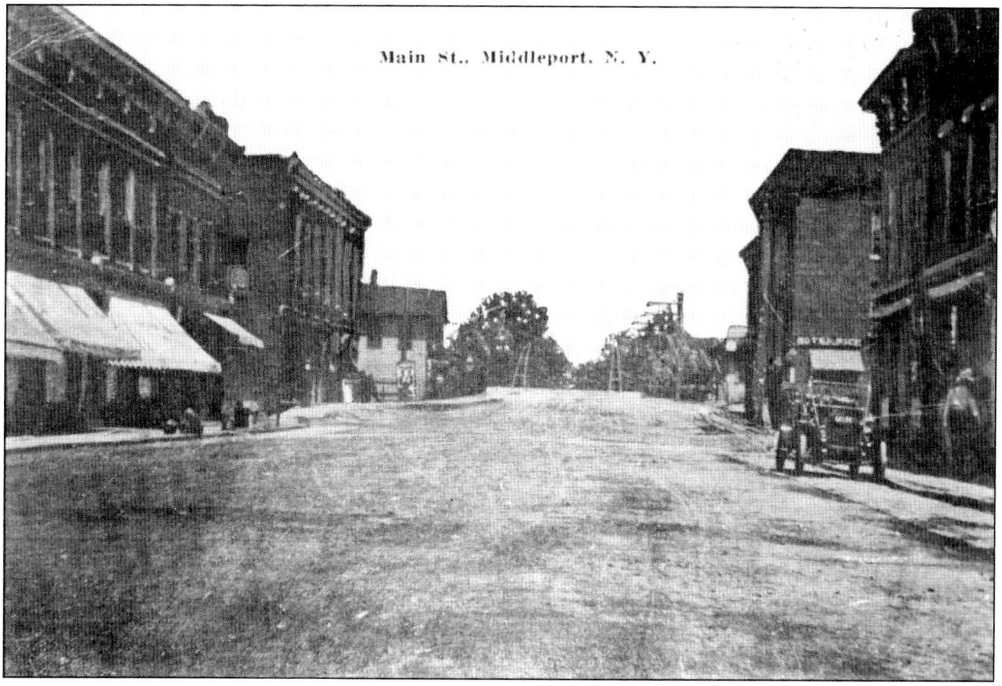

This is another view of Main Street in 1905. The automobile had made its way to town. The picture must have been taken early in the morning, as the area appears deserted. The Hotel Rich is visible on the right side of the street, just before the canal. (NCH.)

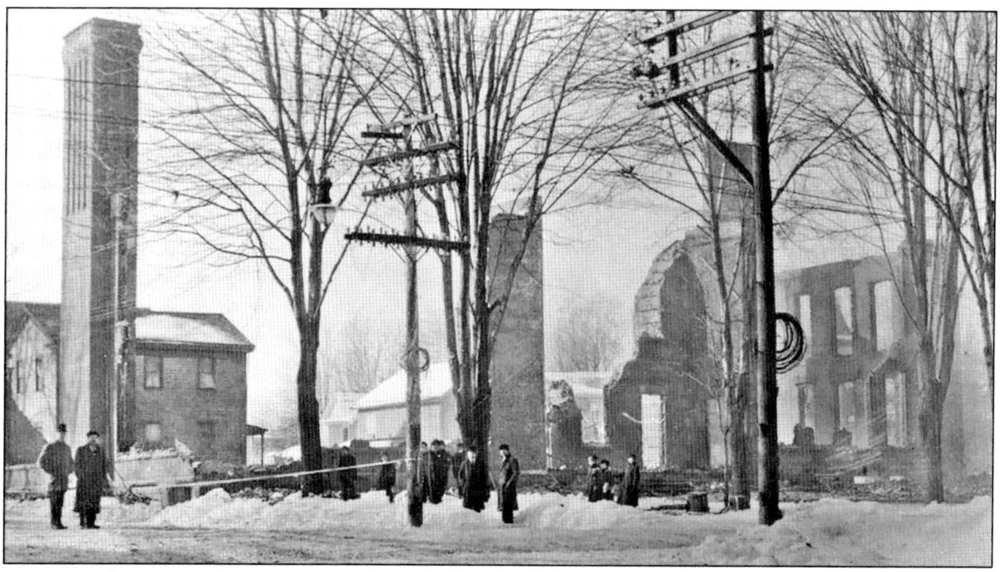

Here are the remnants of the Middleport Union School after the destructive fire of 1910. The house on the left (Vernon Street) side of the photograph is still standing today. The little that remained of the building attests to the intensity of the fire and its destruction. (Niagara County Historian's Office.)

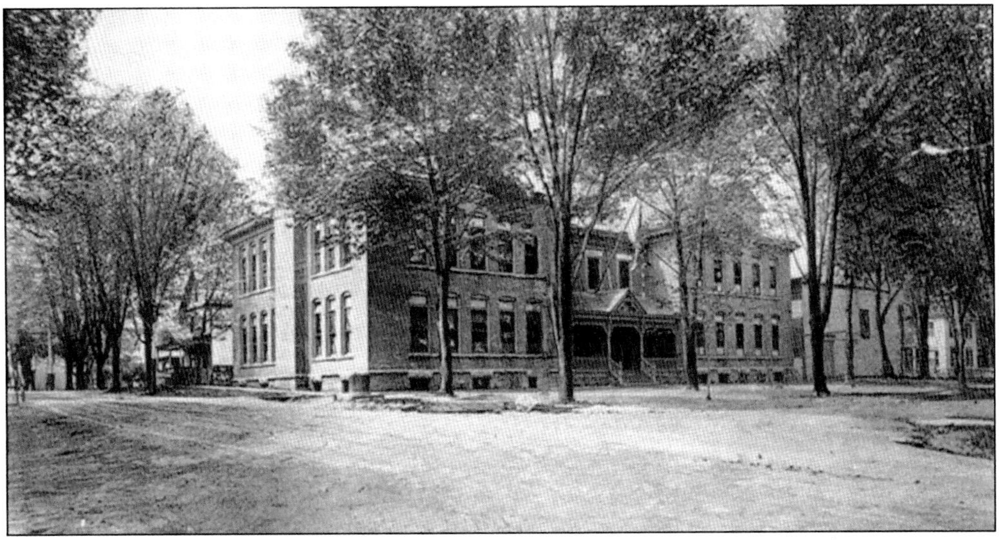

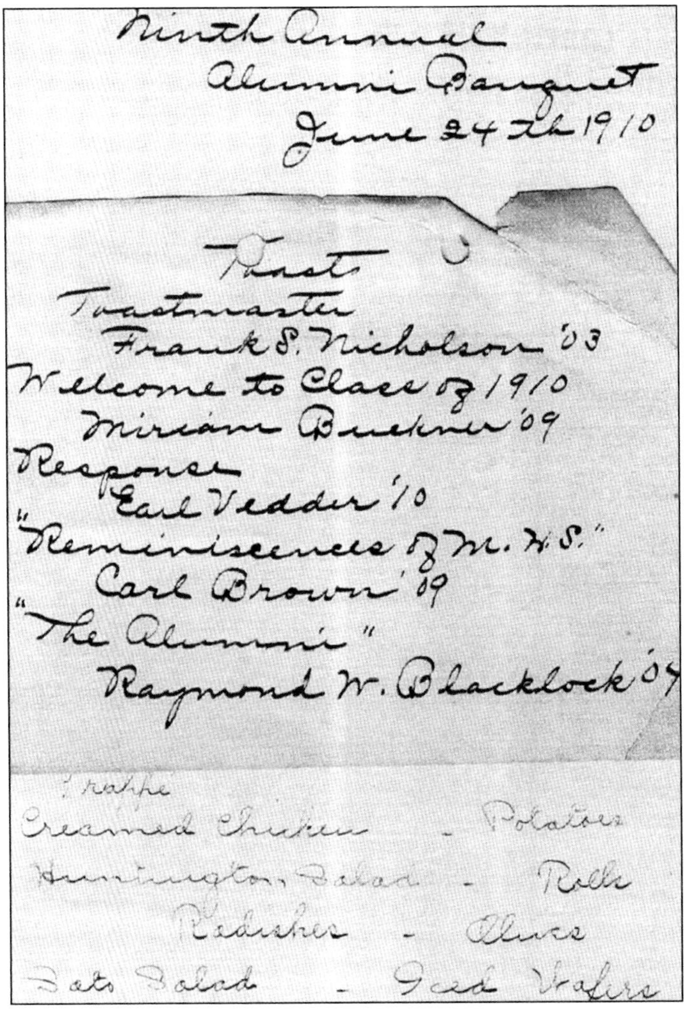

Ninth Annual
Alumni Banquet
June 24th 1910

Toasts
Toastmaster
Frank S. Nicholson '03
Welcome to Class of 1910
Miriam Buckner '09
Response
Earl Vedder '10
"Reminiscences of M. H. S."
Carl Brown '09
"The Alumni"
Raymond W. Blacklock '04

Frappe
Creamed Chicken - Potatoes
Huntington Salad - Rolls
Radishes - Olives
Date Salad - Iced Wafers

The magnificent Middleport Union School No. 1 building was located at the southwest corner of Vernon Street and Park Avenue. It served the community until it was destroyed by fire in the winter of 1910. Although the first school in Middleport was established in 1846, it was not located on this site but rather on Main Street. This building was opened in 1886. Graduating classes from the Middleport Union School usually numbered between seven and 10 students. (MVH.)

The Ninth Annual Alumni Banquet was on June 24, 1910. This is a handwritten invitation for attendance at the event, which was held at the high school. It lists the speakers, with Frank Nicholson, class of 1903, as toastmaster. It also details the lunch menu, which consisted of chicken and potatoes. (Richard Keihl.)

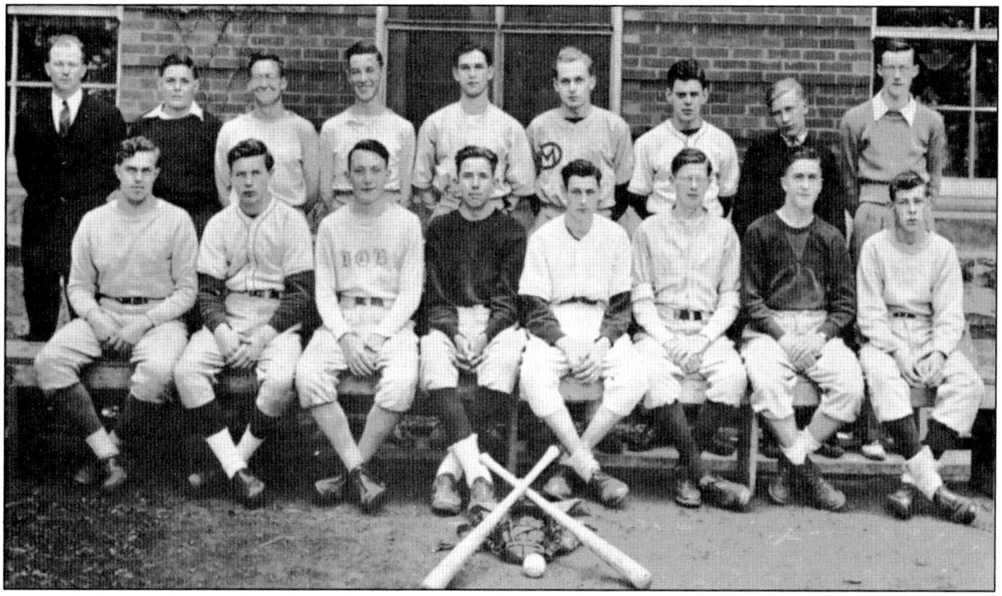

Chris Farrell coached the 1939 Middleport High School baseball team. Many well-known residents of the village were on that team: Roy Wheeler, George Droman, George Mufford, Fran Winters, and Dave March. Chris Farrell coached every sport at Middleport High School for many years and is fondly recalled by those who remember. (Author's collection.)

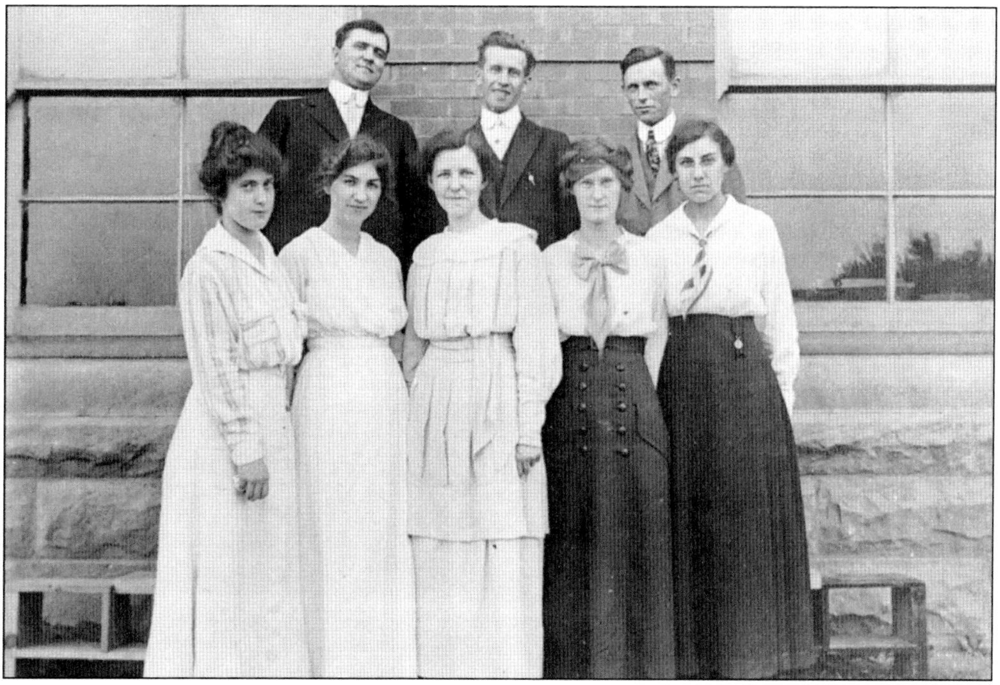

The Middleport High School faculty in 1916 is pictured here. From left to right are (first row) Ms. Smeador, Ms. Moger, Ms. Bernhard, Ms. Swift, and Ms. Yates; (second row) Professor Armstrong, Mr. Devereaux, and Mr. Blanchard. These eight instructors taught all classes to all grades. At that time, there were few students, and even less continued onto high school for eventual graduation. The faculty remained in their positions, usually for their entire working lives. (MVH.)

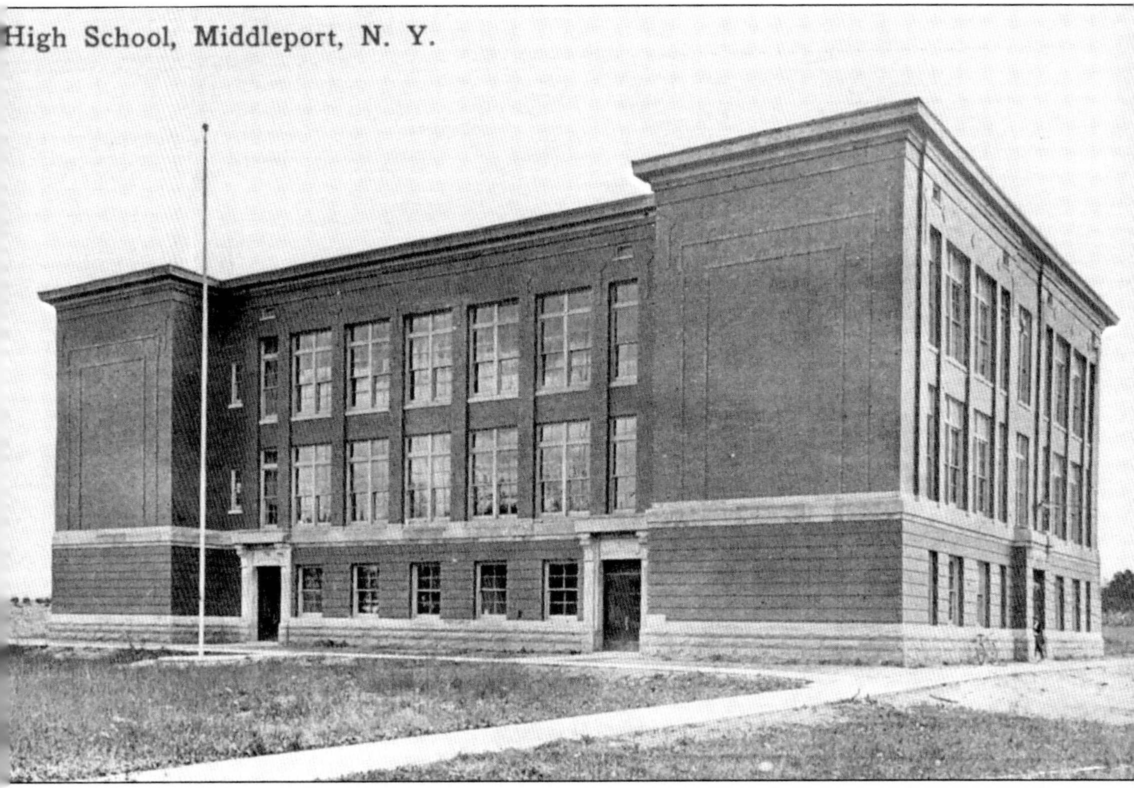

Middleport High School is pictured above. It was opened on September 4, 1911. This part of today's school remains virtually unchanged except that the original front doors have been filled in with cinder blocks. There have been major expansions over the years. The years 1950–1951 saw the addition of the gymnasium and the classrooms in the rear as well as the terraced athletic fields and tennis courts. In 1958, two elementary schools were constructed, one in Middleport and the other in Gasport. In 1963, additional classrooms were added along with the swimming pool. In the 1990s, modifications were made to the 1963 expansion, and finally, in the early 2000s, a small gymnasium was added along with more classrooms along the east side. (Richard Keihl.)

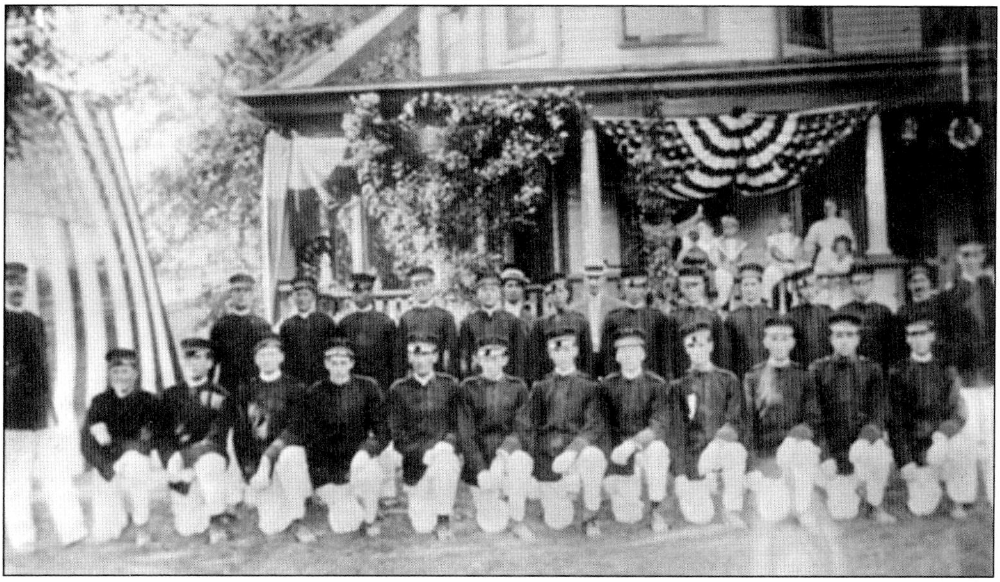

The Middleport Fire Department was established for three different organizations, one of which was the Spaulding Hose Company pictured here. They had their own territory within the village and would assist the others in times of need. This photograph is from 1911, at which time they were participating in the cornerstone celebration. (Richard Keihl.)

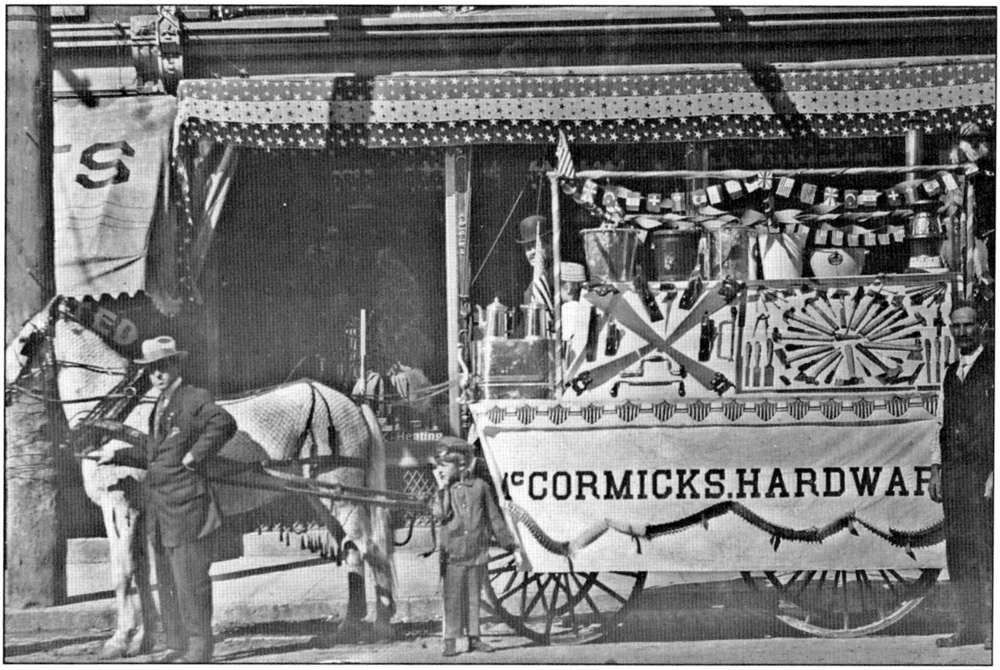

The McCormick's Hardware float is pictured here for the September 4, 1915, parade. The store itself was located on the east side of Main Street, where the Snell Hardware store was later located. The parade was a major event, so many of the local merchants participated. (Richard Keihl.)

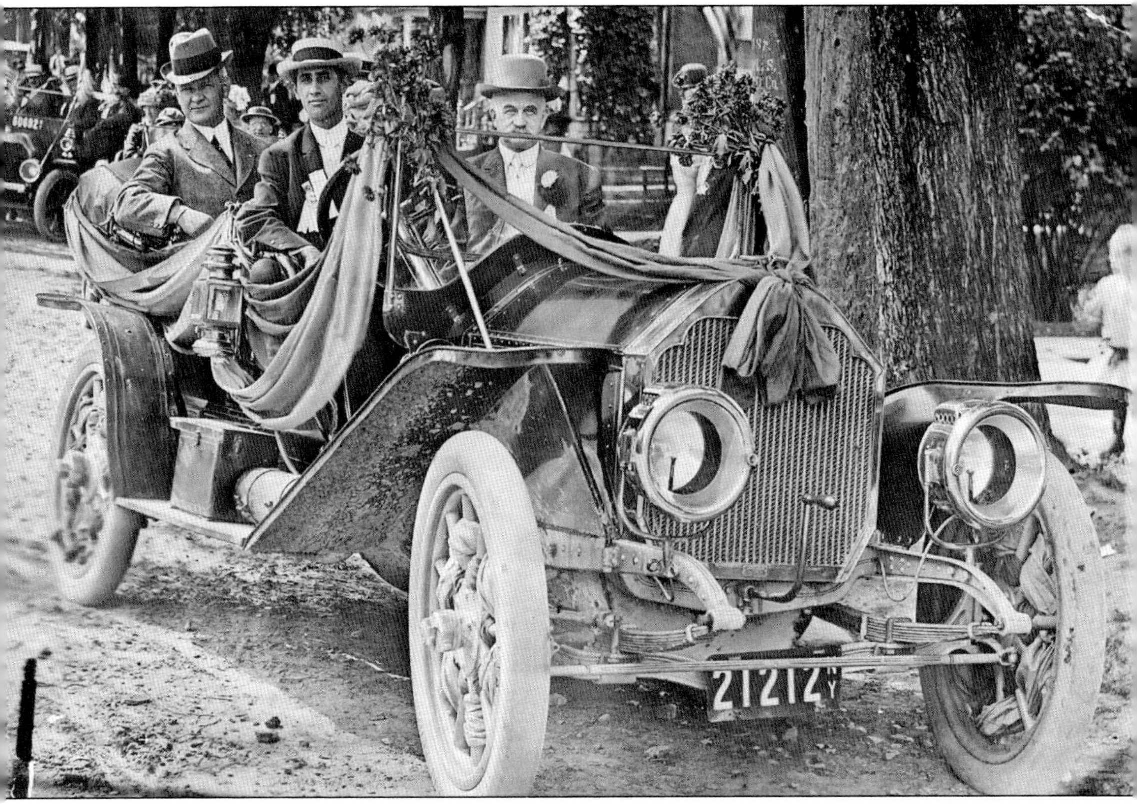

September 4, 1911, was a significant day of celebration. Middleport had major events that occurred almost simultaneously. The new school was dedicated on that date and the widening of the Erie Canal with its changes had been completed. Pictured are the parade officials preparing to lead the event. The changes within the village were monumental in that the configuration and width of Main Street had been altered because of the widening of the canal, the new high school had been completed on the east end of State Street, the electric trolley service had been operative for five years, and new houses were completed on the Park Avenue site of the old high school. (Richard Keihl.)

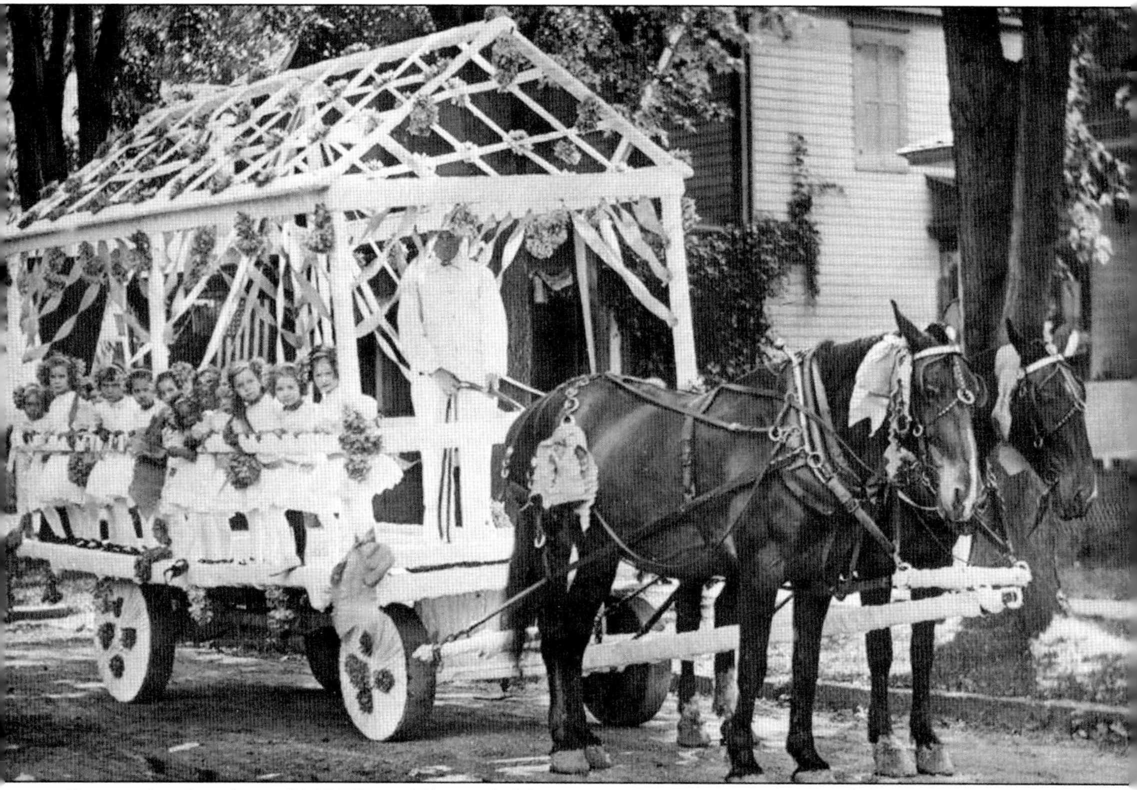

Pictured is the class of 1924 float. These children were the youngest to attend the new school and would have been only five or six years old. There appears to be 11 students in the class—all girls! The photograph was taken on the west side of Main Street, near today's post office. This float was part of the parade celebrating the laying of the cornerstone for the new school on September 4, 1911. These students would have graduated and moved on just prior to the Great Depression, thus escaping Middleport's turmoil during that time. One has to wonder why there were no boys enrolled in school at that time. (Richard Keihl.)

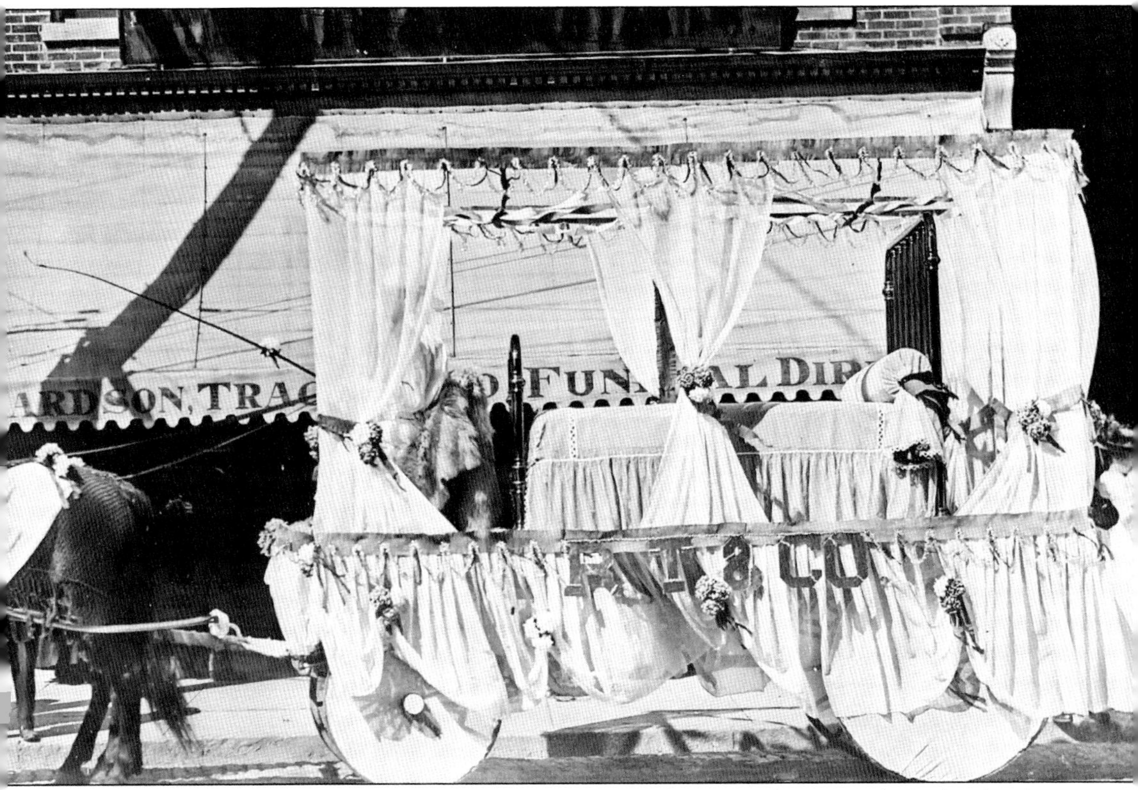

The float for the Richardson Undertakers was entered in the September 4 parade. Richardson's was not located on Main Street; the morticians on Main Street were Taylor and Whited. Richardson's was located on State Street but was prosperous nonetheless. The importance of the Richardson enterprise is demonstrated by the grandeur of its float. Sadly, however, the Richardson Undertakers failed during the Great Depression and left Middleport forever. The fact that so many photographic postcards were produced demonstrates the importance of the day. Seemingly, anyone with a commercial interest created a means of advertisement for the event. (Richard Keihl.)

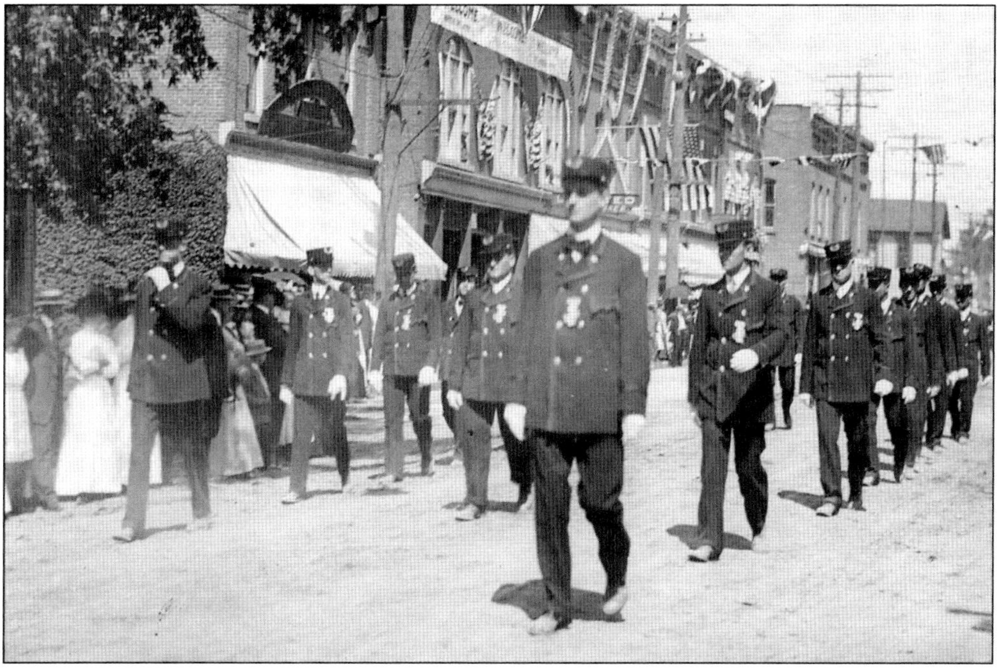

The fire department, or in this case, one of the fire departments, has always been a major component of Middleport events. The September 4 celebration was no exception, as these firemen proudly march in full uniform. The fact that there were three separate fire departments at this time made the event more exciting, as well as competitive. (Richard Keihl.)

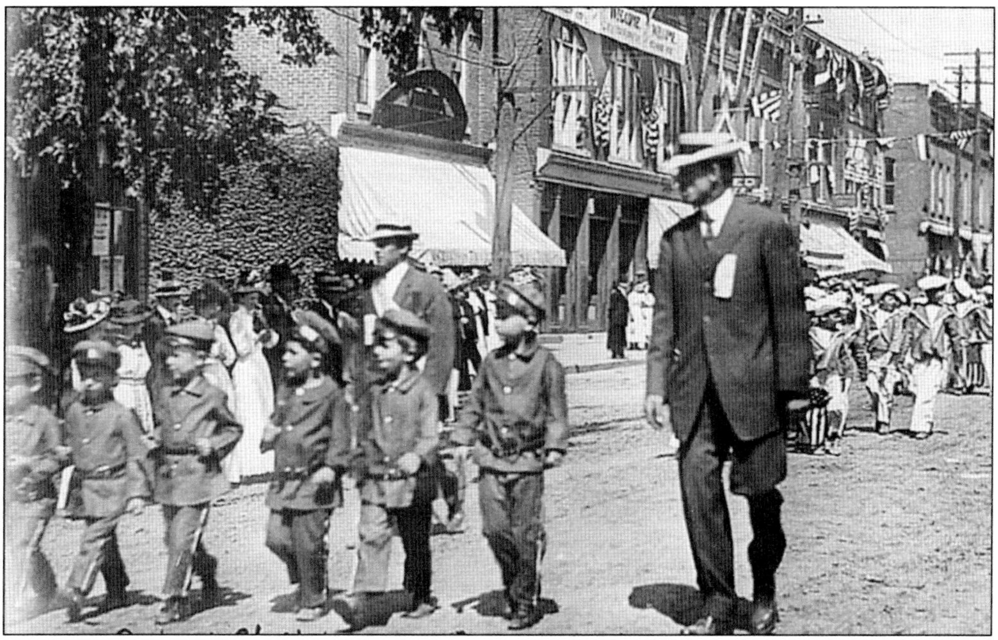

These schoolboys were part of the September 4 parade. The young men in the lead wore their military-style uniforms, while the trailing group wore sailor-styled uniforms. The picture is truly symbolic of the times with the men in suits with hats, the ladies dressed in gowns, and the children clad in uniforms. (RTH.)

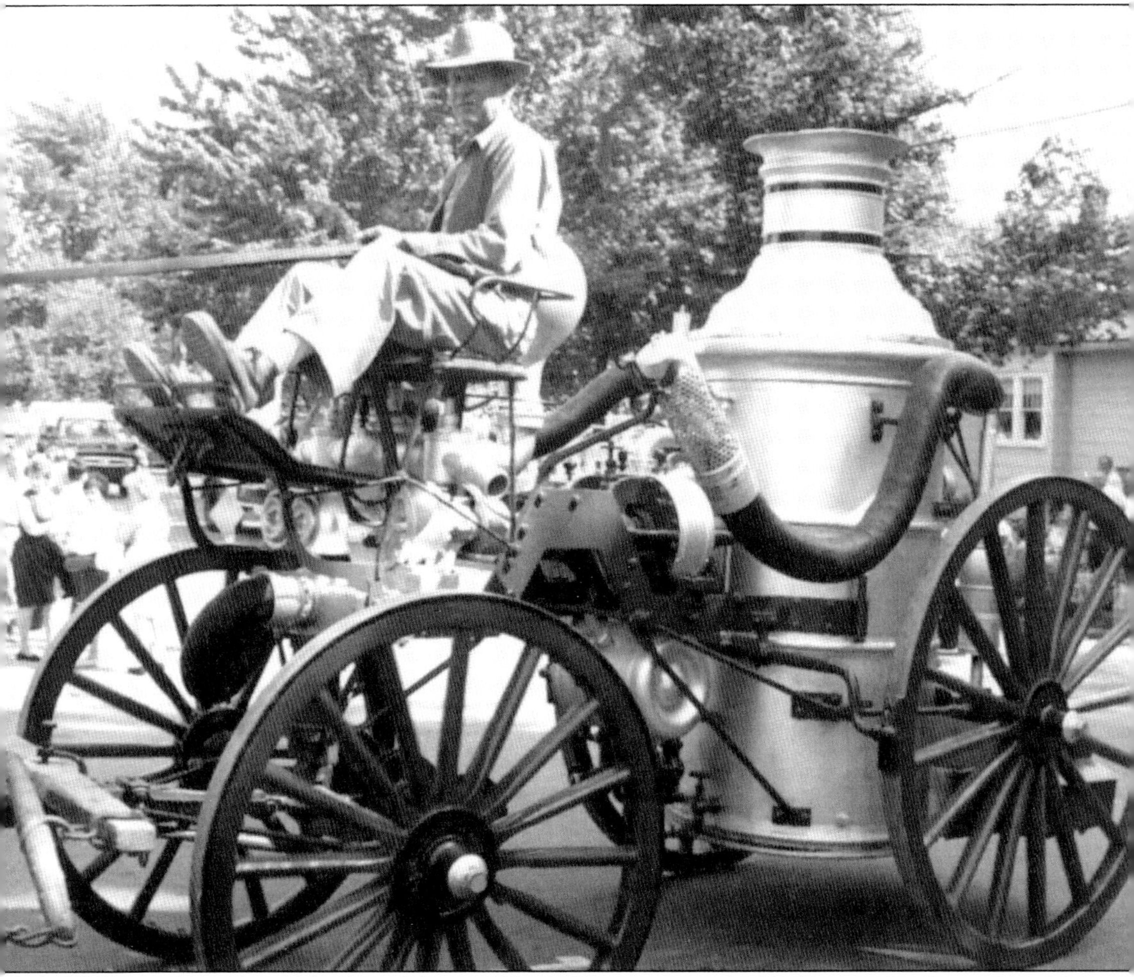

One of the enduring aspects of the Middleport fire companies over the years has been the 1893 steam fire engine shown in this photograph. During the late 1800s, there were no pressurized water lines readily available for use, so the method of the day was to use steam to propel the water. That was accomplished through a device like the one shown. Middleport has preserved this particular piece of firefighting equipment and it is still in excellent condition. It can be viewed at the Middleport Fire Hall on Main Street. Very few of these engines remain anywhere in the United States, so Middleport is indeed fortunate to have it. It would probably be more difficult to find a set of draft horses to pull it down the street. (MVH.)

The Universalist Church was the first church to be constructed in the village. The exterior is of the local cobblestone style. The parsonage is connected directly to the church. During the 1950s, the church itself was rented to the local school for use as classrooms while the school was being expanded. Today the church is still used as a religious site and continues to be one of the architectural gems of the village. (MVH.)

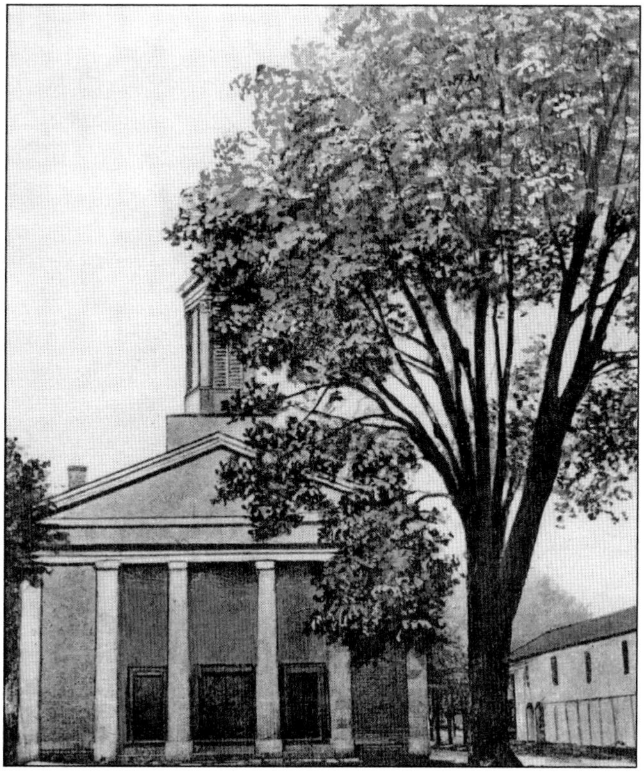

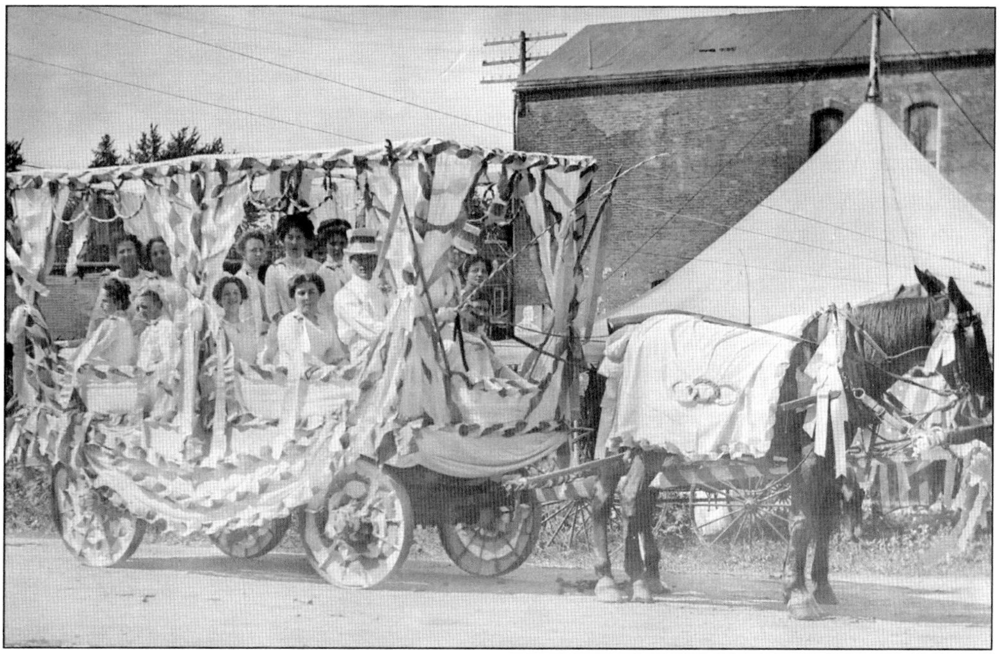

The Purity Rebecca Lodge float is pictured in the September 4, 1911, parade. This was a social organization with religious backing. The interesting aspect of this picture is the building in the background. It was located at the southwest corner of Vernon and State Streets and was both an opera house and Ford automobile dealership before it was demolished. (Richard Keihl.)

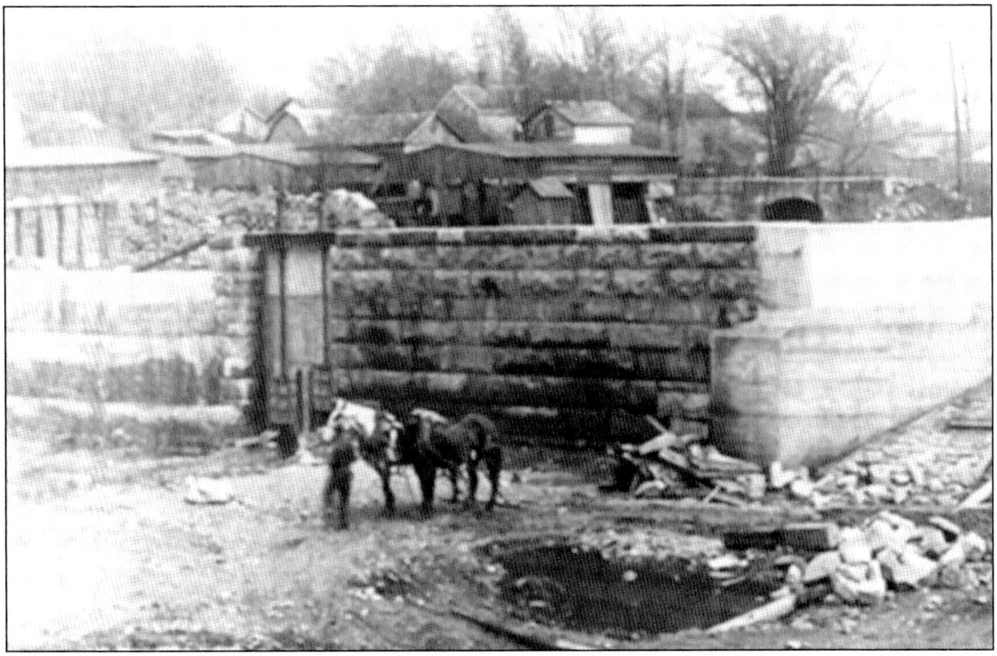

When the last expansion of the canal occurred in 1910 and 1911, a spillway was constructed on its south side to accommodate any overflow. This structure is in use today and is located off Church Street at the juncture of the canal and Jeddo Creek, into which it flows. (RTH.)

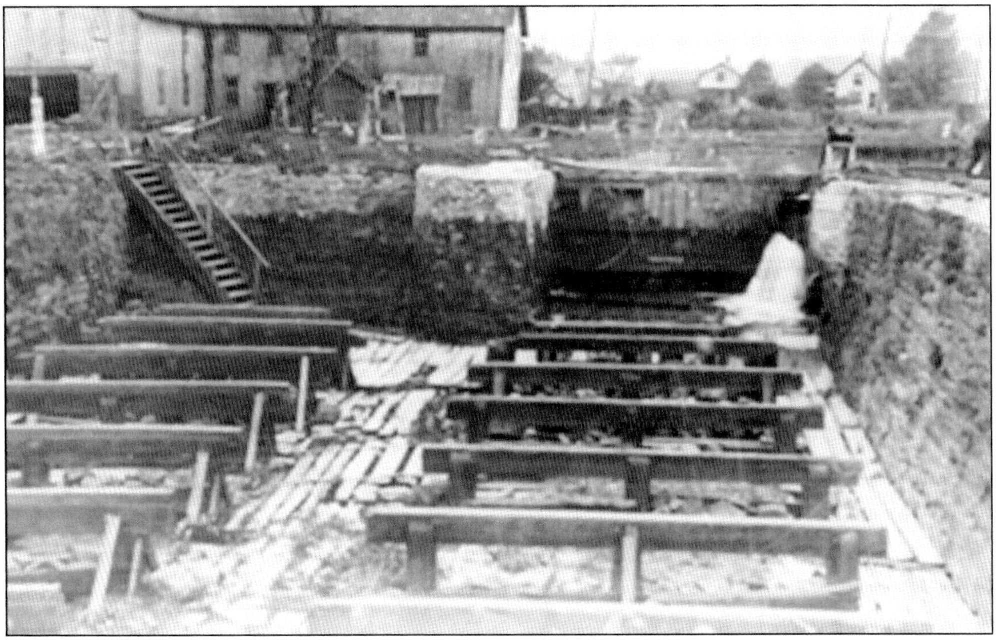

The C. J. Haines dry dock was located off Church Street and Watson Avenue near today's Basket Factory Restaurant. The lock from the canal actually emptied from the Log Pond behind the restaurant. The facility was used to repair barges and was a casualty of the widening of the canal. (RTH.)

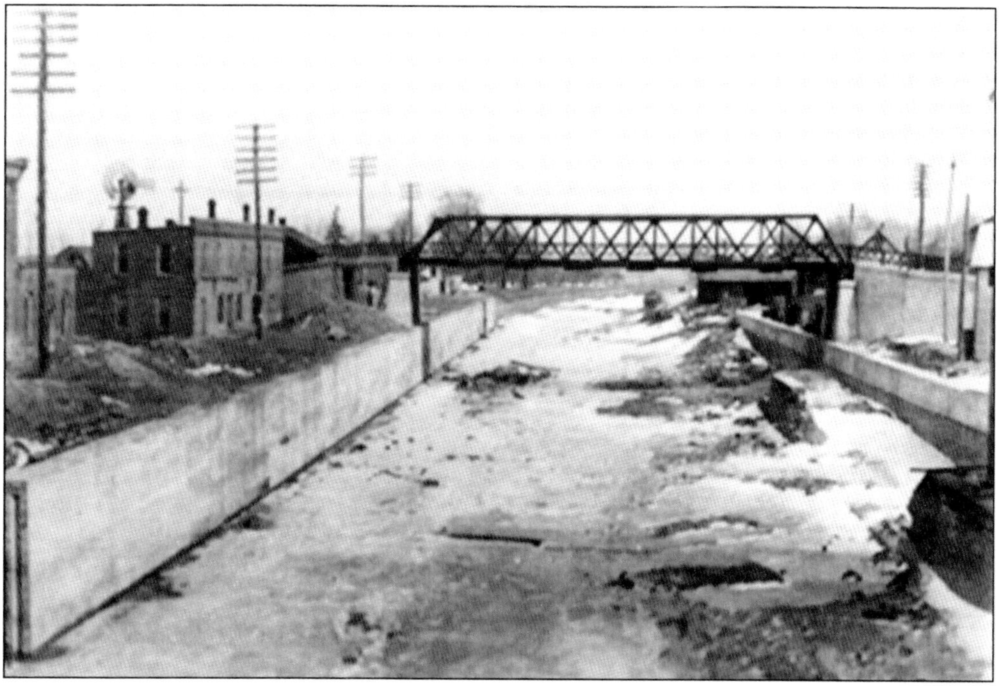

Pictured is a view of the recently completed Vernon Street Bridge in 1911. On the right side of the picture, some of the old width canal wall has yet to be removed. On the north end of the bridge is a building that would become Tony's in the 1930s. The bridge remained until the early 21st century. (RTH.)

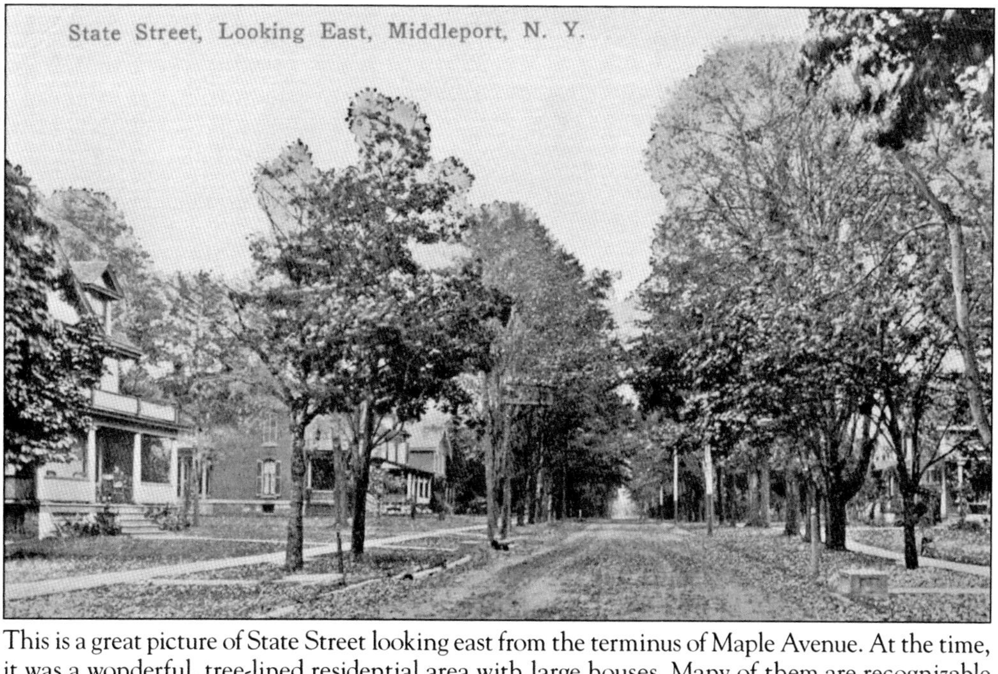

This is a great picture of State Street looking east from the terminus of Maple Avenue. At the time, it was a wonderful, tree-lined residential area with large houses. Many of them are recognizable today. Robertson Street does not appear between the two houses on the left, indicating that it probably was not there at the time, around 1910. (Richard Keihl.)

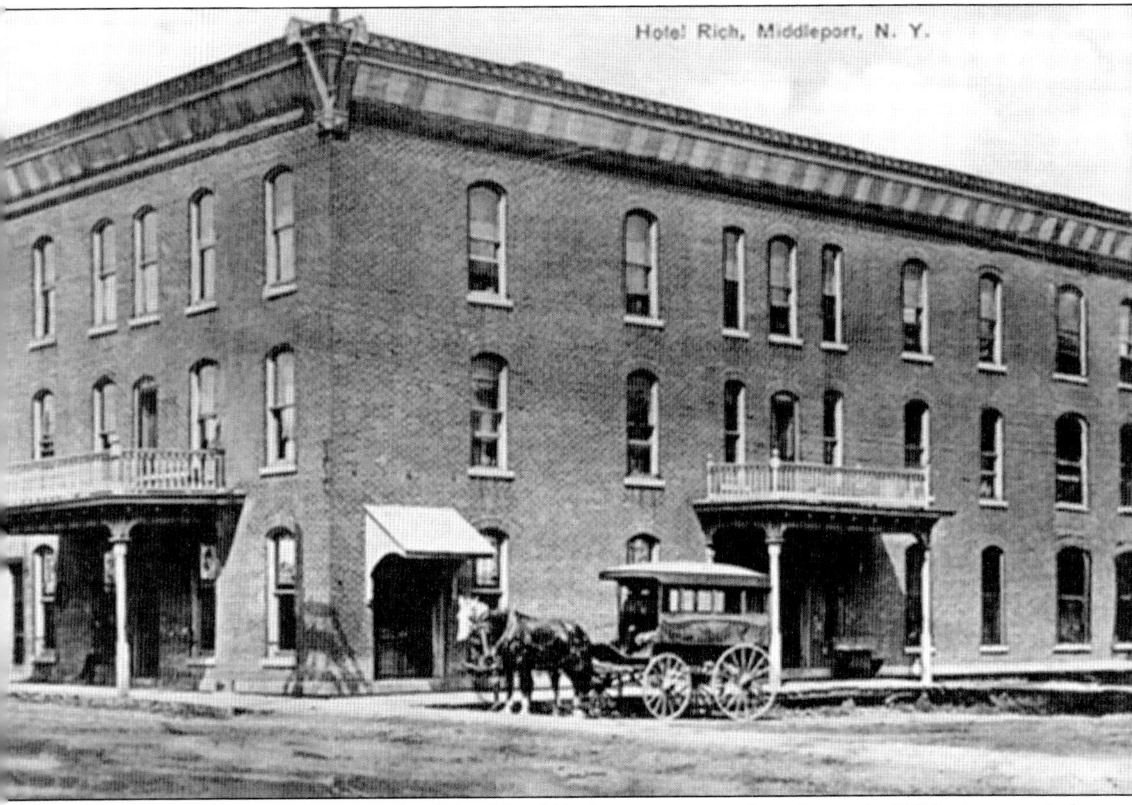

This is a wonderful photograph of the Hotel Rich as it appeared in the early 1920s. It occupied the northeast corner of Main and State Streets. It was a huge building for a small village. The horse and carriage brought patrons from the railroad station to the hotel. From the 1890s until the 1960s when it was demolished, it was known as the Rich, the International, and the Fenton Hotel. Various businesses occupied the ground floor, such as the Middleport Savings and Loan, Jackling and Shaw Insurance, and Fowler's Barber Shop. The rear of the hotel occupied the south canal bank. The intersection of the road was the busiest in the area since the original Route 31 came south of Main Street and east on State Street. In the 1940s, the Greyhound bus service made its Middleport stop in front of the hotel. This lasted until the hotel was taken down. (RTH.)

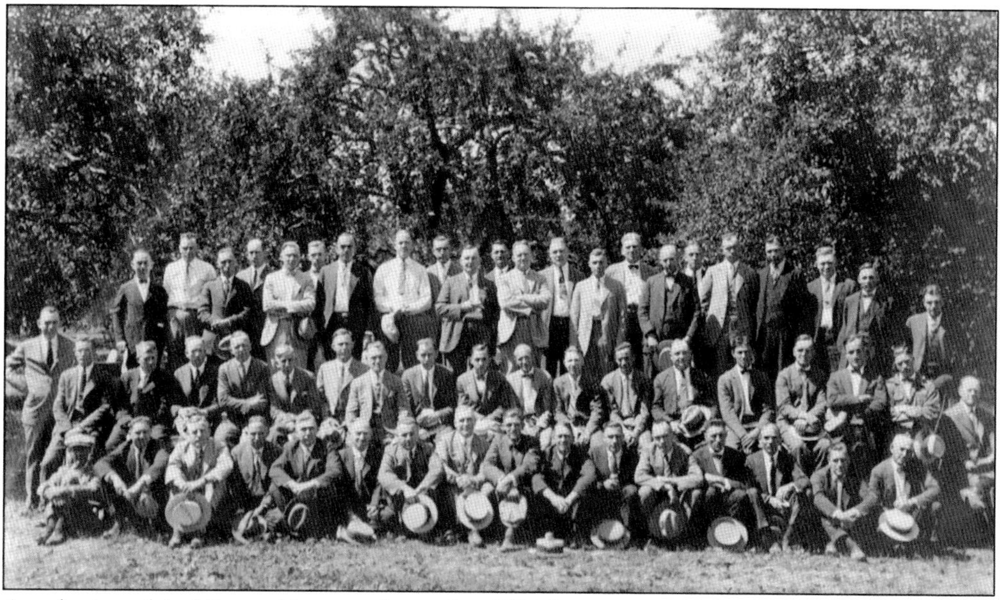

A gathering of the Niagara Sprayer sales staff in 1926 demonstrates the size of the company and its influence upon Middleport. As a local business, it had a dramatic impact upon the area in terms of employment, either directly or because of its peripheral contracts with other local businesses. It became Niagara Chemical in the 1940s and still employed a large number of people. (MVH.)

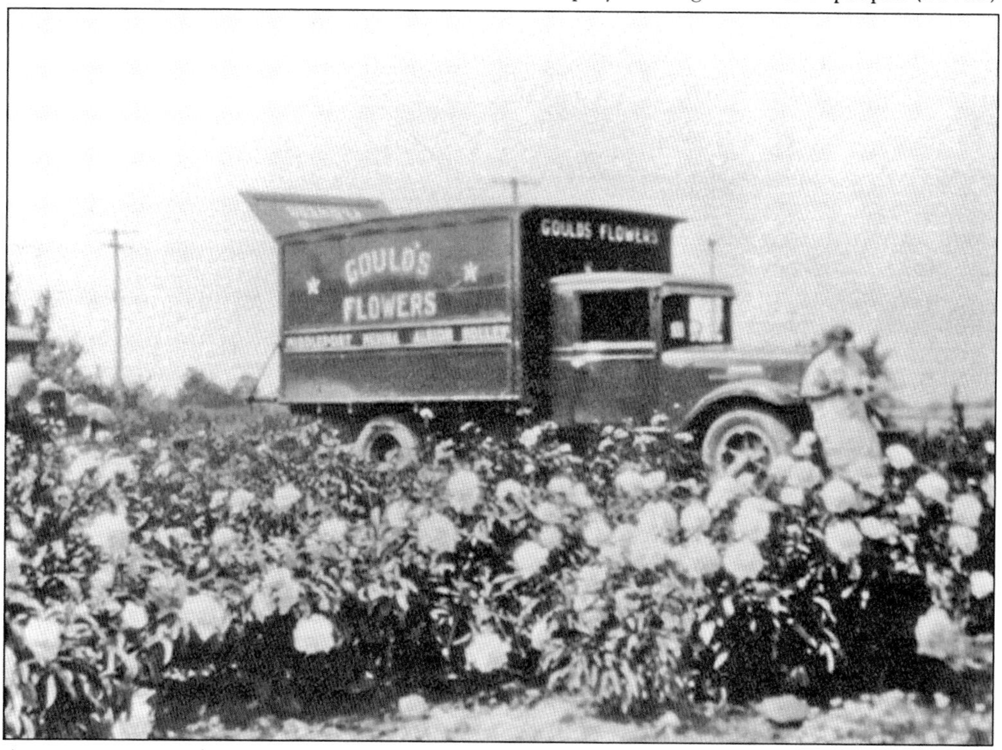

A major commercial concern within the village was Gould's Flowers, which had massive greenhouses located between Mechanic and Sleeper Streets and offices on North Hartland Street. Gould's also had shops in Lockport, Medina, and Albion. (MVH.)

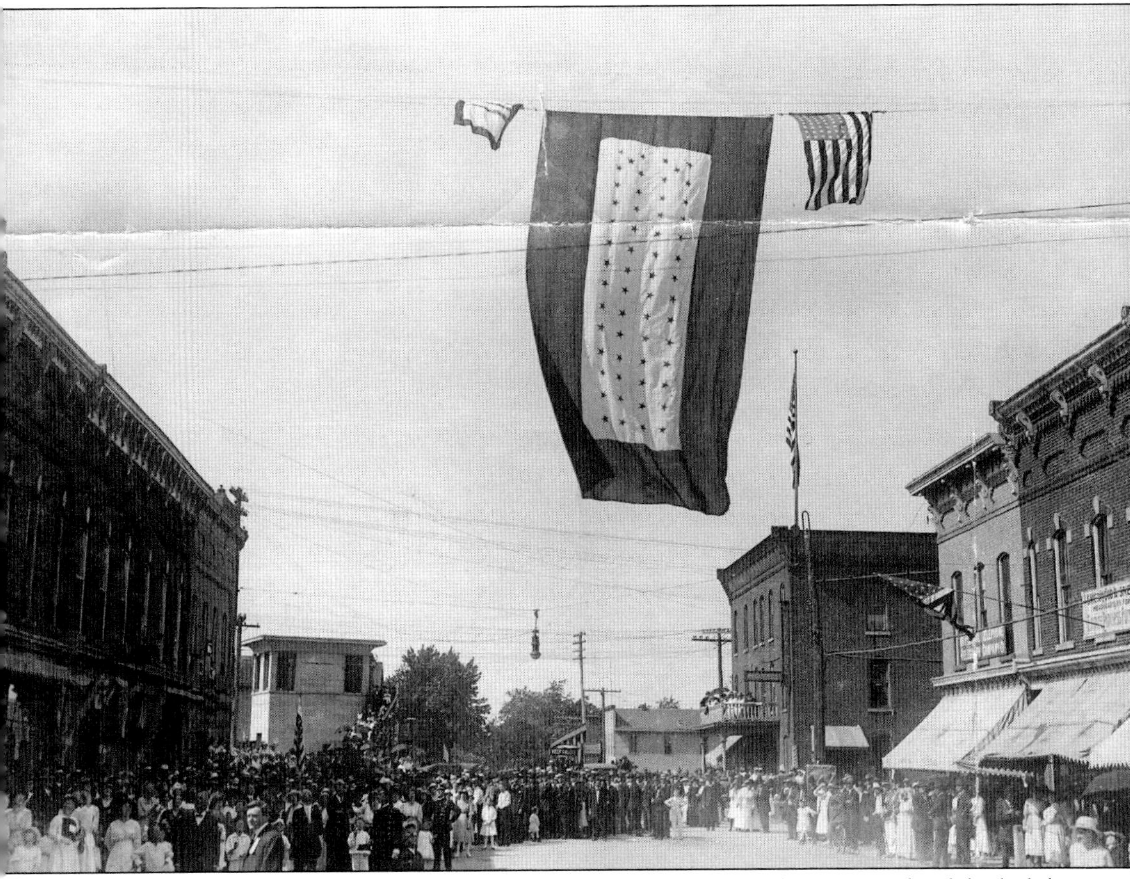

Middleport's Fourth of July celebration in 1914 was a gala event. The magnitude of the holiday was enhanced by the fact that the New York state senator for the district was George Thompson. Not only was he a Middleport resident, he was also president of Niagara Sprayer Company, the largest enterprise in the village. In the picture, the sign on the large building in the rear says "International Hotel," and the lift bridge was raised to half-height. This would indicate that there were probably many boats either in the village or passing through as part of the event. Note the tremendous number of people occupying the downtown for the occasion and their attire. The women are dressed in their finest gowns, while the men are equally dignified for the event. The people are even fully occupying the stairway to the bridge tower. George Thompson was elected for two terms. (Richard Keihl.)

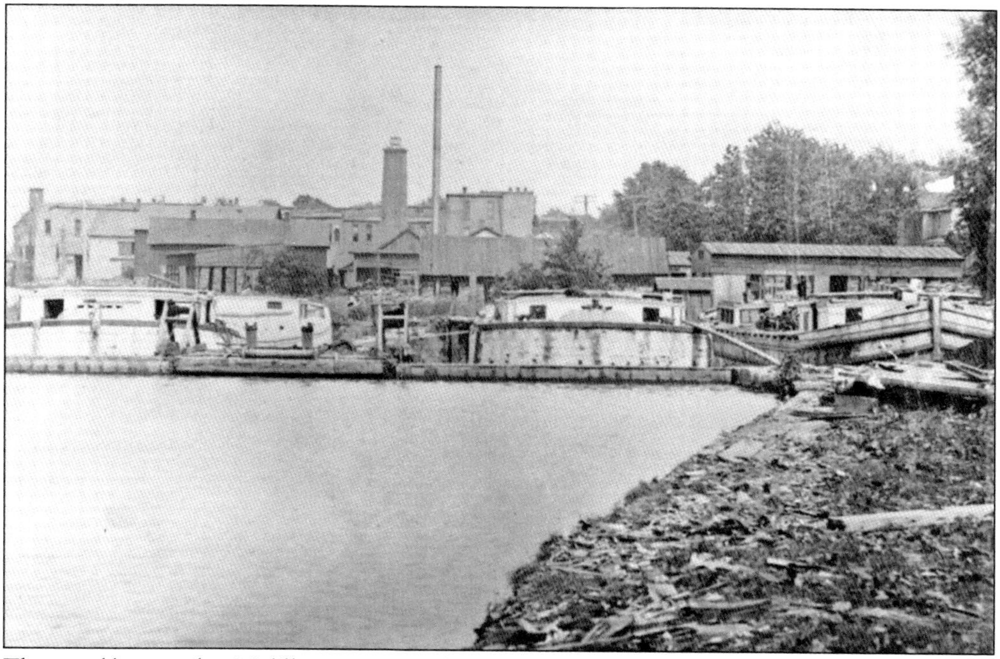

The canal boatyard in Middleport occupied the area immediately behind Main Street on the west side. Later much of this canal "wide water" area would be filled and the boatyard would disappear. This photograph is from 1880 and shows what appear to be barges under construction. (MVH.)

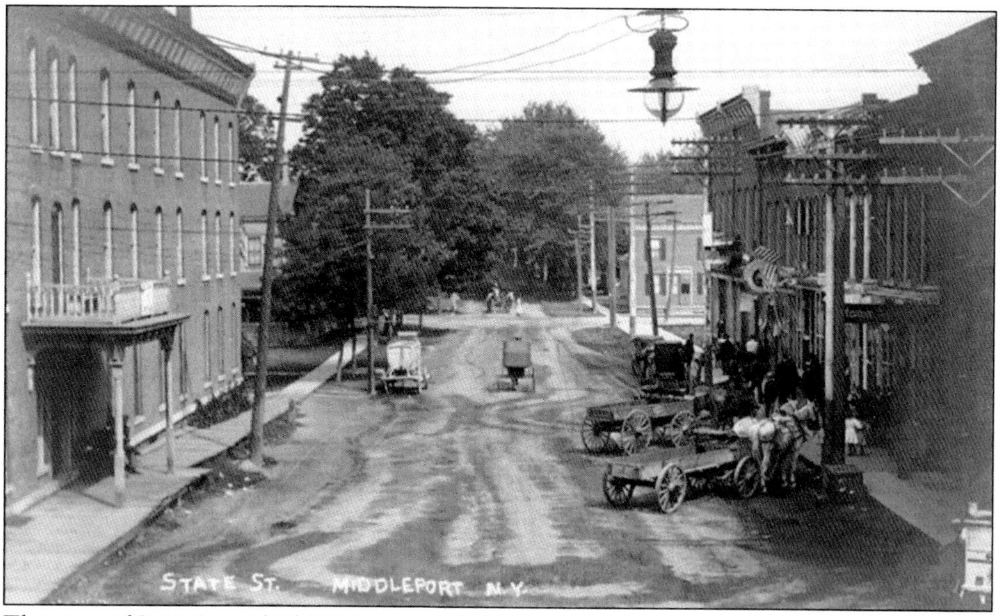

This view of State Street looking east around 1900 was used for the sesquicentennial painting on the State Street building in 2009. The merchants along the south side appear to have a great deal of business the day the picture was taken. Even the dirt street has traffic leaving town. (MVH.)

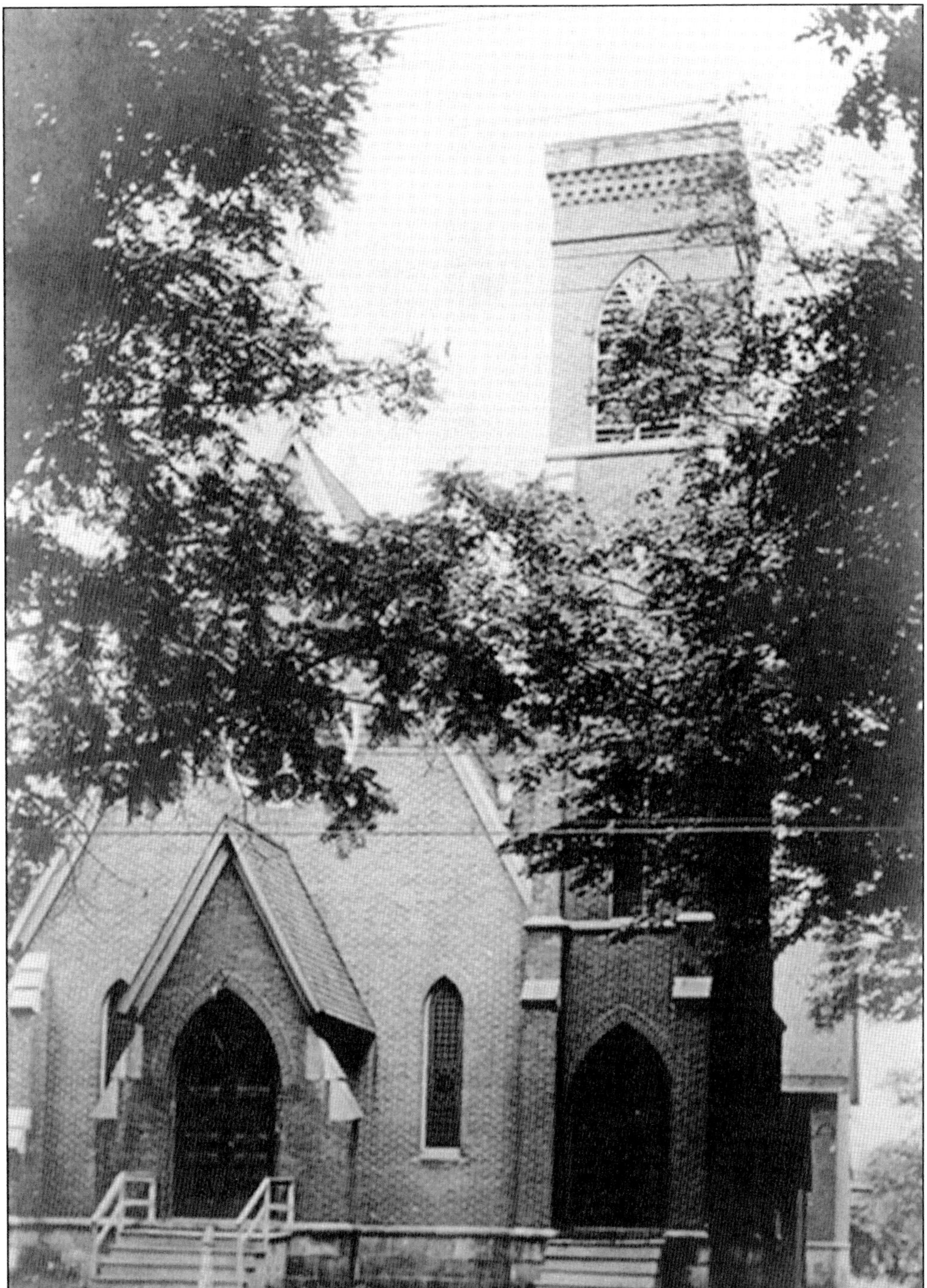

The original Episcopal Church was located on Main Street, south of Church Street on the west side. The building is still a church today. Interestingly, after the bell tower was completed, the Village of Middleport paid $25 a year in rent to use it as a fire observatory. (MVH.)

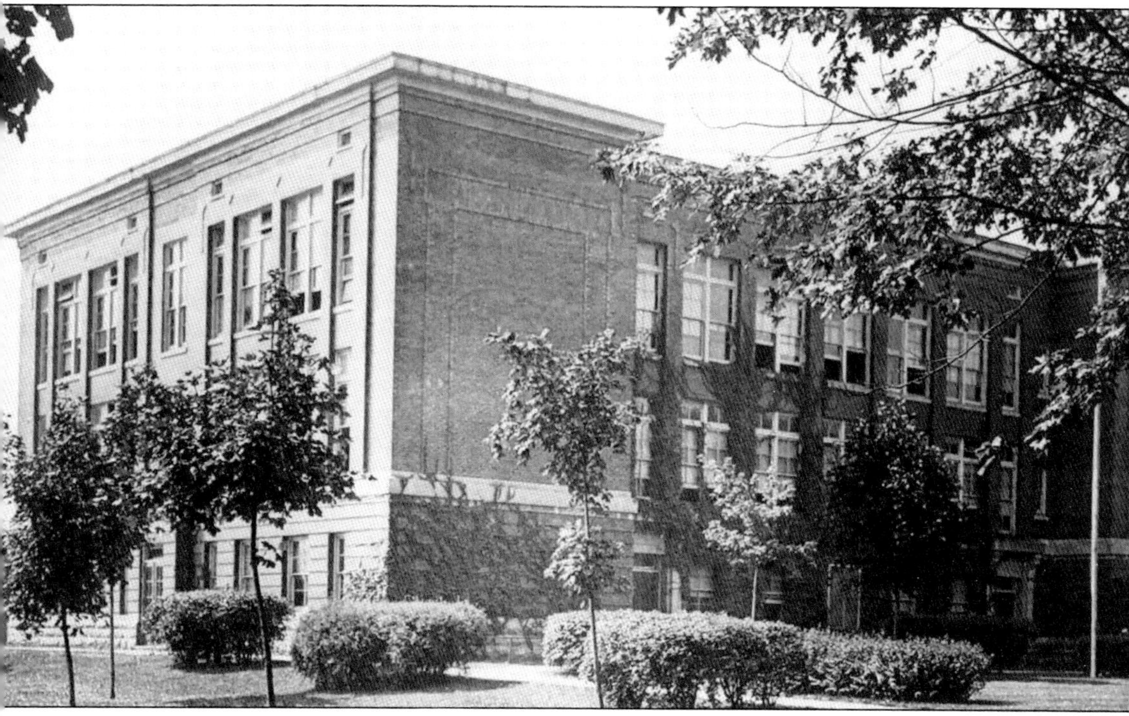

The new Middleport School was completed and dedicated in 1911. Little has changed in the building to the present day, except there have been numerous additions. The two front entrances were blocked in during the 1950 expansion and that remains the only change to the original edifice. Until 1958, this building housed the entire student body, kindergarten through 12th grade. Until 1950, the auditorium and the gymnasium were the same room (very low ceilings for basketball!). That room today is the media center on the first floor. From 1911 until 1946, the building was the Middleport School, but from 1946 until 1958, it was the Middleport School of the Royalton Hartland Central District. In 1958, it had no elementary students, and from 2005 onward, it has housed only high schoolers. (NCH.)

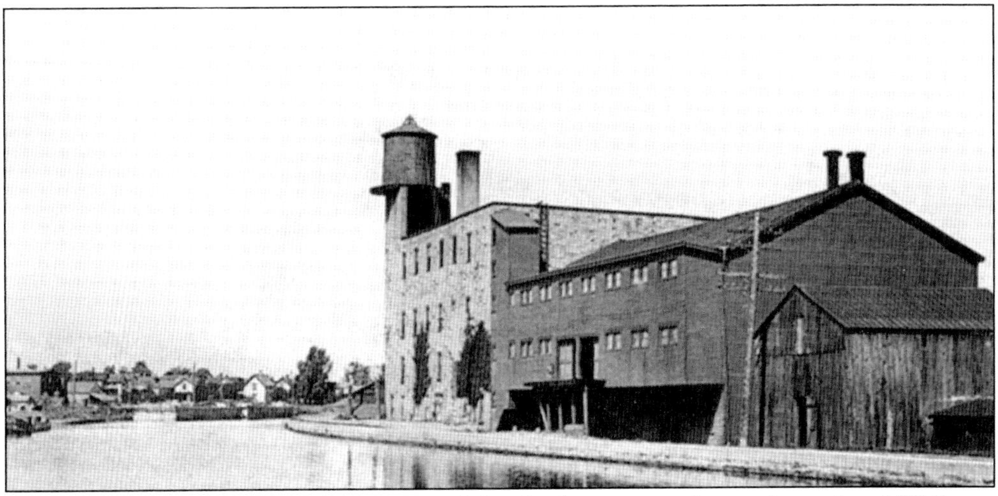

The Batavia Preservation Company operated this food-processing factory located on Mill Street at its intersection with North Hartland Street. It took the local produce and either prepared it or shipped it by canal barge to markets along the canal route. By the 1950s, it had been purchased by Longview Farms of Gowanda, New York. It was lost to fire a few years later. (NCH.)

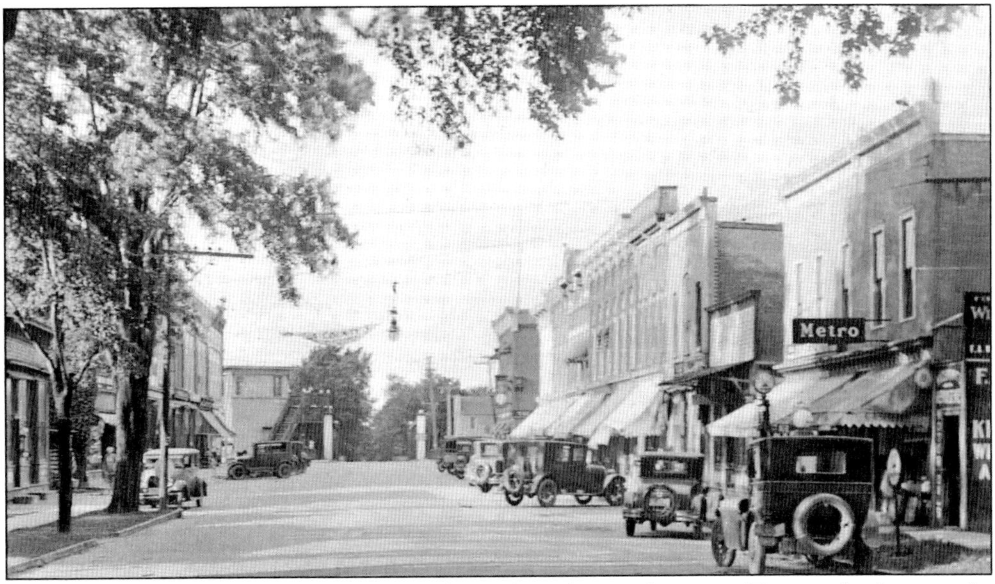

The Main Street of Middleport has changed significantly over the years. These early photographs show many buildings, which can still be distinguished, but probably more structures that no longer exist. The devastation to the downtown during the 1960s when many buildings were demolished in anticipation of a mini-mall has never been eased by its non-existence. (MVH.)

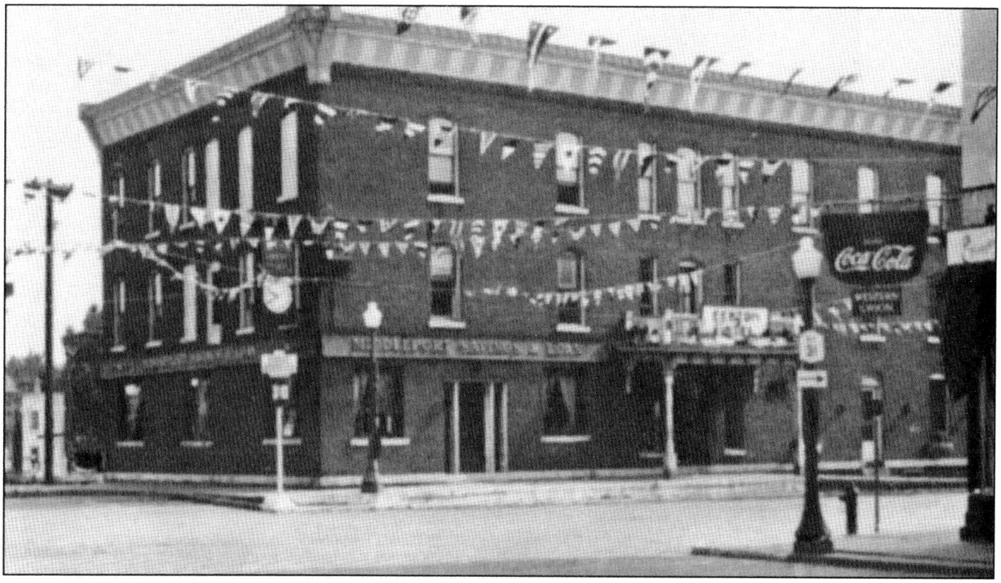

Pictured here is the Fenton Hotel as it appeared during its most prosperous period—the 1940s. As the original Rich Hotel, it eventually became the property of George Fenton. The Middleport Savings and Loan occupied much of the ground floor, along with a barroom and a dining room. It contained a full-service restaurant. Of course, many of Middleport's finest gatherings were held at the Fenton. (MVH.)

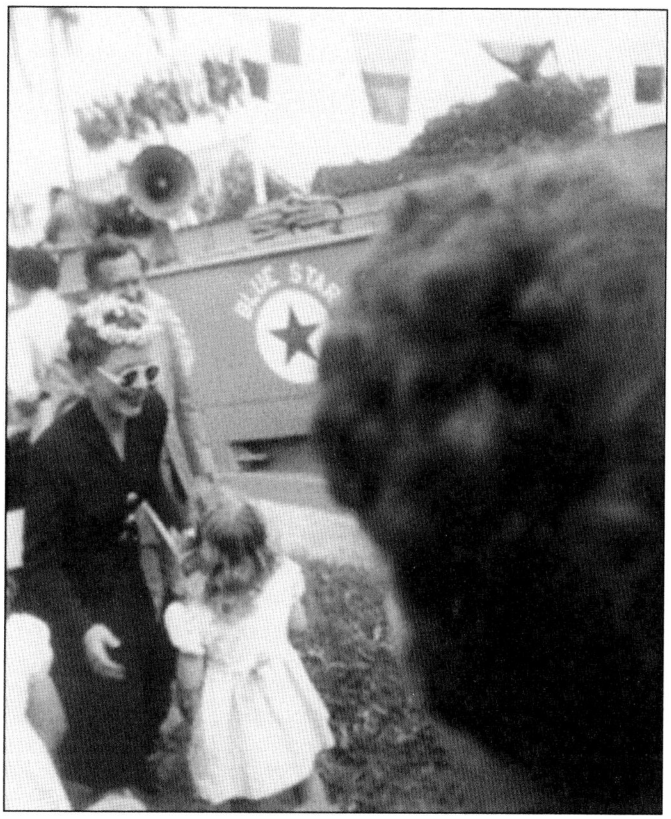

Middleport was as patriotic as any American community during World War II as evidenced by the names on the Veteran's Memorial on Park Avenue. During June 1944, the Hollywood actress Helen Hayes visited the community as part of a U.S. bond drive to support the war effort. Fittingly, she arrived in town on a Blue Star barge in the Erie Canal. (MVH.)

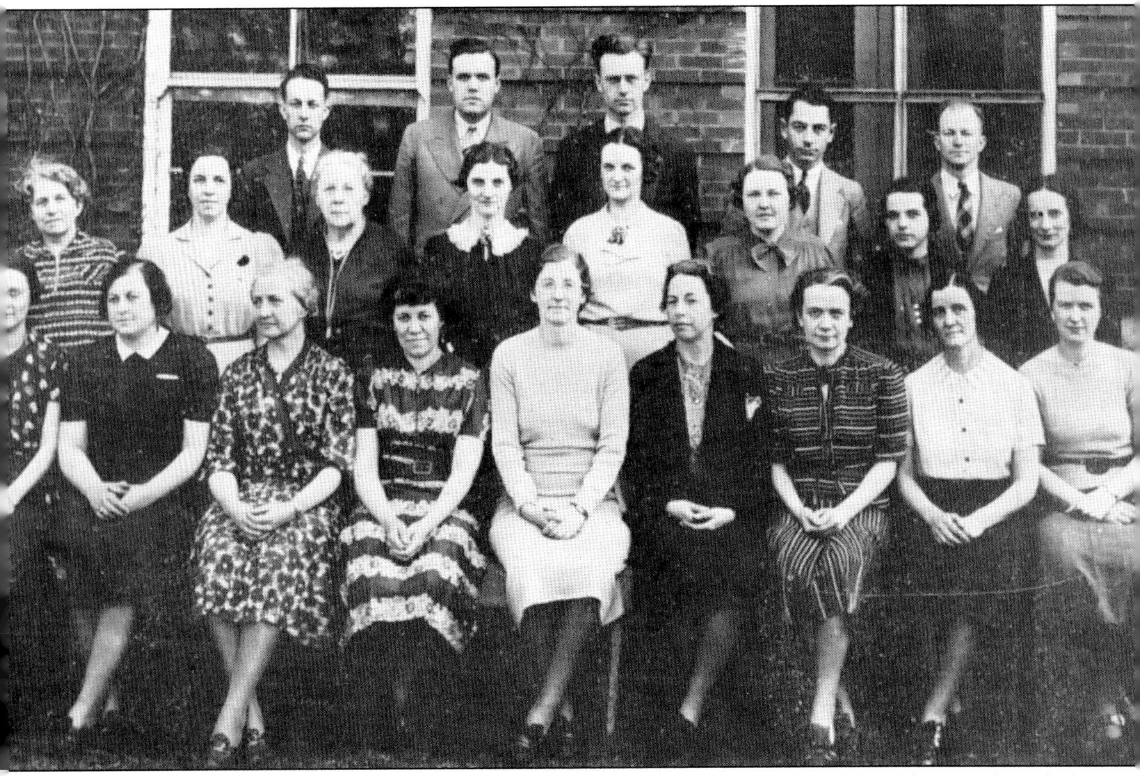

The school faculty for the Middleport School is pictured above. Many teachers, who are identified by today's residents, include Chris Farrell, Mary Mack, Jane Mather, Jane Bland, Vera Vollmer, Catherine Cramer, and Margaret Mahar. These instructors provided life skills for generations of Middleport students. Five of the six mentioned above were still teaching well into the 1960s. They usually taught the same grade levels throughout their entire teaching careers. A few, such as Vera Vollmer, became administrators and served as principal. (Author's collection.)

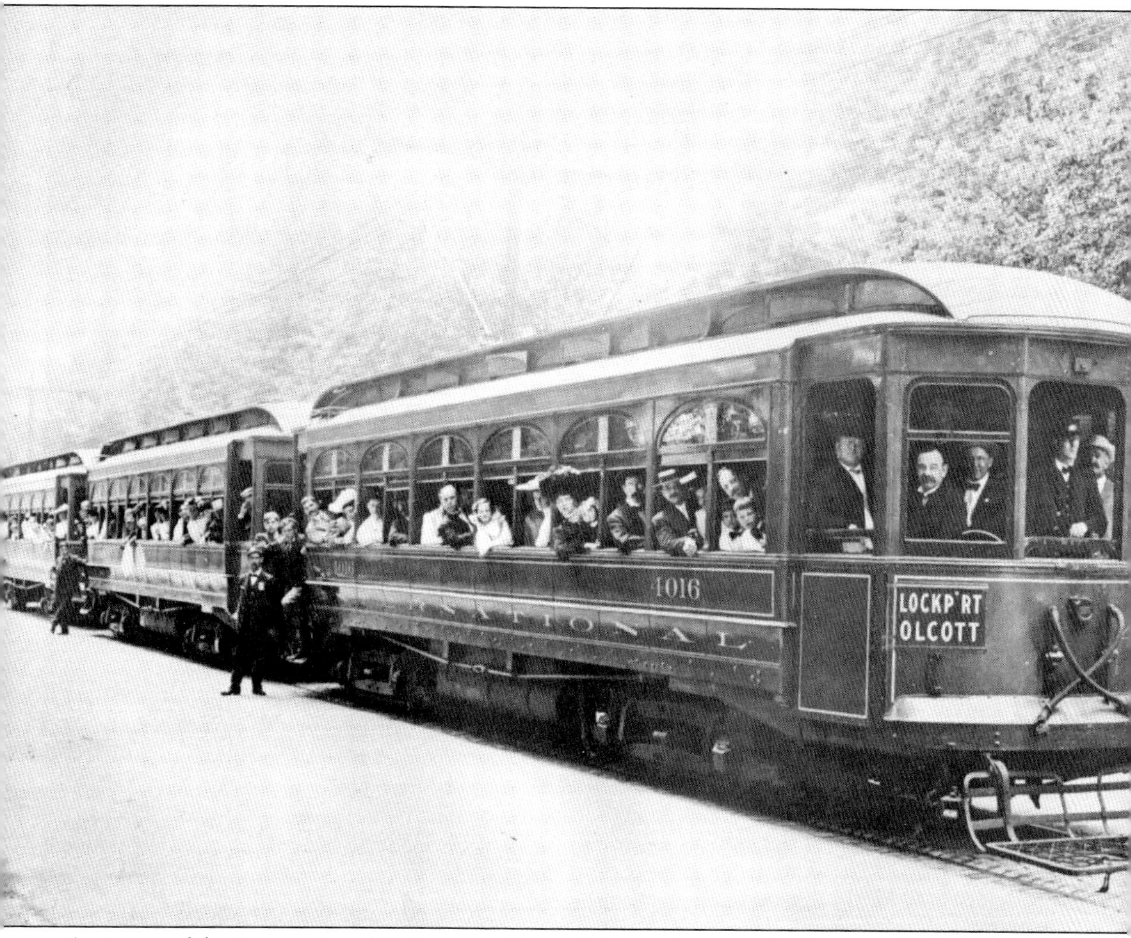

A picture of the International Railways trolleys, which ran between Lockport and Olcott Beach, offers insight into the comfort that was afforded to the passengers. The route ran somewhat parallel to Route 78 on its east side. Near Burt there remains an old trolley bridge. The trolley company worked in tandem with the lake ferry and the Olcott Beach Hotel. (Author's collection.)

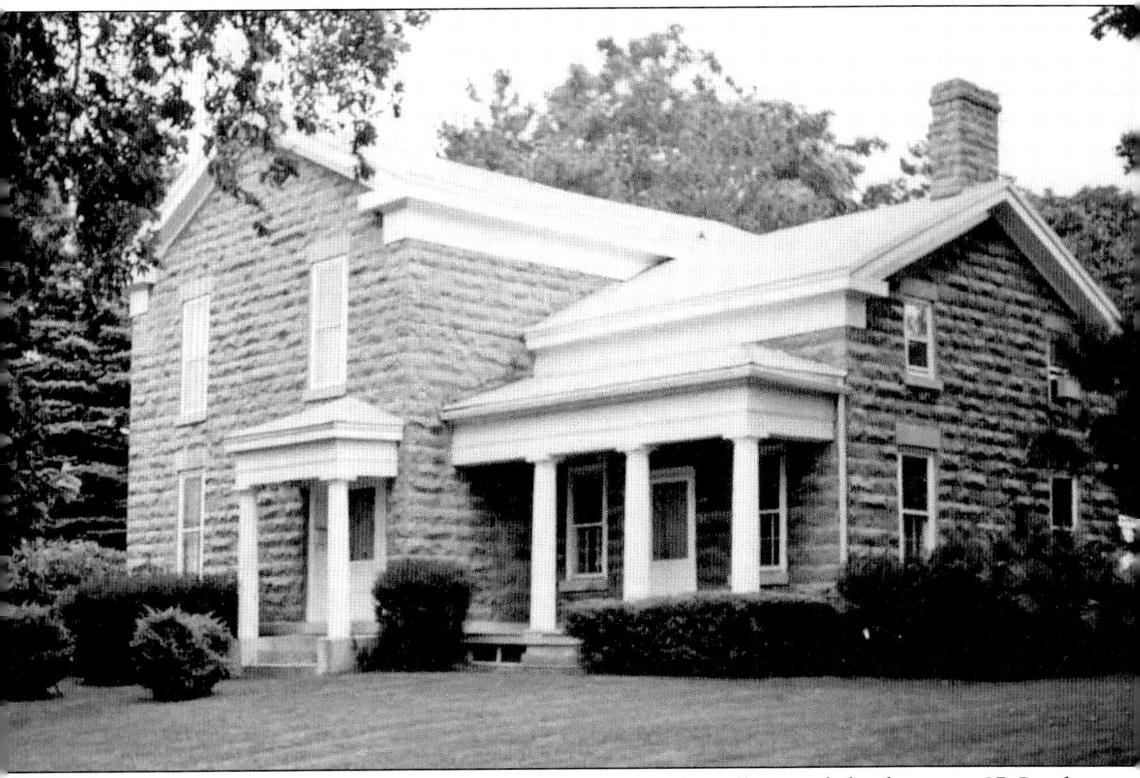

There are many architecturally attractive residences in the village and this house at 97 South Main Street is one of them. It was built in the Greek Revival style in the mid-1800s and is situated next to Jeddo Creek. The house has changed a great deal through the years. When the Hammond family moved into the house in the late 1950s, the rear of the house still contained remnants of the stables that were part of the property. Naturally, they were removed, and an exterior porch currently occupies the space. The interior of the house has never been reconfigured, but the motif has been changed often. The circular driveway, which had been removed years ago, has been replaced. (MVH.)

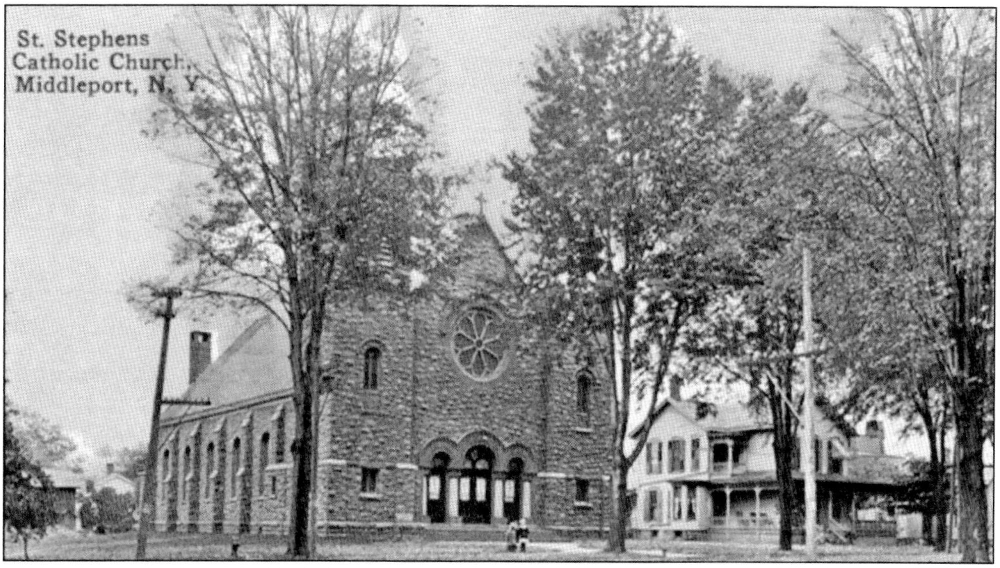

The property for St. Stephen's Roman Catholic Church was acquired from the Presbyterians in the late 1800s. Prior to the present structure, a small wooden building provided a place of worship. The rectory next door, with its open porches, looks nothing like it does today. The angle of this photograph suggests that it was taken around 1912, as it was taken from a vacant piece of property formerly occupied by the high school. (MVH.)

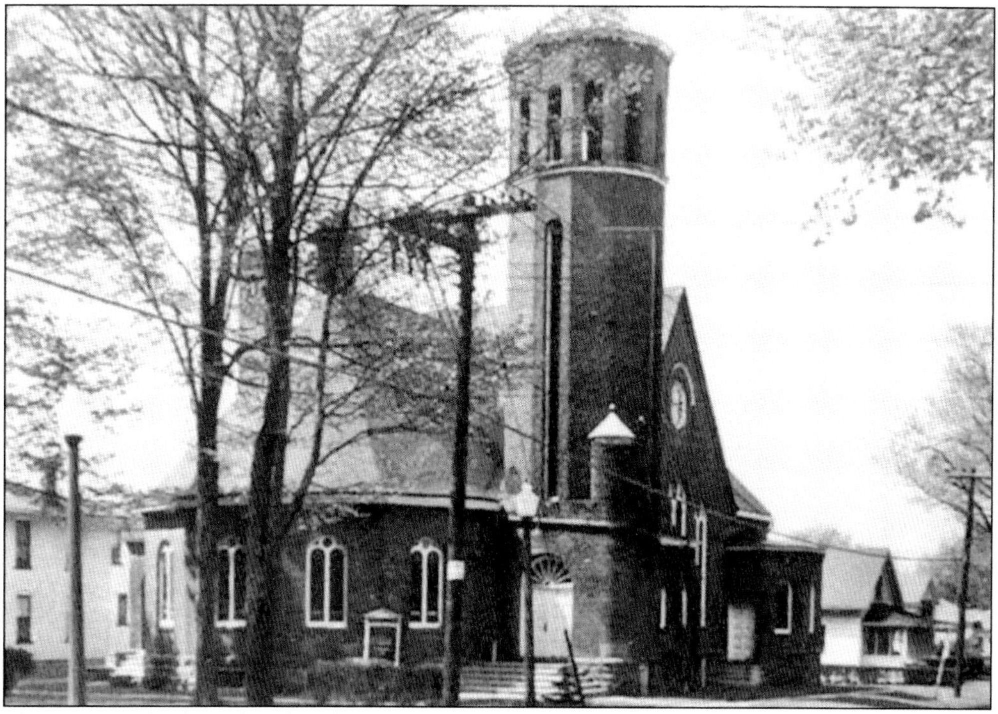

The First Methodist Church is located on the corner of Park Avenue and Vernon Street, with its parsonage two doors away on Park Avenue. The bell tower was removed in the 1950s and the rooms on the back of the Vernon Street side were also added later. During the 1950s and 1960s, the church bells would chime at 6:00 p.m., and the kids always knew they had missed supper! (NCH.)

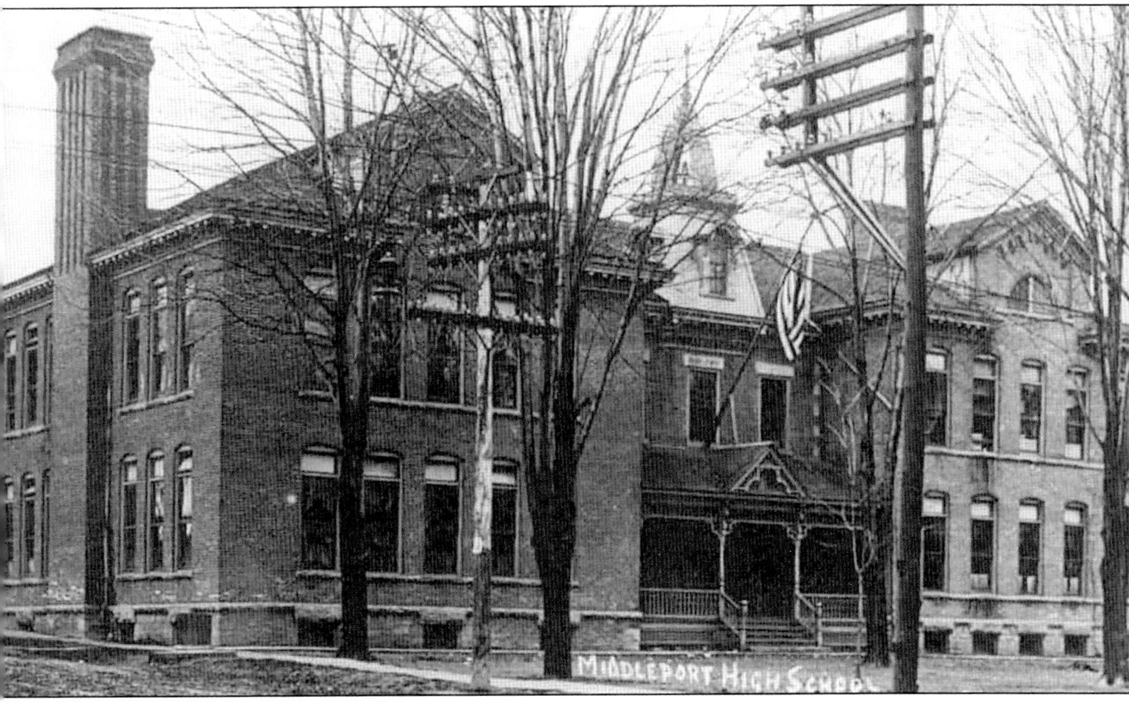

The old Middleport Union School has been viewed before, but this is a different perspective, which offers the opportunity to see much of the fine workmanship that the structure contained. As the building sadly disappeared in 1910, the picture is probably from about 1907. The porches on the exterior are truly very attractive, and one can only imagine the detail of the interior as no photographs of that part of the building have surfaced over the years. As the earlier faculty photographs indicate, there were probably only eight classrooms in the school. (MVH.)

Four

Middleport and Gasport in the 1950s

During the first half of the 20th century, both towns grew. With the canal, the trolley, and the New York Central Railroad, the movement of people and goods was easy and convenient.

The Erie Canal became the Barge Canal, a designation mandated by New York State. During this period, a lamplighter had a state boat anchored at the log pond in Middleport behind today's Basket Factory Restaurant. There was also one in Gasport. The operators would leave at dusk and light the kerosene lanterns that marked the canal banks at night. In the morning, they would repeat the route to extinguish them.

During the first part of the last century, most residents worked in or near the villages. There were many industries and farms to employ the population. In the years prior to women seeking full-time employment, food-processing plants offered work to women on a seasonal basis. The Middleport Cold Storage, and later Longview Farms, would employ numerous women.

Factories such as Niagara Sprayer, Loud and Wendel, E and M Enterprises, and Monroe Electronics and Plastimold provided many jobs in Middleport, while Friend Manufacturing, Duracraft Homes, Lobee Pump, and the numerous cold storage facilities in Gasport did the same there. As World War II ended and the automobile became available to more people, citizens took jobs at Harrison Radiator in Lockport and Bell Aircraft in Niagara Falls.

Each community was self-sufficient during these years (1930–1960). There were grocery stores, clothiers, new car dealerships, hardware stores, farm stores, numerous gasoline stations, three coal yards, two lumberyards, movie theaters, and of course, numerous taverns and bars located within the two communities. Middleport had two hotels, and Gasport had one.

Sadly, however, just as with many small towns in the area and across the country, prosperity brought shopping malls, the suburbs, and relocation for many family members, who were assisted in their move by the interstate highway system. In the massive change, which culminated in the 1960s, both Middleport and Gasport lost most of their businesses and places of employment, but not their character.

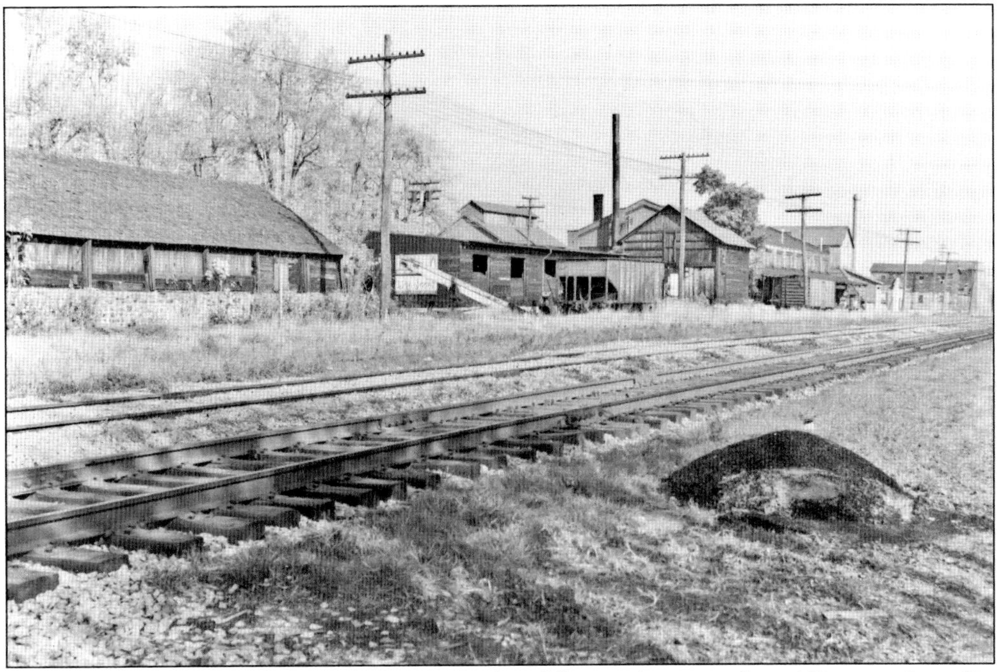

The Niagara Sprayer has been a major part of Middleport for more than 100 years. Initially, it was a factory that designed and produced agricultural spraying equipment. Later it would become Niagara Chemical Company. Most people in the village today think that the site of the Niagara Sprayer was on the south side of the railroad where it is located today. Actually, the Niagara manufacturing site was on the north side of the railroad and stretched all the way from the old Norco building to the high school football field. Moving from Vernon Street and the Wheeler Coal Yard on that street, Niagara had production buildings, a sulfur mill, offices, and warehouses. Beyond the last warehouse was a fruit orchard, which Niagara used for testing their sprayers and later their chemicals. Little remains from the original site today. (Niagara County Historian's Office.)

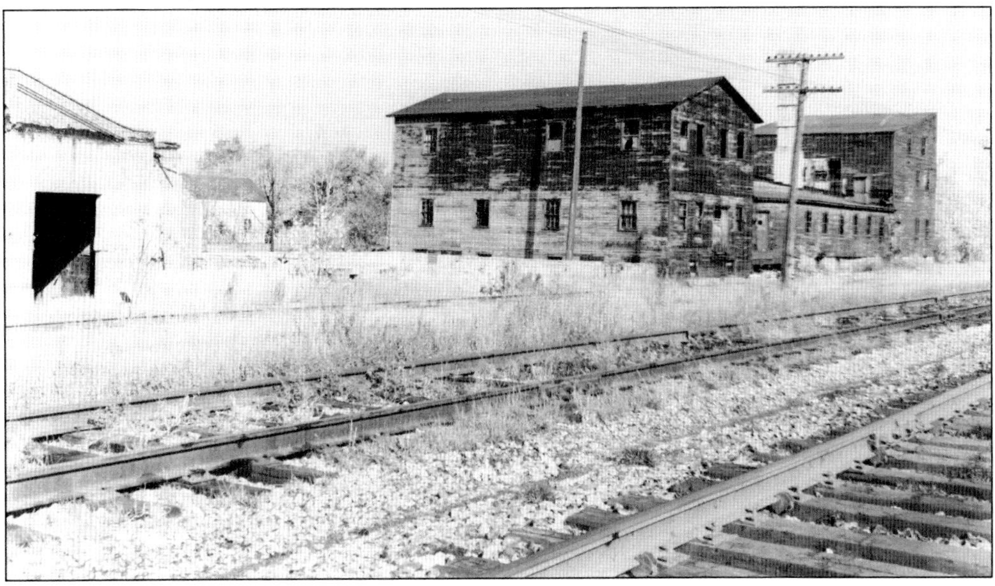

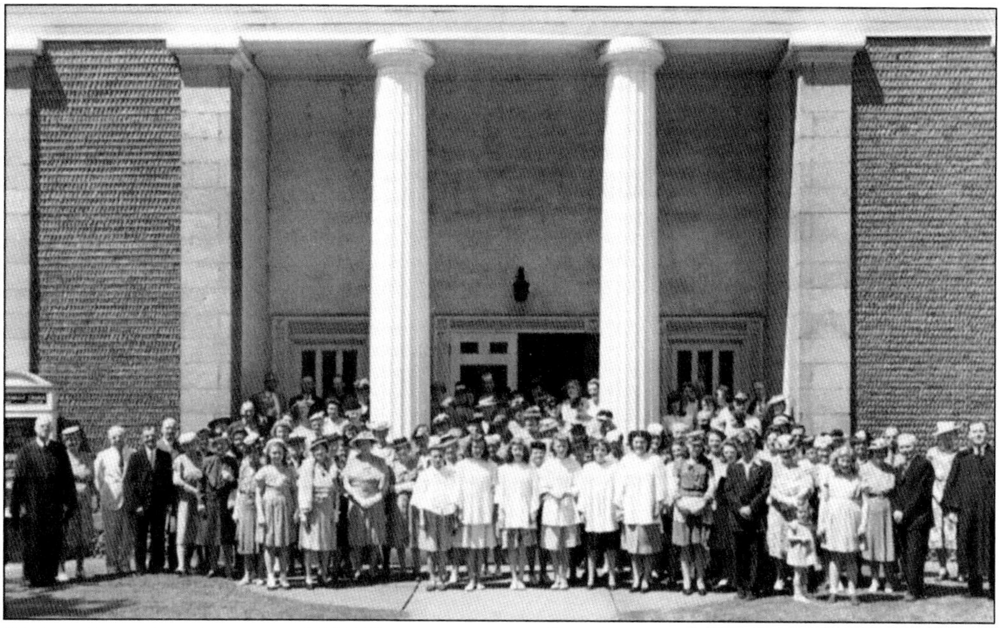

Quite often, the churches of Middleport join together for united services. The congregation pictured above in 1946 was a joint service between the Methodist and Universalist Churches held at the Universalist Church on Main Street. Surely, the subsequent united service would have been held at the Methodist Church on Park Avenue. These days, ecumenical services are often held to include any member of any church. (MVH.)

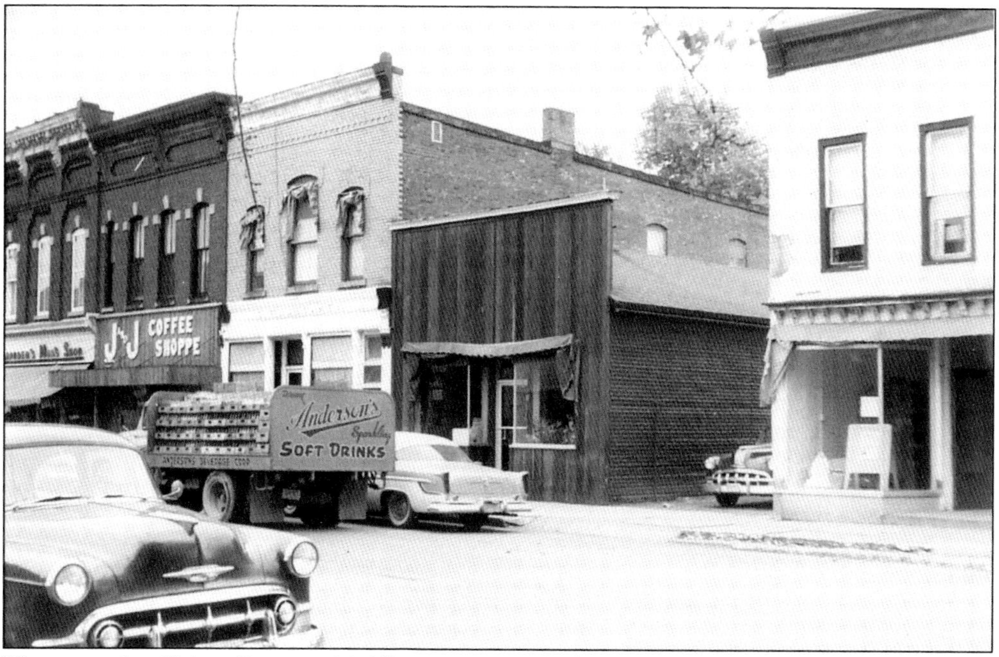

The east side of Main Street in Middleport in 1958 looked different than it does today. Most of the visible buildings have been razed. The alley between Jackson's and the shoe repair shop is no longer there, nor are the buildings mentioned. There were many businesses in the village a half century ago. (RTH.)

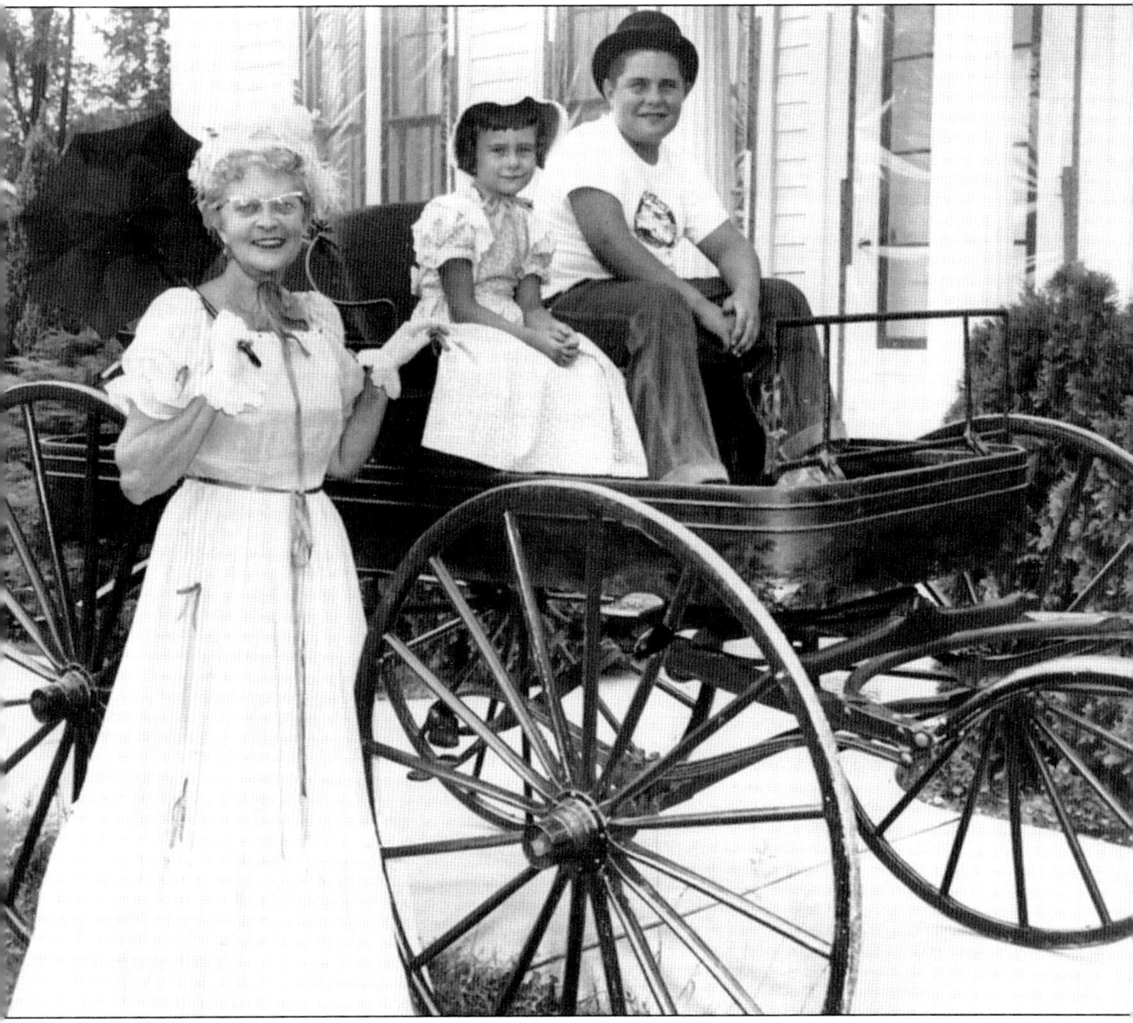

Middleport celebrated its centennial in 1959 and held a grand, yearlong celebration. Many men of the village grew beards for a contest (the winner for the longest beard was Floyd Fierch) and there was a grand parade in August of that year. The major events were held on the high school grounds and a souvenir centennial book was produced. There were old-time floats and exhibits in the parade. The queen of the centennial celebration was Mary Nicolia. The village also issued "wooden nickels," which were valid for trade at many of the local stores. The majority of the village residents seemed to enjoy the retro costumes of the centennial. In those days, Middleport also hosted a three-day Fireman's Field Day event over the Labor Day weekend, making the weeks of August and early September very spirited times. (MVH.)

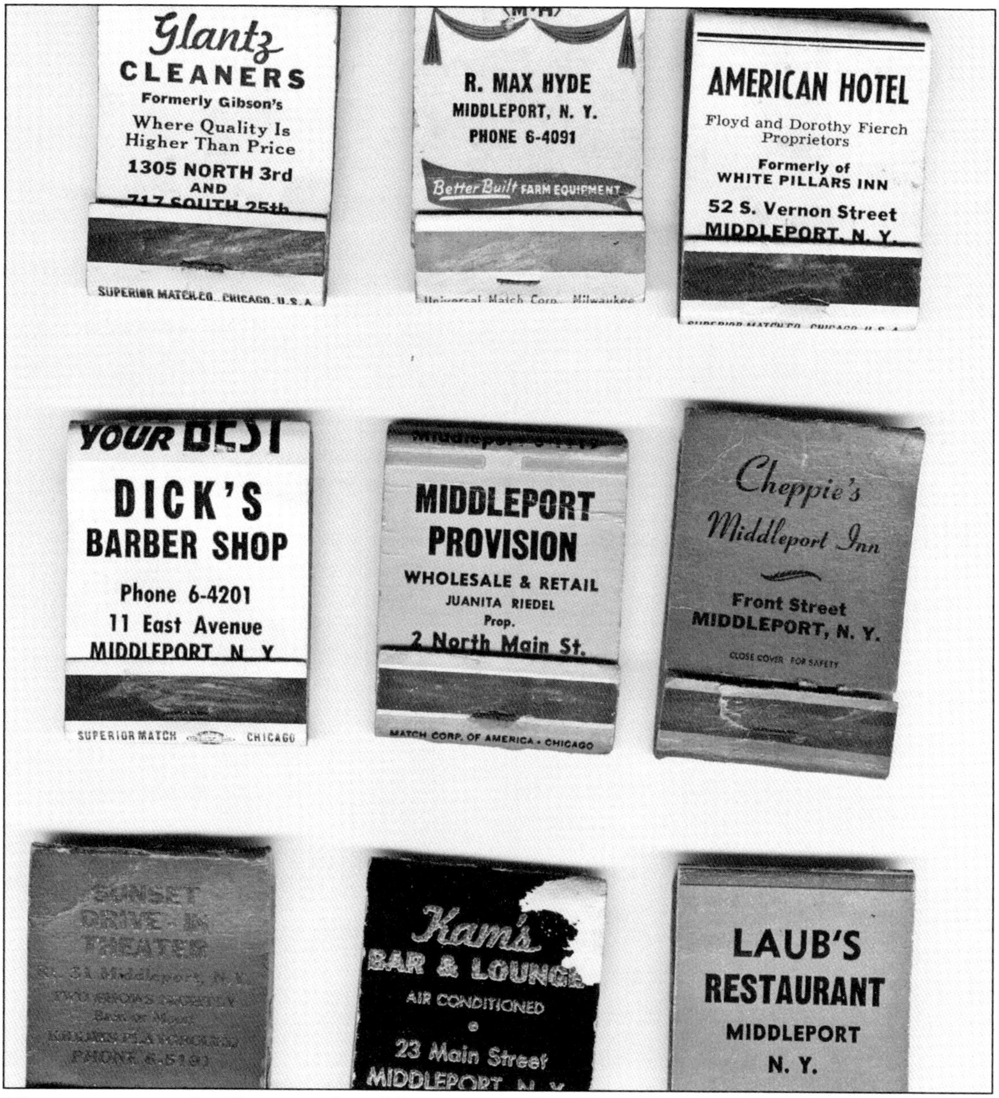

There were many fondly remembered businesses in Middleport in the early 1950s and some not so easily recognizable. The Sunset Drive-In opened on August 31, 1950, and was an immediate hit. Middleport Provision was a short-lived enterprise on Main Street, immediately across the bridge on the right. Cheppie's Middleport Inn was the name given to Tony's by a lessee in 1953. It did not last long. Laub's Restaurant was an institution located on State Street, and later became part of Plowie's. Ma Laub managed her 12-foot bar, despite having to walk with a cane. Kam's Bar and Lounge was owned by Art Kam and was on Main Street. It later became Mr. Ed's. The American Hotel was located on Vernon Street. Glantz Cleaners was on Main Street between the pool emporium and Whittaker's. R. Max Hyde sold farm equipment on South Main Street, while Dick's Barber Shop was on East Avenue. (Author's collection.)

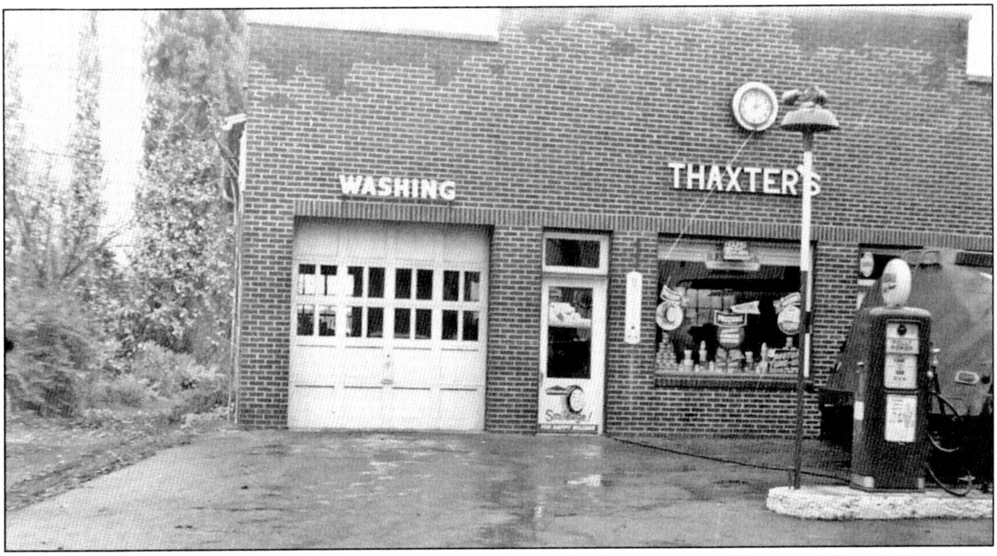

Located on State Street near its intersection with Maple Avenue was Thaxter's Kendall service station. This site was much larger than most stations in the village and able to accommodate five to six vehicles at a time. It was later owned and operated by Allen "Hoppy" Oliver and then sold to become a motorcycle garage, Peterson's.

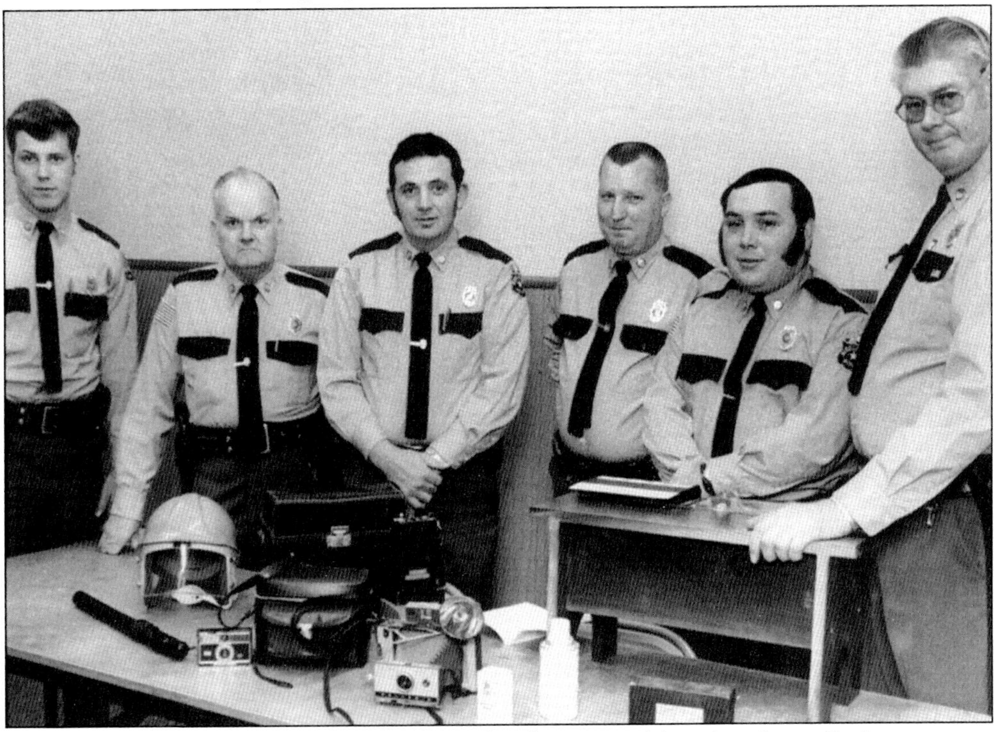

The village of Middleport has always seemed to have a sizable police force. Early on, it was comprised of Charlie White, Frank White, Frank Kubatek, Tim Lahey, and Ray Wienke. That was the entire force for about 25 years. By 1975 (the date of this picture), there were six officers. Pictured here are, from left to right, Phil Gang, Dick Keihl, unidentified, Elroy Fuller, Doug Webber, and Earl Woodworth- Chief. Middleport was always safe! (MVH.)

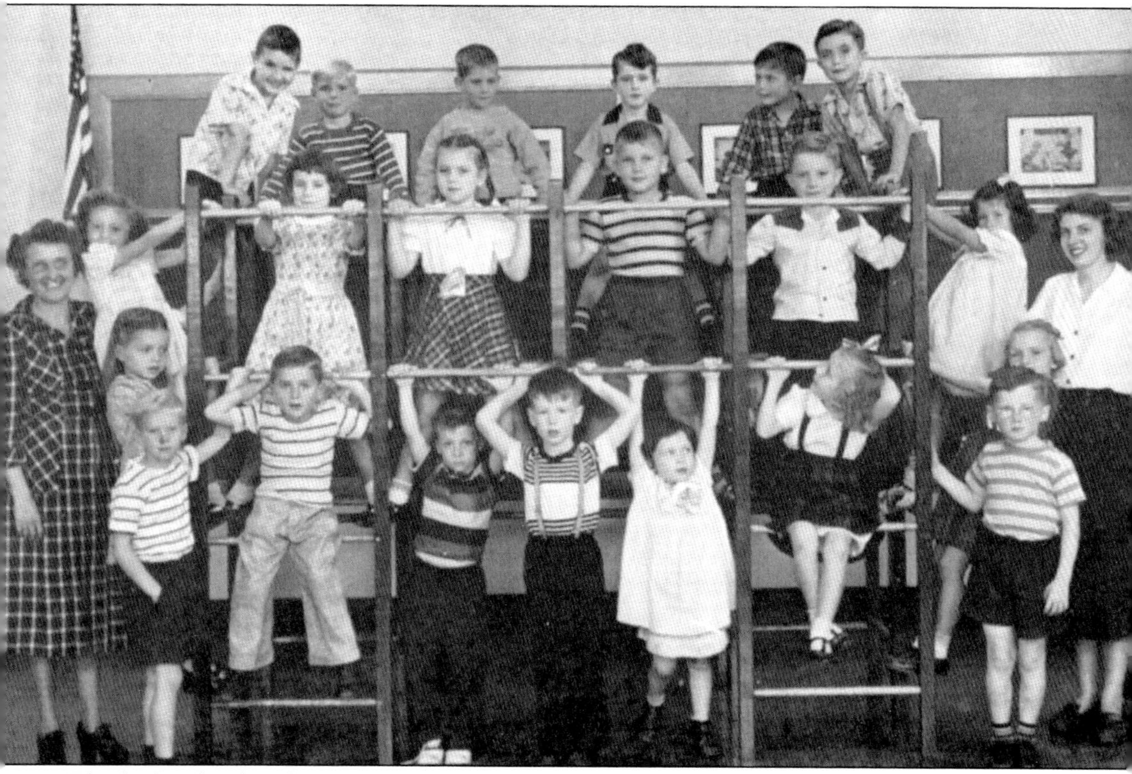

The high school underwent extensive renovation during the school years from 1949 to 1951. New classrooms were added in the back of the building, a new front entrance was added, a new gymnasium and locker rooms replaced the auditorium as a part-time gymnasium, and the fields behind the building were terraced into athletic fields. At that time, Royalton Hartland Central was still playing six-man football. (It would not expand to 11-man football until the 1953 season.) This photograph shows the newest group of students to enter the school under the new renovations. This was Fern White's kindergarten class and would become the class of 1962. This was the first kindergarten class to attend school for the full day. The students were given blankets for "naptime," which was done on the classroom floor. All students who lived within a mile of the school walked, as there was no bus service within the village. The same system was used at the Gasport branch of the school. (Author's collection.)

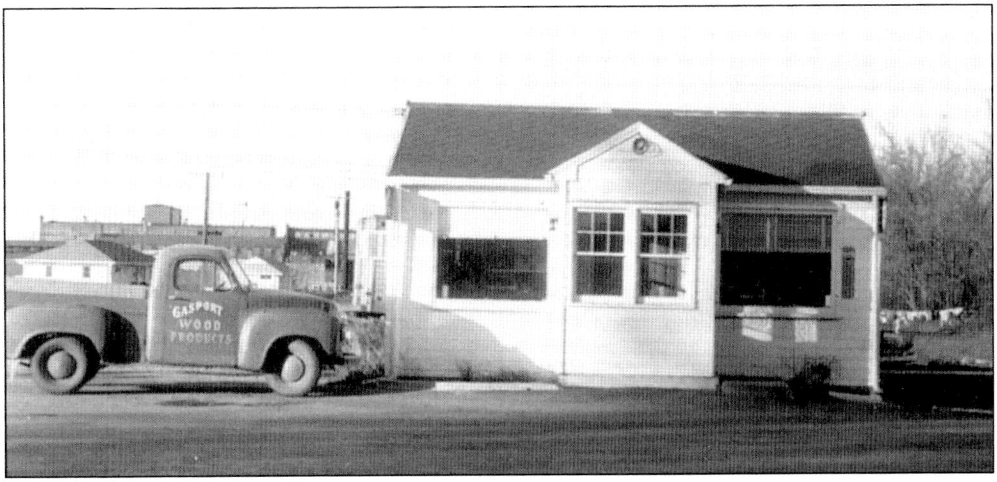

The Green Kettle Restaurant was located on the corner of Route 31 and Kelly Avenue. Most residents remember Marge cooking and waiting on the counter and Margaret McCauley making the pies. It is truly hard to believe that the original building was this small. Eventually, the place would become Murph's and undergo a major expansion in the early 1980s. It would later become Darrell's Place. (RTH.)

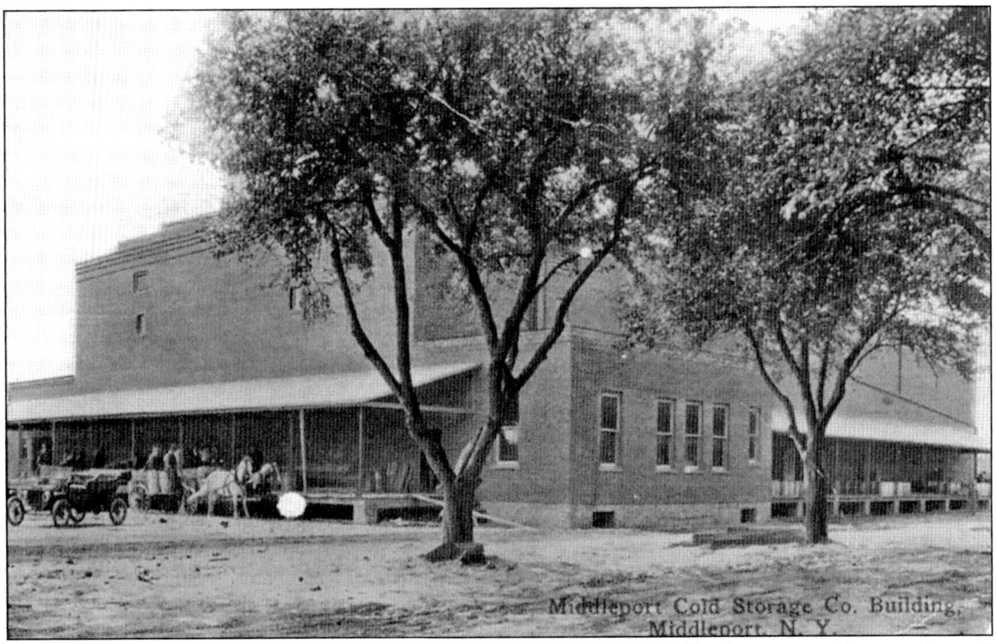

The Middleport Cold Storage was a multiuse facility located on Kelly Avenue, and most of it still stands today. Produce was stored at the site, and before the wide-scale use of refrigerators, blocks of ice were produced and sold for food preservation. In the early 1950s, George Ferris and Jeff Boardwell ran a fruit-canning operation in the summer months. Many women were employed in the processing of cherries, peaches, pears, and apples. (MVH.)

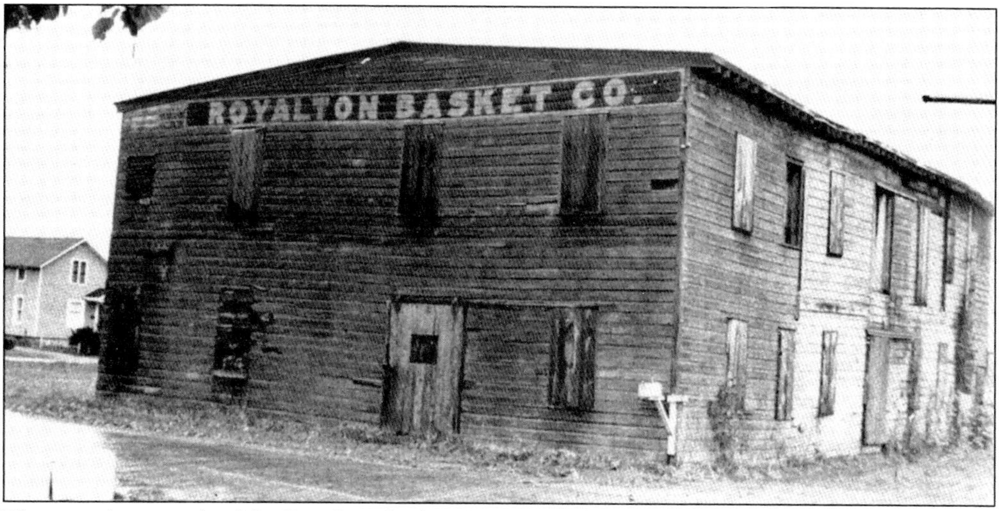

This is a photograph of the Royalton Basket Company's facility on Watson Avenue as it appeared in 1959. It had long ceased operation and was boarded up, probably awaiting demolition. The small body of water behind the building was known as the Log Pond and its only use for years seemed to be a docking place for the canal lamplighter's boat. Of course, it would become today's Basket Factory Restaurant. (RTH.)

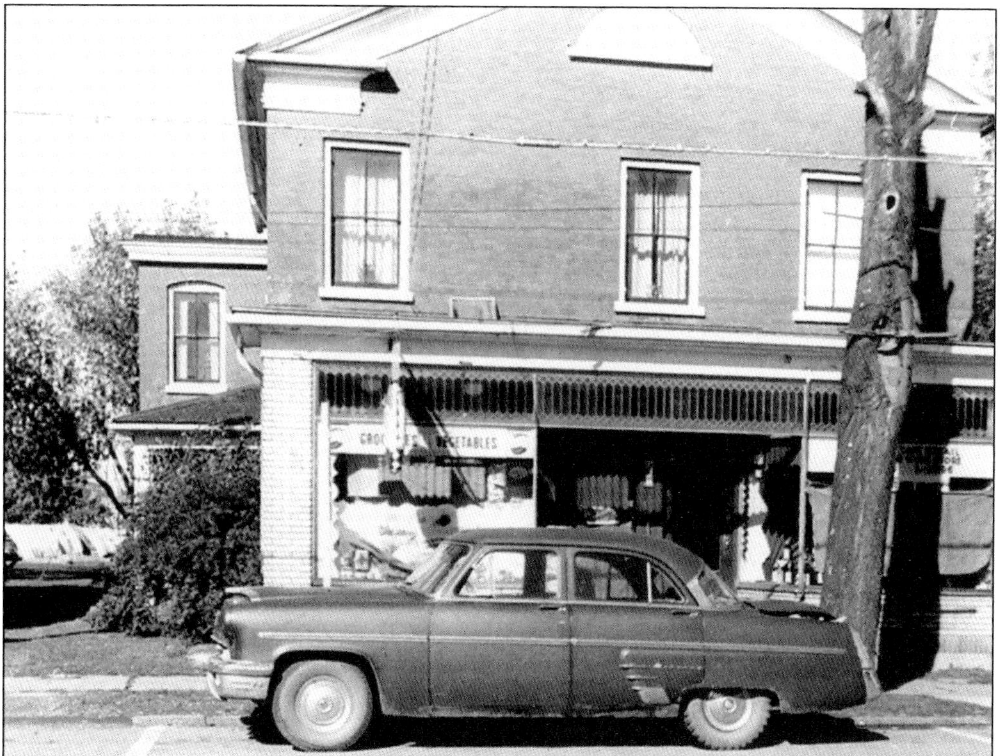

Bortain Gracey and his wife owned this dual-purpose storefront, located on State Street next to the high bridge. The west side of the store was a grocery emporium, while the east side was Middleport's liquor store. The Graceys had the store configured so that they could enter either store from the rear, therefore working the entire operation with just one person if needed. (RTH.)

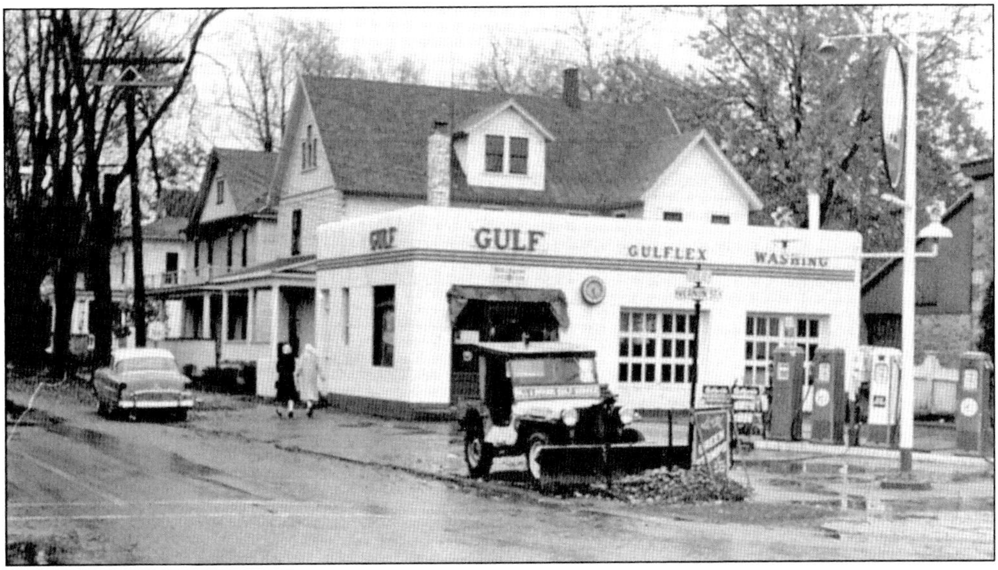

Middleport had numerous gas stations, each selling a different brand of gasoline. All of them offered repair services and car washing in addition to fuel. The Gulf station on the corner of State and Vernon Streets was originally known as Bill and Don's. Eventually, Don left, and Byron Scott purchased his half, with the station becoming Bill and Byron's. In the 1960s, Byron owned it himself. (RTH.)

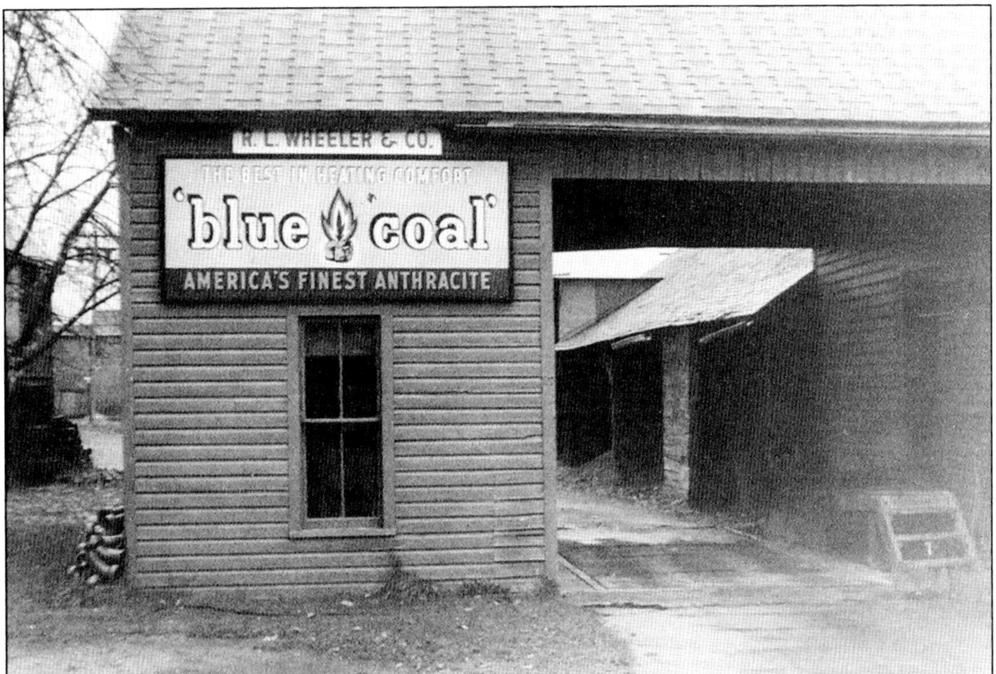

There were two coal yards in Middleport, one of them being R. L. Wheeler and Company located on Vernon Street next to the railroad tracks. Leighton Wheeler had assumed ownership from Roy Wheeler Sr. in the early 1950s after a fire had destroyed the round coal supply bin. The two men who delivered the coal were George Altman and Doug Whitney. (RTH.)

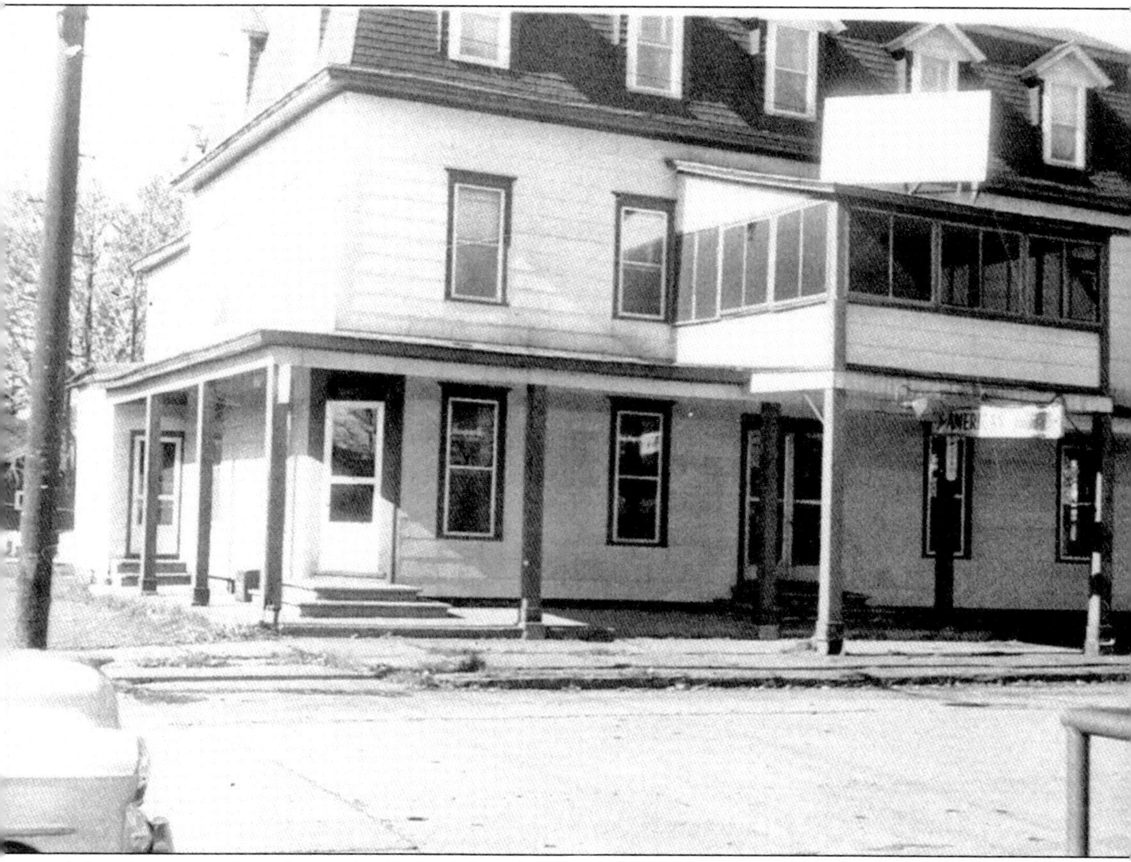

The American Hotel was the "other" hotel in Middleport. It was known as the Vernon House in the late 1800s and had a great location next to the New York Central Depot. There were still passenger trains passing through the village right up until 1955. After World War II, the Antonuccis, the Martellis, and the Fierchs owned it in succession. In 1951, live radio broadcasts were aired from the site, making those programs only the second time live radio was done from Middleport. Activities within the village, which were shared by the American Hotel, were participation in shuffleboard leagues and euchre leagues. These filled any place that had a team on game day and were reported in the Middleport *Herald Record* newspaper. There were two huge barns behind the hotel, which were once stables. One of them burned to the ground in 1951. The other, which for a time was used to house a fire truck, was demolished in 1954. (RTH.)

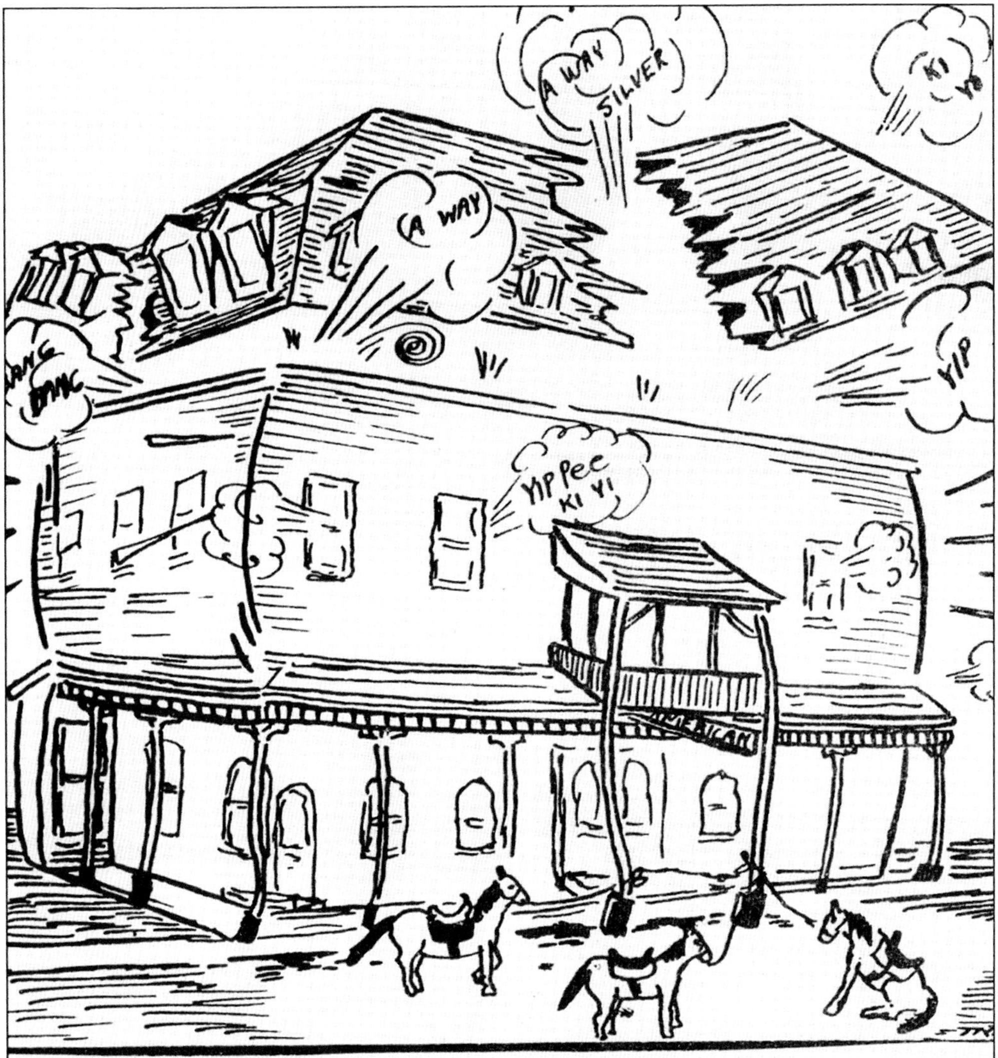

The Komodey Kowboys are now appearing at the American Hotel on Vernon Street on Saturday nights.

The Middleport *Herald Record* was the local newspaper, which was under the ownership of Roy Wheeler and Bill Holahan from 1950 through 1951. The paper was entirely local; it only had Middleport area news and occasionally Gasport information. It highlighted all activities in the village and in its weekly form carried cartoons drawn by a local artist, Ted Kirkpatrick. Ted's regular occupation was at Niagara Sprayer, where in his later years he was in charge of the boiler (and the four daily toots of the whistle 8:00 a.m., 12:00 p.m., 1:00 p.m., and 5:00 p.m.). The cartoon shown celebrates the radio broadcasts on Lockport's WUSJ. The emcee for the programs was Pat Fagan. The biggest draw for the live music sent along the airwaves was the Komodey Kowboys, who played at the American Hotel every Saturday night. Fridays at the American featured boxing on television, as the hotel had the first television in town. (Author's collection.)

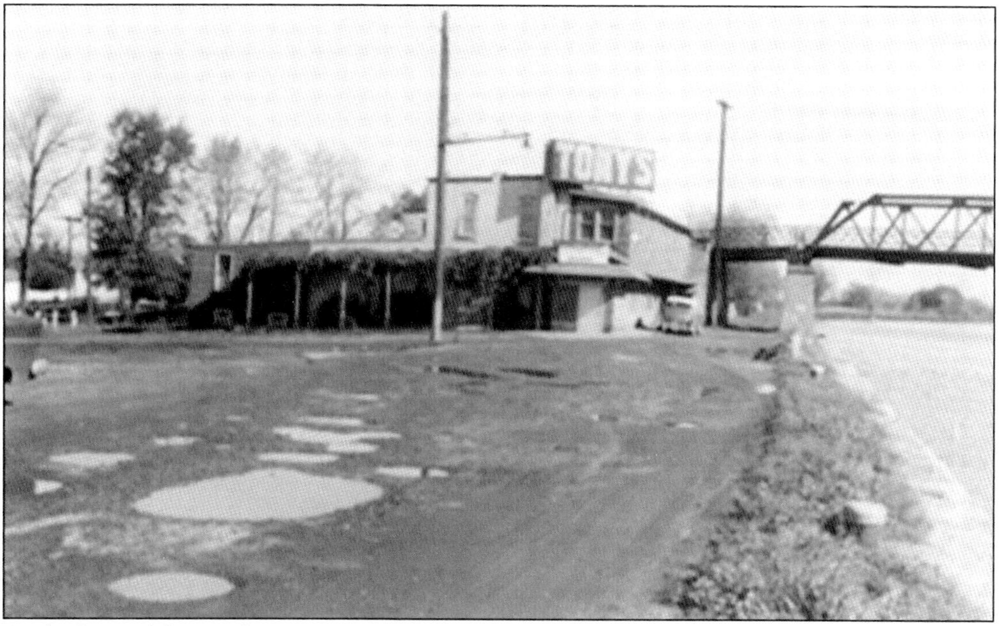

At the base of the northern approach to the high bridge sat Tony's, a restaurant and bar established by Tony Nicolia in the 1930s. It was a unique place in that it sat directly on the canal bank, had two full apartments upstairs, and had the largest dining room in town. The taproom contained a three-sided bar and the foot rails were enclosed and had running water going through them to clean out the mud and butts. (RTH.)

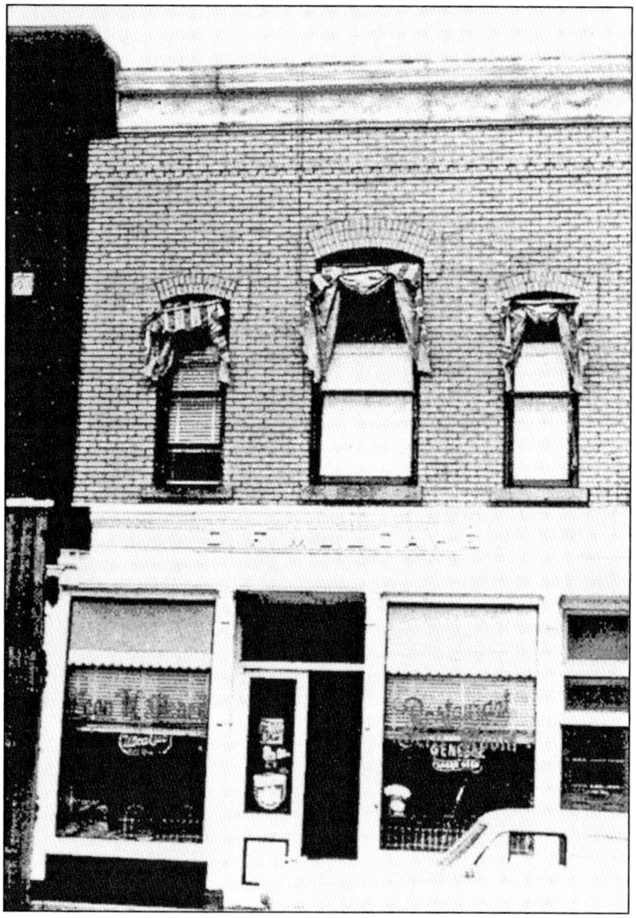

Dan Mulcahey owned this building early in the 20th century. It was literally a traditional Irish workingman's tavern during those years. It was sold to Leon Mears, who operated the bar into the 1960s. He in turn sold it to the Hill family. Later they sold it to Ruth Turrell. In the 1990s, it changed hands a number of times, finally closing in 2008. (RTH)

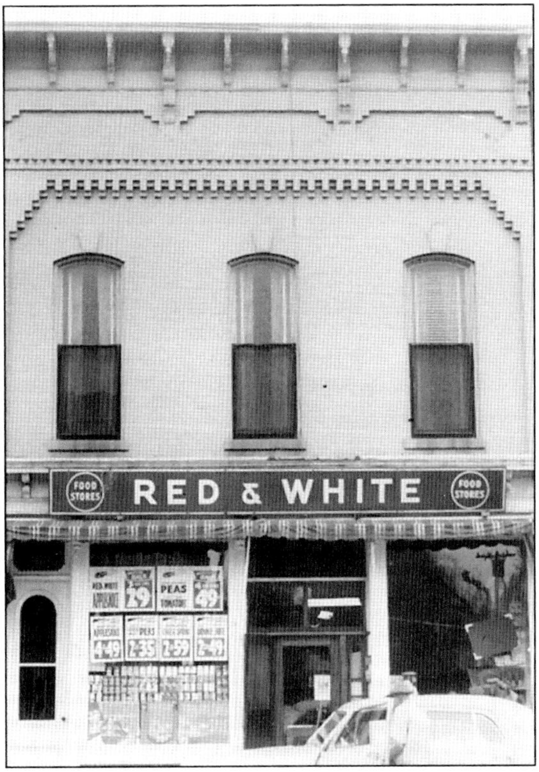

The primary full grocery store in town was Germain's Red and White located on Main Street next to Western Auto. Although small by many standards, it carried every food item a housewife needed. It had a fresh meat counter in the back with a cutter on duty. The store lasted into the 1960s, when, like many other retail outlets, box stores hastened their demise. (RTH.)

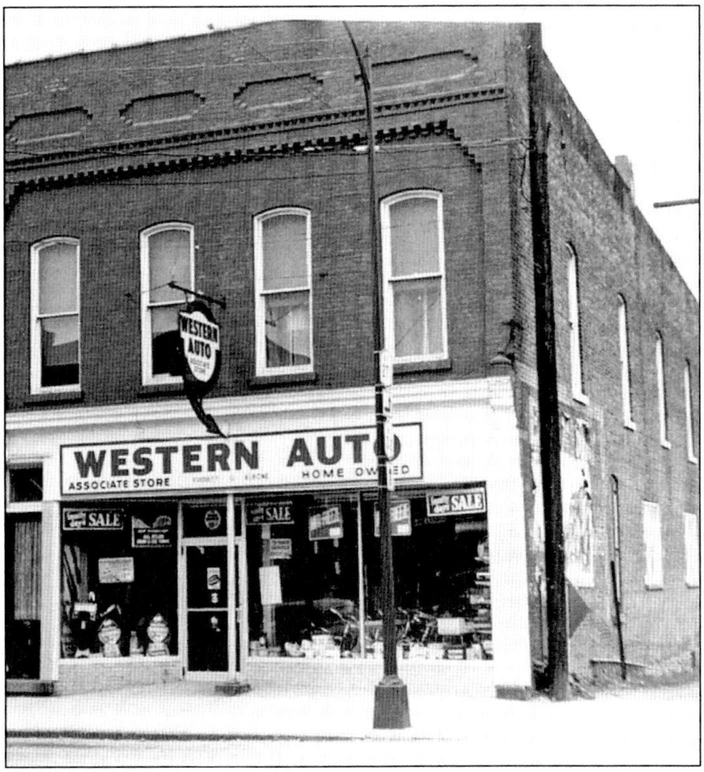

At the end of Main Street just before the canal, sat the old Middleport *Herald Record* building. It was vacant for a few years until Everett Albone bought it and put a Western Auto franchise there. The store was a joy. He kept the new bicycles in the front window to entice the kids who delivered their newspapers from next door at Westy's. The store stocked seemingly everything, including lawn mowers. It changed hands a couple of times, going to Bill Pritchard and finally to John Kenyon. (RTH.)

On the east side of Main Street on the corner of State Street stood the Peterson Drug Store. This was another emporium where one could find more than the prescription counter. There seemed to be every imaginable item for sale. When Don Swift acquired the franchise, he moved it first to Vary's Garage on Vernon Street and later to its new location on Route 31. (RTH.)

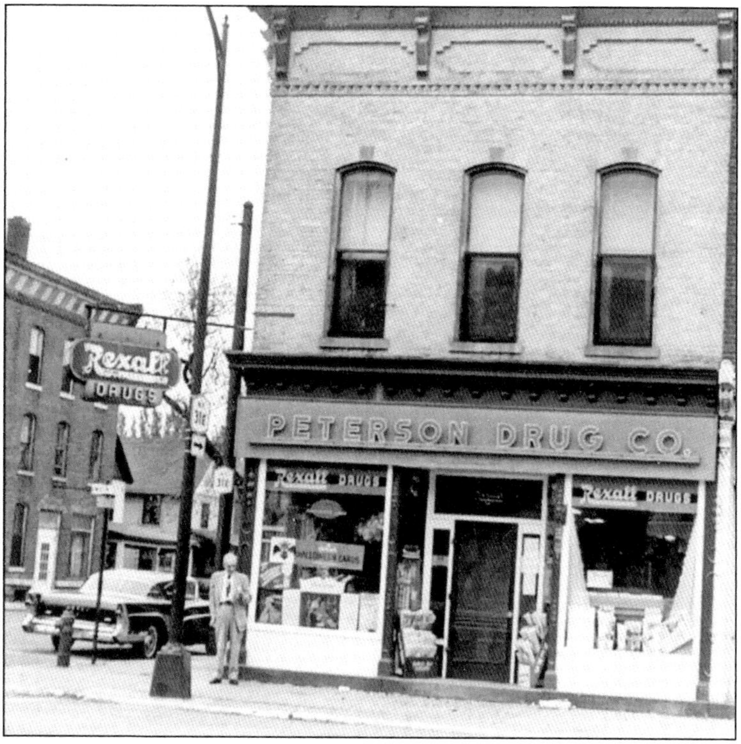

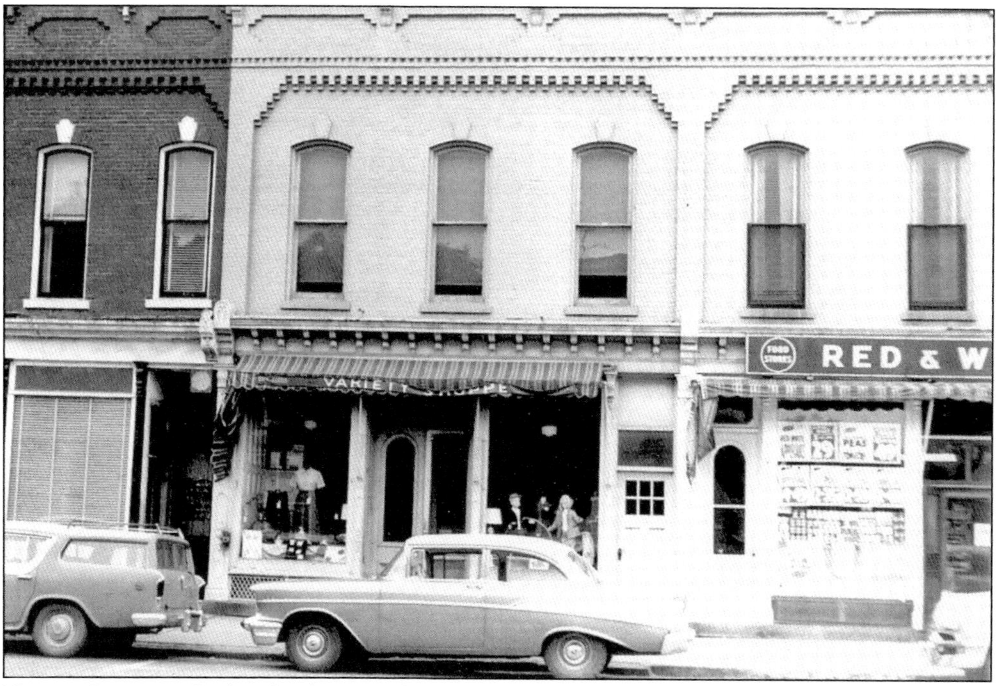

Next to Germain's Red and White stood June Hall's Variety Shoppe. This store was really symbolic of the times, as it carried cloth and threads, items that many people would not know how to use today. There were all types of household goods in the store, and it was a real asset to the community. After Hall left the business, the store did not remain viable for very long. (RTH.)

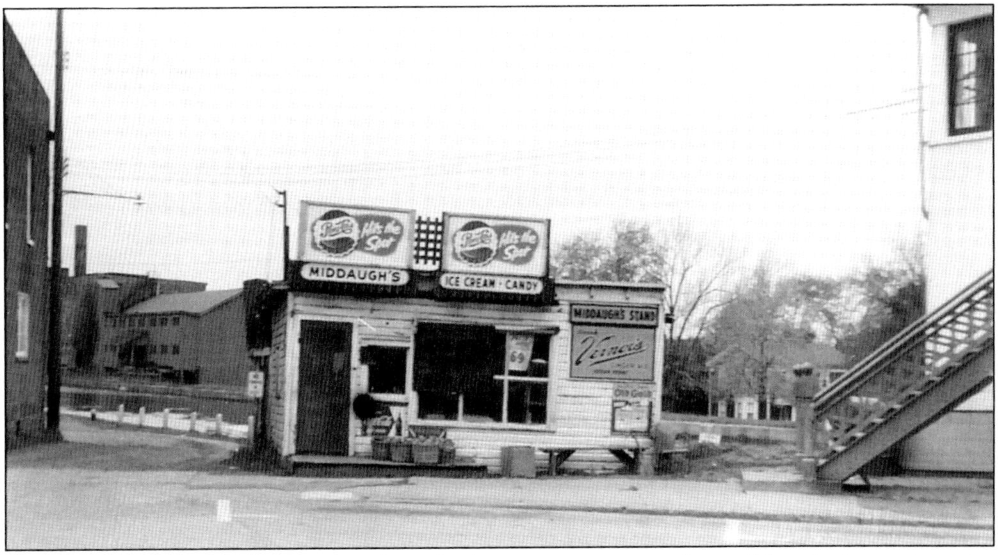

The most notorious place in the village (at least through rumor) was Westy's, located on the canal bank. Westy was really Ray Middaugh, a Canadian by birth who came to Middleport from Alberta (thus Westy). The bench in front of the stand provided seating for the men who provided commentary on the happenings of the village. In the back room, however, the card games went on by the hour. (RTH.)

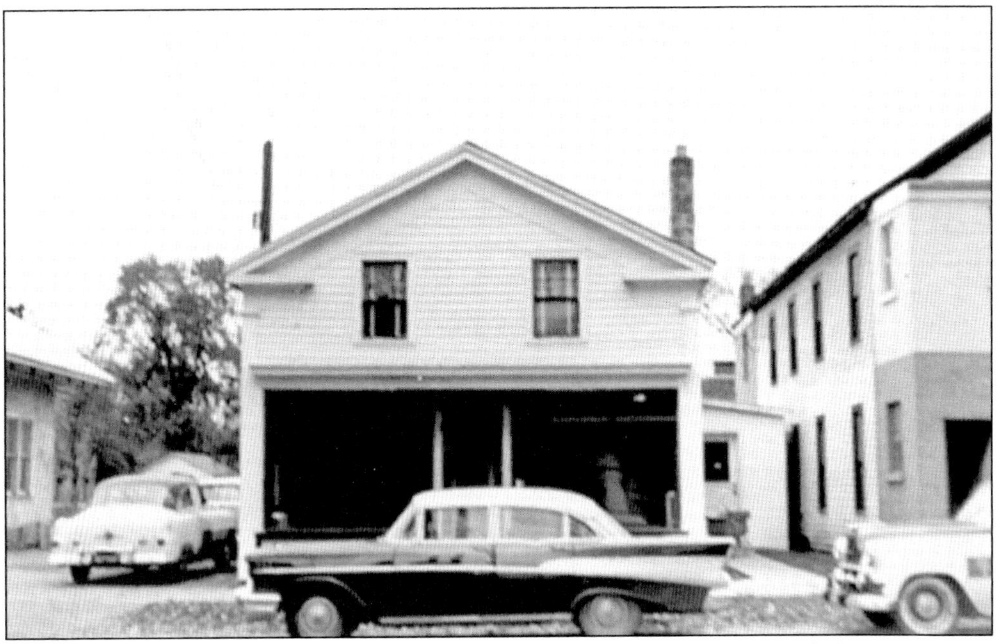

While Westy's catered to the "day trade" in town, Jimmy Aiken's poolroom provided entertainment for the youth during the day and space for the gamblers at night. There was a large card room upstairs, which was entered by the visible door on the right side of the building. Rumor has it that when the building was sold, stacks of unused punchboards were in the cellar. (RTH.)

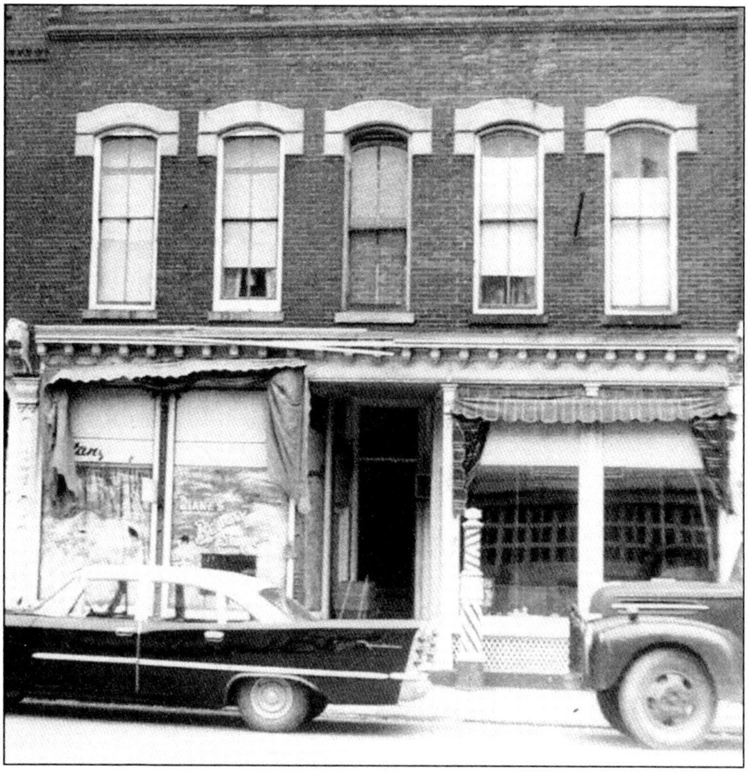

This building once housed Luke Stangland's small grocery store and a barbershop next door. In this picture, the store occupying the left side of the building was Diane's Beauty Salon, while on the right was Cy Roberts's barbershop. Cy was a very active country singer who had his own band. On occasion, he would warble to the clientele. He remained in this shop until retirement in the 1980s. (RTH.)

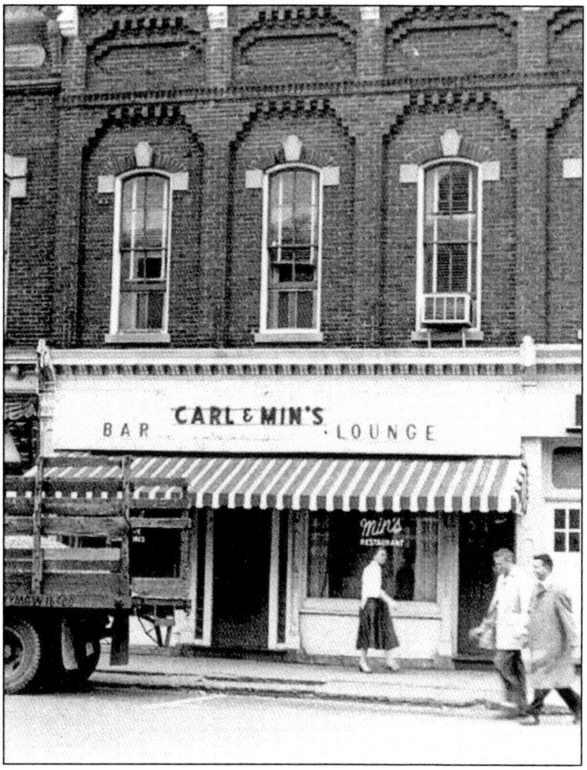

Carl and Min's was the "sophisticated" bar in the village. Originally, it was known as Kam's and owned by Art Kam. Carl's in-laws were bar owners all over the county, controlling Don's Grill in Gasport, Reggie's in Lockport, Cecil's in Newfane, and Clack's in Johnson Creek. This bar would be sold to Don Fink and later to Ed McCabe where it became Mr. Ed's. (RTH.)

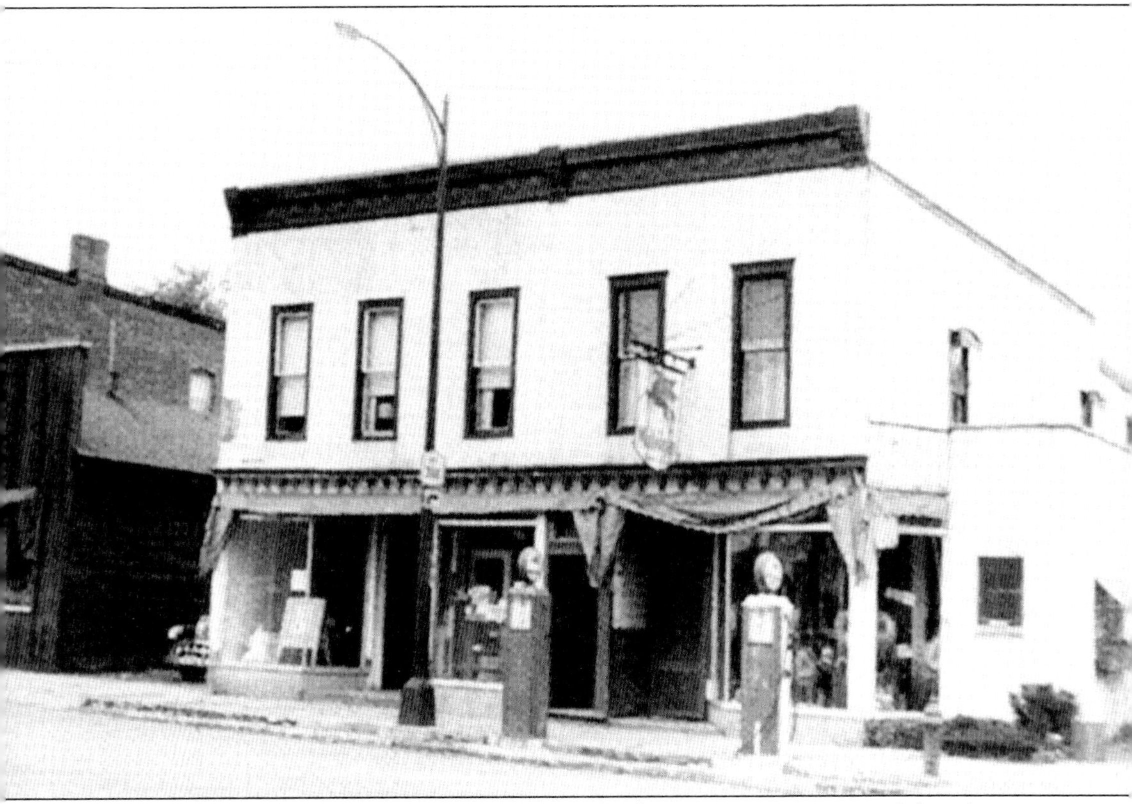

This building occupied the middle of the eastern side of Main Street. It contained three businesses with an alley on the north side. From north to south, the businesses were Coppa Shoe Repair, the Cake Box, and Whittaker's Mobil station. Coppa Shoe Repair also had another shop in Medina. Not only did they repair shoes, but they sold musical instruments as well. The Cake Box was a very interesting place in that Sid Flatt sold baked goods from Corky's in Medina and was a popular hang out for kids after school. He also collected money for the telephone company and the electric company. Bill Whittaker owned the gas station, which also dealt in oil furnaces and was the local dispenser of home heating oil. Whittaker also owned another gas station on the corner of State and Vernon Streets. The building was demolished when a mini-mall was proposed for downtown Middleport in the late 1960s. (RTH.)

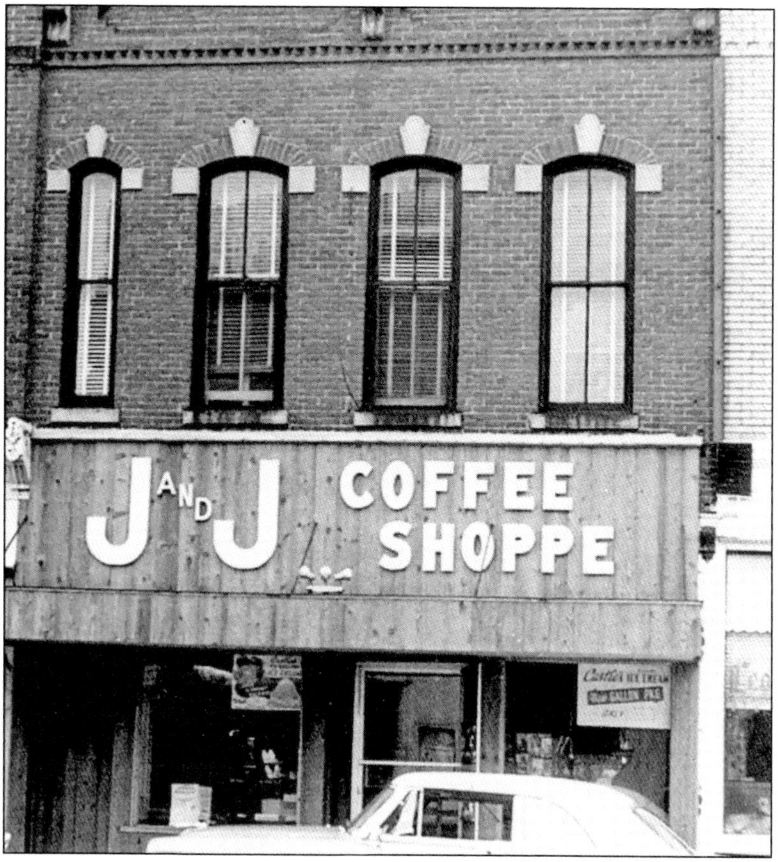

For the teens in Middleport in the 1950s and 1960s, J and J Coffee Shoppe was the place to go. Originally called Smiler's, it was purchased by Jim and JoAnne McCormick. The continuity between the two owners was the ever-present Edith Schilling. J and J catered to the working people in the morning and at lunch and to the high schoolers after 2:30 p.m. (RTH.)

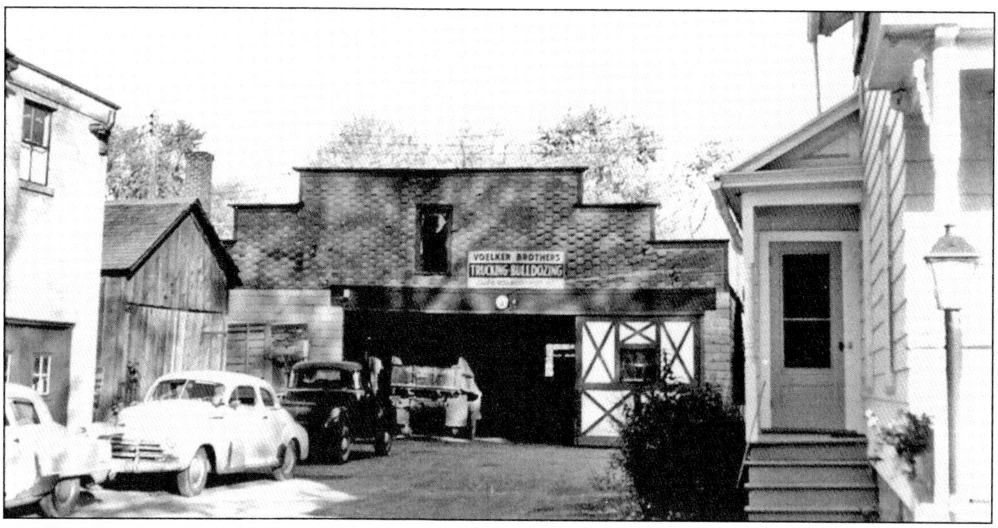

Voelker Brothers Trucking provided all of the major equipment work for the village as well as hauling houses for Barden Homes in the 1960s. Voelker's plowed the streets as well. There were four brothers: Alvin, Louis, Willie, and Fred. The business continued into the 1980s with Fred as the last brother working. Its building remains, two doors north of the bank. (RTH.)

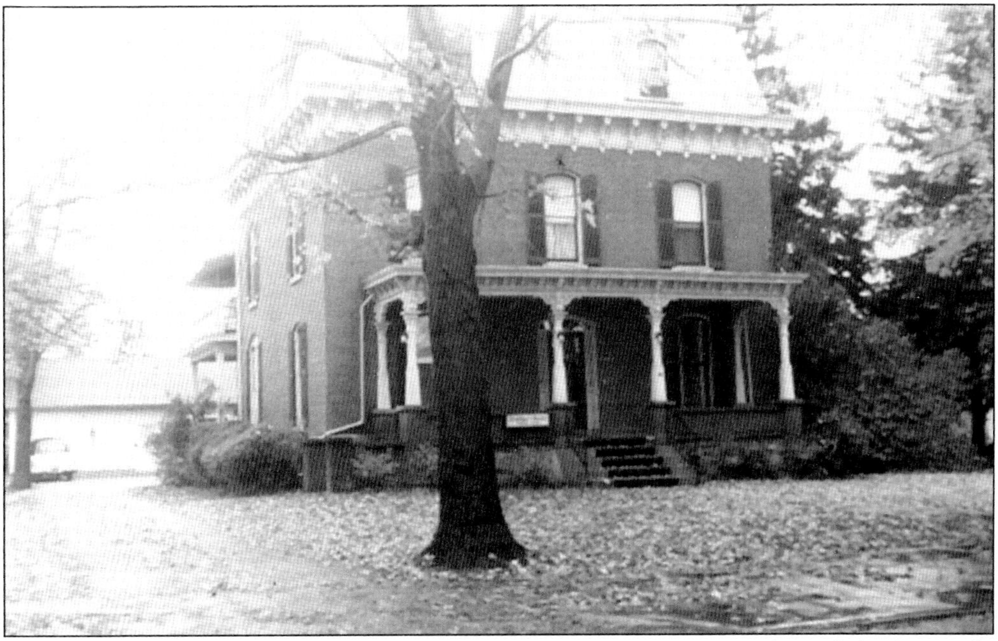

The Wallace and Heath Funeral Home has been a fixture on State Street for a while. Originally owned by Warren Wallace and Donald Heath, the structure has changed little over the years except for the front porch enclosure. It became Bates, Wallace, and Heath, when purchased by Dennis Bates. It is still a very vital part of the community. (RTH.)

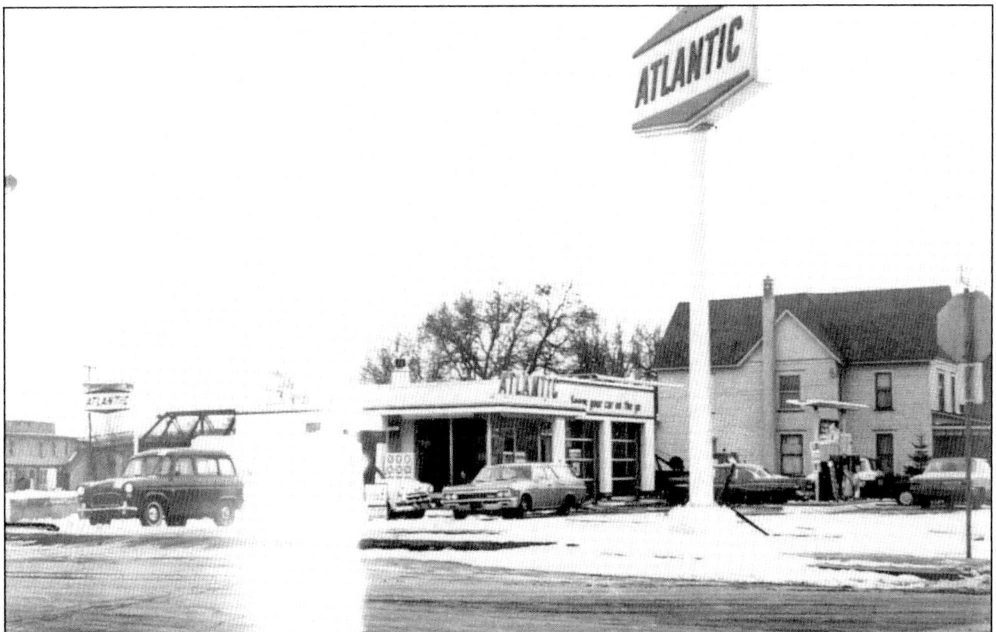

This building is located on State Street between Main and Vernon Streets. At the time of this photograph, it had just been built on the former site of the Fenton Hotel. It would remain an Atlantic station for a short time before becoming Fred's Import Repair shop. Not long after, the site would again have a new replacement building, the Middleport Savings and Loan. (RTH.)

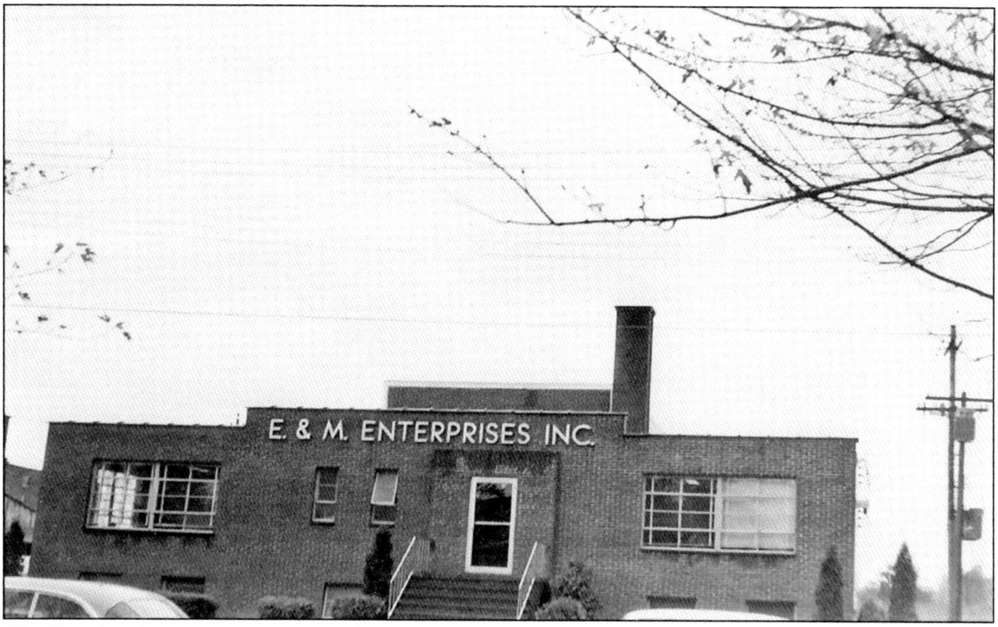

The E and M Enterprises, Inc., was located on Kelly Avenue next to the Middleport Cold Storage. It was founded by Art MacDonald and was a very large machine shop. Over time, it acquired the land to the north, which included Cliff Allen's truck garage and his house. The house was demolished, but the garage was connected to the main building and used as a machine shop. (RTH.)

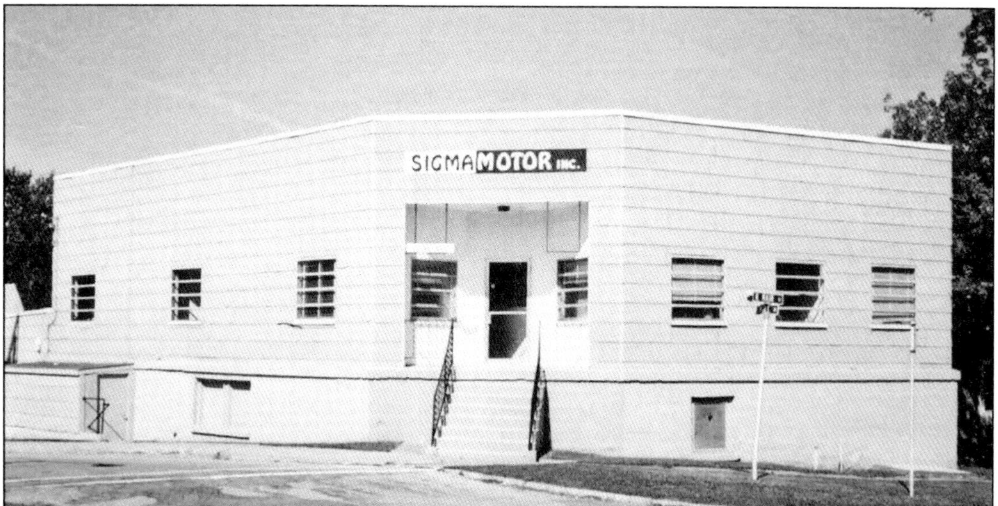

This Sigma Motor factory was located on the corner of North Main Street and Mill Street. Originally, it housed a very specialized manufacturing facility, which produced medical pumps. Later Sigma would move and, after being vacant for years, the building was used as an office by Dr. Douglas Gilbert. Later it again became a production facility. (RTH.)

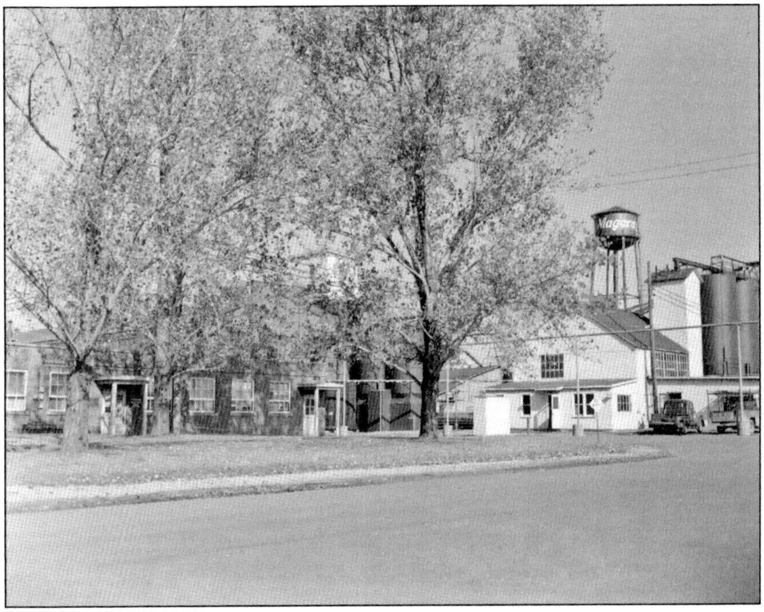

This photograph is from the early 1960s and shows the Niagara Sprayer/FMC production facility. What makes the picture special is that it is dated 1960, after Niagara became part of FMC, yet the water tower had yet to be changed from Niagara. Later there would be an FMC logo on the tower. (RTH.)

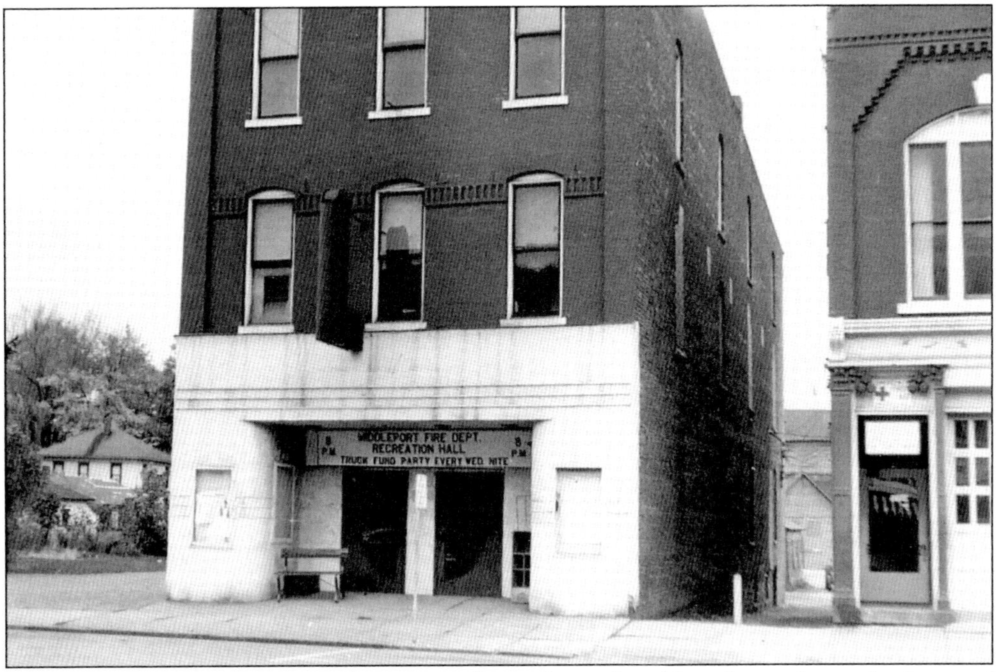

Until 1950, Middleport had an indoor movie theater located on Main Street. It was the Star, and the Stornelli family owned it. A kid could attend a matinee on Saturday afternoon for 10¢ in 1950. The structure was later purchased by the fire department, used for a while as a recreation hall, and later demolished to make way for the new fire building. (RTH.)

The bank has stood at the corner of Park Avenue and Main Street for at least the last 70 years. Initially, it was the Middleport Savings Bank, then Marine, and Marine Midland, and finally, HSBC Bank. The chief bank officer in the 1950s was Warren Snell, who lived two doors away to the south on Main Street. Except for the awnings, the building looks the same today. (RTH.)

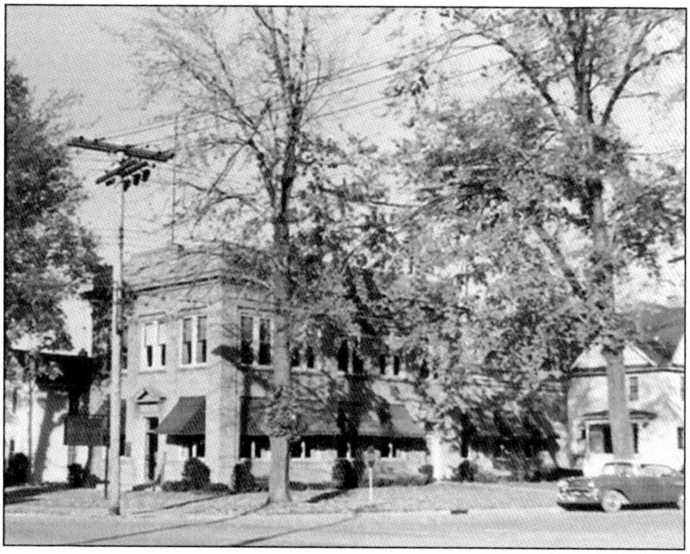

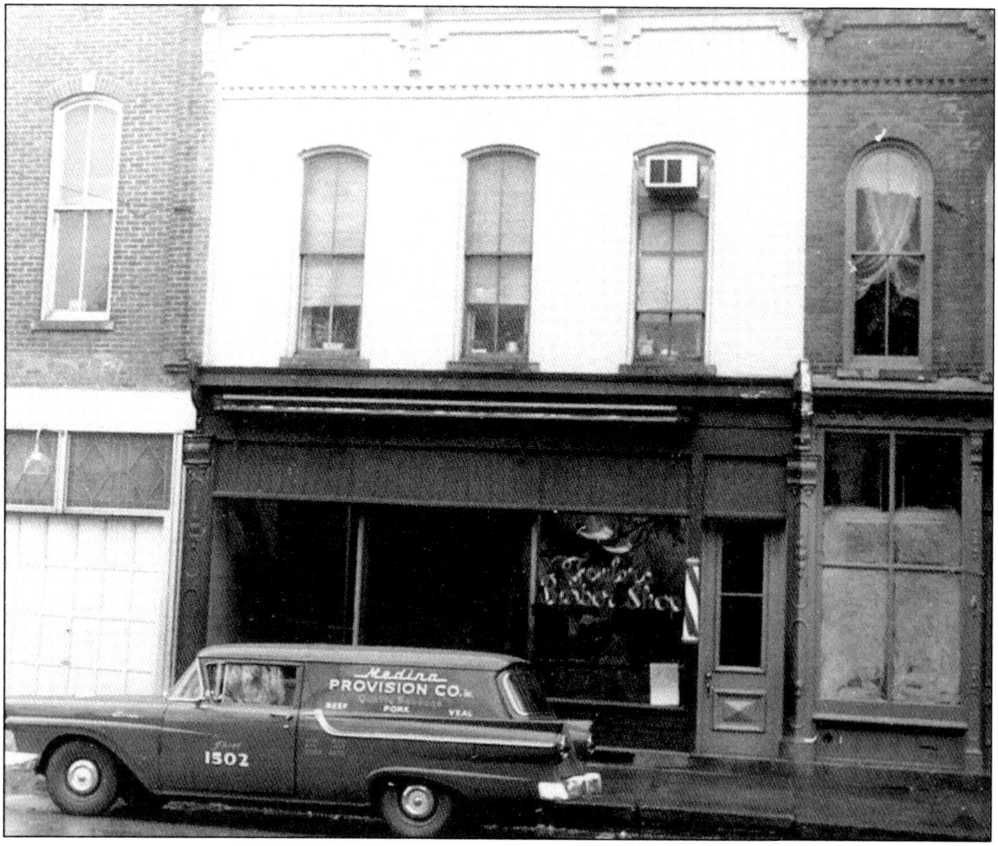

This building is located on State Street between Main and Vernon Streets. At the time of this photograph, it had two businesses: on the right, Norm Fowler's Barber Shop and on the left, owner Paul Hammond's Insurance Company. Two men, Norm Fowler and his young employee, Mike Reale, staffed the barbershop. This was one of four barbershops in town, which included Cy Roberts, Barnum, and for a short while, Dick Menzel. (RTH.)

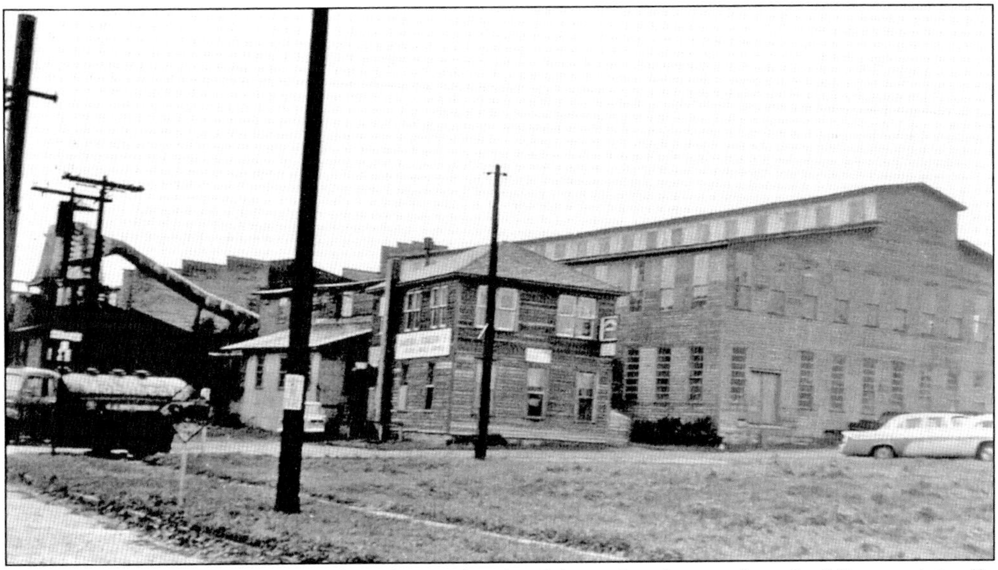

Located on Kelly Avenue, situated on the south side of the railroad, were these buildings, originally named the Barden and Robeson Company. Beginning in the late 1950s, it became Barden Homes and would eventually become one of the largest producers of prefabricated houses in the northeast. At its peak, the factory could complete two full houses a day. (RTH.)

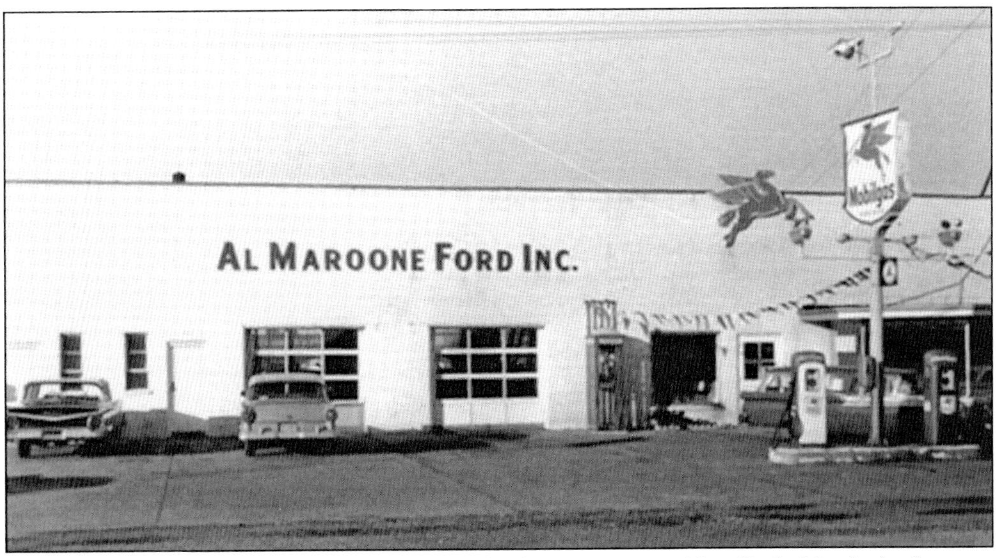

Al Maroone owned one of the largest Ford dealerships in western New York. His dealership was not always a huge enterprise. He began in Middleport with this building, which he had constructed on Route 31. The dealership did not just sell automobiles but was also a full-time Mobil gasoline station. The franchise would later move to Transit Road in Clarence, but a Ford dealership did remain in town until the 1980s. (RTH.)

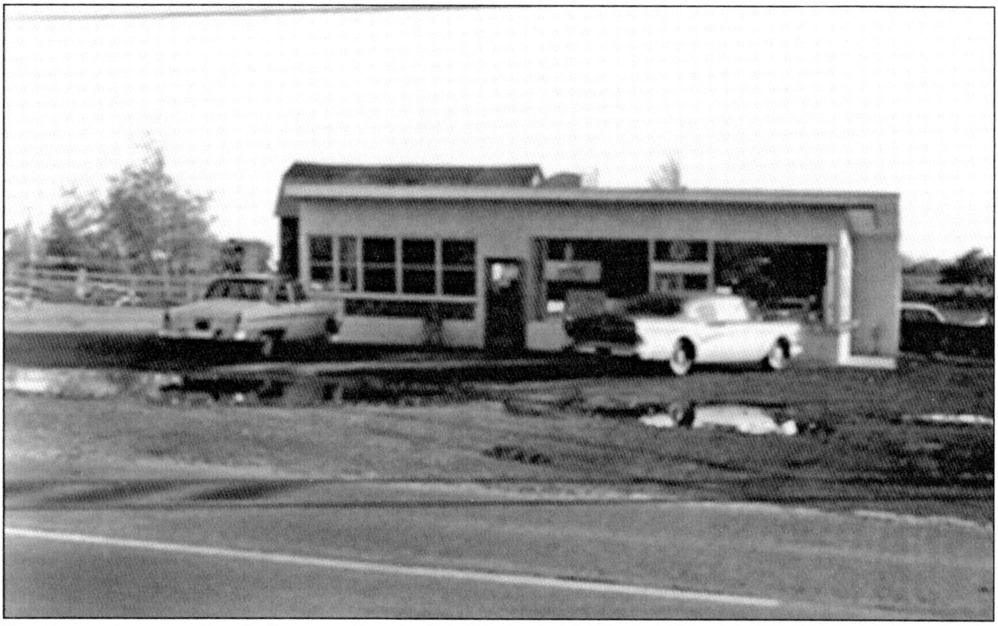

Doc Lewis began a family favorite, located on Route 31, in the 1960s. It was called the Milk House and featured ice cream, hot dogs, hamburgers, and French fries. It remained a dairy-snack bar until about 1970, when it was converted into a bar called the Scottish Piper. It was quickly lost to a fire, purchased, and rebuilt into Pizza Place II, which it remains today. (RTH.)

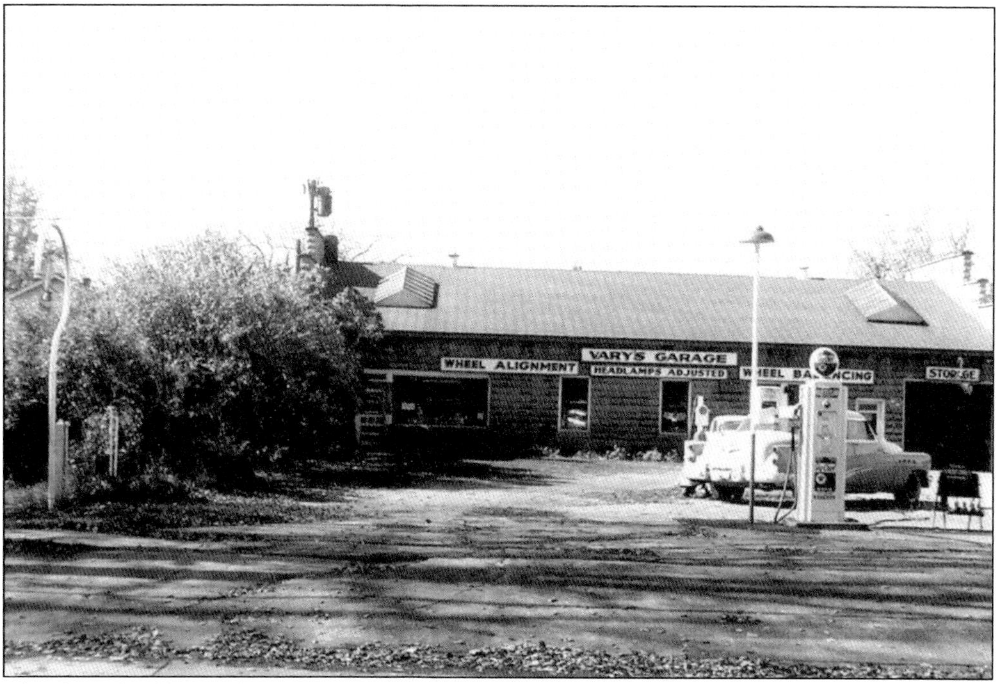

This large building is located on Vernon Street and was originally an automobile repair shop owned by Elmer Vary. Vary was also an inventor who held patents on fruit-peeling equipment. The site would be used over the years as Peterson Drugs and Mr. Bill's convenience store. It has been vacant for some years. (RTH.)

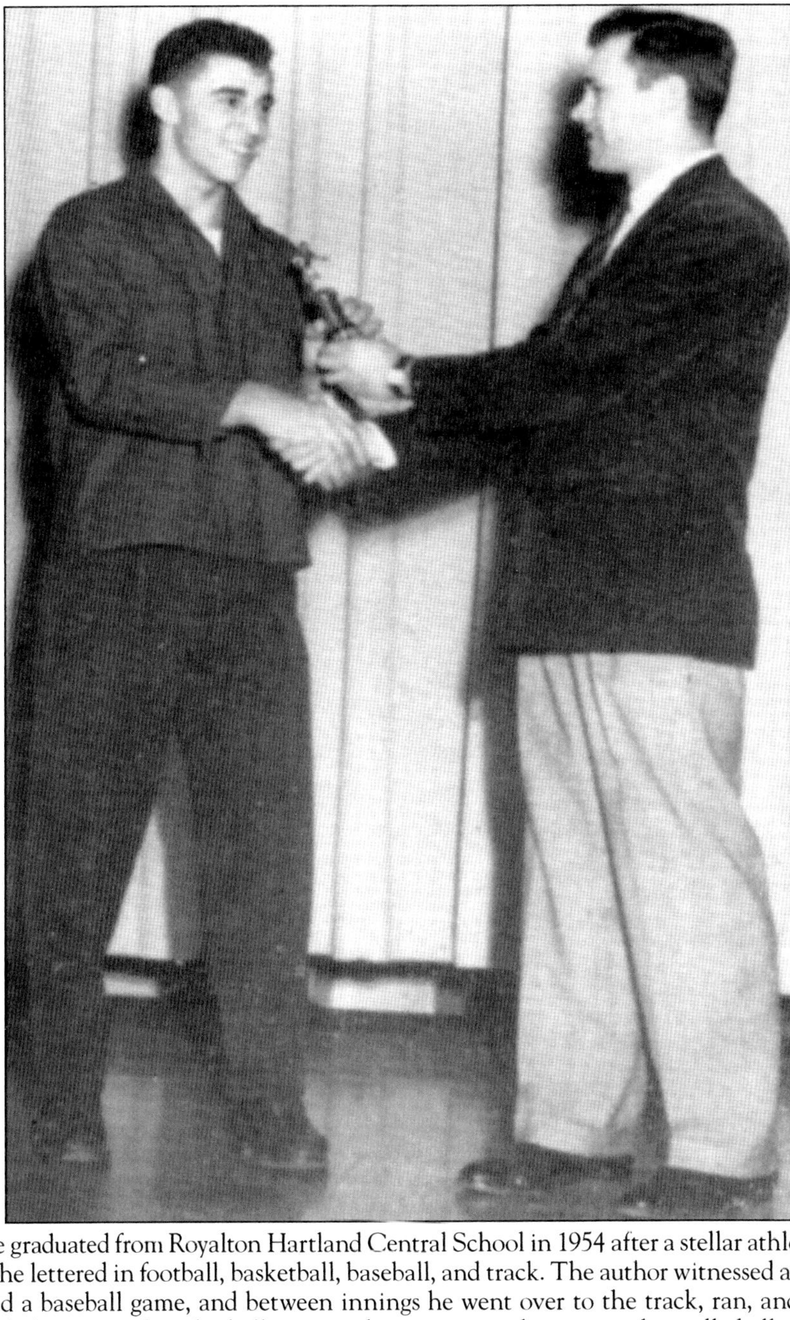

Lou Reale graduated from Royalton Hartland Central School in 1954 after a stellar athletic career in which he lettered in football, basketball, baseball, and track. The author witnessed a day when he pitched a baseball game, and between innings he went over to the track, ran, and won the 100-yard dash, returned to the ball game to hit a towering home run that rolled all the way to the goal posts on the football field! He next attended the University of Buffalo where he started as fullback his first two years before switching to center his last two seasons. In his senior year, the 1958 football season, UB won the Lambert Trophy, symbolic of being the best small college team in the East. For that, they were offered their first bowl bid, but they declined, as they would not have been able to play their African American players in the southern part of the U.S. It would be 50 years before UB would receive another bowl invitation. Lou Reale was cocaptain of that UB team. (Author's collection.)

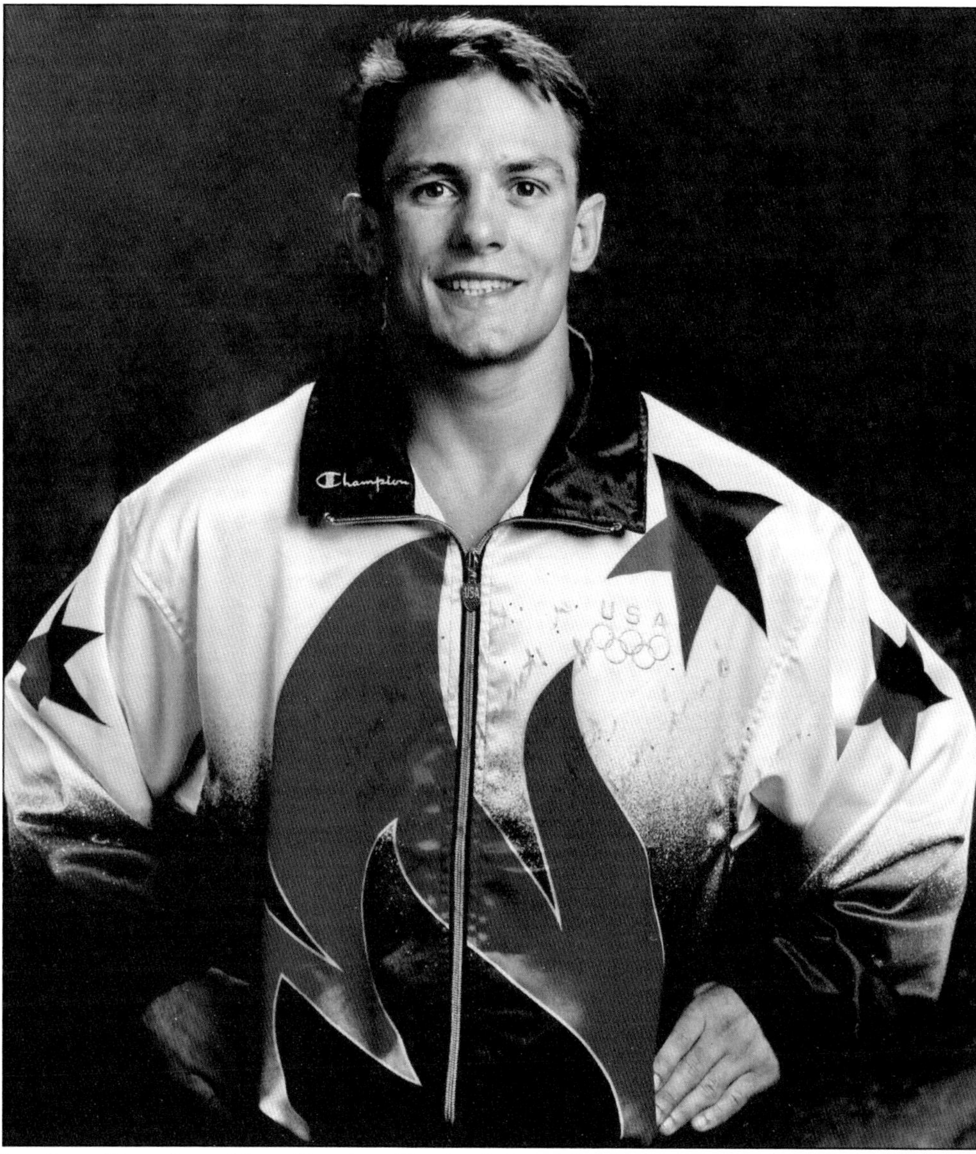

Lou Rosselli graduated from Royalton Hartland Central School in 1988, where the gymnasium carries his name. During his time there, he was a Niagara Orleans All-League wrestler five consecutive seasons and a New York state champion in his sophomore and senior seasons. He still holds numerous school records. Upon graduation, he earned a scholarship to Edinboro State University in Pennsylvania. While there, he earned All-America honors for an excellent series of college teams. In 1996, he wrestled his way through the Olympic trials onto the U.S. Olympic team. He wrestled at the games in Atlanta, Georgia. During one of his matches (which he was winning), he suffered multiple fractures in his arm but finished the match. Naturally, he could not continue in the games and finished 11th in the world. He returned to Edinboro where he served as a coach. He is now an assistant coach at Ohio State University and runs many well-respected clinics for wrestlers. (Author's collection.)

EFFECTIVE APRIL 24, 1955

New York Central System

LOCAL TIME TABLES

The Time shown herein is
STANDARD TIME
add one hour for
DAYLIGHT SAVING TIME

New York
Poughkeepsie
Albany
Schenectady
Utica
Syracuse
Rochester
Buffalo
Niagara Falls
and intermediate stations
also
Auburn Road Branch
Falls Road Branch
Niagara Falls Branch
Albany—Troy

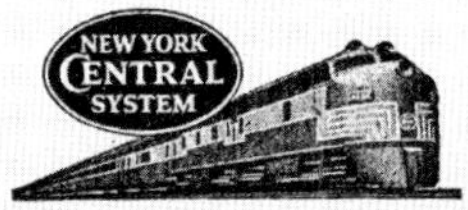

FORM 100

Buffalo to Niagara Falls

Miles		◆ 681 Daily	217 Sun. only Note	207 Ex. Sun. Note	◆ 683 Daily	◆ 685 Daily	◆ 687 Daily
		BEELINER AM	AM	AM	BEELINER AM	BEELINER PM	BEELINER PM
0.0	Lv **Buffalo (Central Term.)** ... (E.T.)	4 55	6 35	7 20	10 00	2 00	4 21
3.0	Lv **Buffalo** (Exchange St.)	5 02	6 44	7 29	10 07	2 07	4 28
6.9	Ar Black Rock	5 10	f6 51	f7 36	10 15	2 15	4 36
14.1	Ar North Tonawanda	5 21	7 08	7 53	10 25	2 26	4 47
20.1	Ar La Salle	......	f7 16	f8 01	......	......	4 58
22.9	Ar Echota	......	f7 21	f8 06	......	......	......
25.1	Ar **Niagara Falls**	5 40	7 30	8 15	10 45	2 45	5 07
26.9	Ar **Suspension Bridge**	5 45	7 50	8 35	10 50	2 50	5 11
		AM	AM	AM	AM	PM	PM

217: Will also run May 30, July 4 & Sept. 5
207: Will not run May 30, July 4 or Sept. 5

Niagara Falls to Buffalo

	◆ 680 Daily	358 Daily	◆ 682 Daily	◆ 684 Daily	246 Daily	◆ 686 Daily
	BEELINER AM	AM	BEELINER PM	BEELINER PM	PM	BEELINER PM
Lv **Suspension Bridge** ... (E.T.)	6 00	7 28	12 10	2 55	8 20	9 40
Lv **Niagara Falls**	6 05	7 37	12 15	3 00	8 45	9 45
Lv Echota	......	......	......	......	......	......
Lv La Salle	6 15	......	......	......	......	......
Lv North Tonawanda	6 23	•8 00	12 32	3 18	9 10	10 03
Lv Black Rock	6 36	......	12 46	3 31	......	10 16
Ar **Buffalo** (Exchange St.)	6 43	•8 27	12 53	3 38	9 32	10 23
Ar **Buffalo** (Central Term.)	6 50	8 35	1 00	3 45	9 40	10 30
	AM	AM	PM	PM	PM	PM

Rochester — Suspension Bridge via Falls Road

49 Daily	Miles			42 Ex. Sun.
PM				AM
4 45	0.0	Lv **Rochester** ... (E.T.)	Ar	7 30
5 04	10.9	Lv Spencerport	Lv	6 39
5 15	17.9	Lv Brockport	Lv	6 25
5 23	22.5	Lv Holley	Lv	6 17
5 40	31.4	Lv Albion	Lv	6 00
5 49	37.1	Lv Knowlesville	Lv	5 45
6 05	41.2	Lv Medina	Lv	5 37
6 14	45.7	Lv Middleport	Lv	5 25
6 24	50.7	Lv Gasport	Lv	5 15
6 40	56.6	Ar Lockport	Lv	5 05
6 50	56.6	Lv Lockport	Ar	5 05
7 05	67.3	Lv Sanborn	Lv	4 38
8 05	75.7	Ar **Suspension Bridge**	Lv	4 25
246 Daily				
8 20	75.7	Lv **Suspension Bridge**		......
8 45	77.5	Ar **Niagara Falls**	Lv	......
9 10	88.5	Ar North Tonawanda	Lv	......
9 32	99.6	Ar Buffalo (Ex. St.)	Lv	......
9 40	102.6	Ar **Buffalo** (Cent. Term.)	Lv	......
PM				AM

New York to Rochester via Syracuse and Auburn Road

99 Ex. Sat.	29 Sat. Only	Miles			6 Daily
PM	PM				AM
①1035	10 10	0.0	Lv **New York** (Grand Central Terminal) . (E.T.)	Ar	6 50
......	......	142.2	Lv Albany	Ar	......
①4 04	3 16	289.5	Ar Syracuse	Lv	1 28

① — Will not operate from New York May 29, July 3 or Sept. 4—Passengers use Train 29 leaving New York 10:10 p.m.

3 Ex. Sun.	7 Sun. Only	Miles	*Auburn Road*		18 Ex. Sun.	8 Sun. Only
5 00	5 30	0.0	Lv **Syracuse**	Ar	10 55	11 05
5 20	f 5 48	8.6	Lv Camillus	Lv	......	......
5 29	f 5 53	10.8	Lv Martisco	Lv	......	......
5 46	6 05	17.5	Lv Skaneateles Jct.	Lv	10 02	10 25
6 06	6 19	26.1	Ar **Auburn**	Lv	9 49	10 10
6 16	6 25	26.1	Lv **Auburn**	Ar	9 34	10 03
6 36	6 44	36.9	Lv Cayuga	Lv	9 18	9 45
6 49	6 54	41.6	Lv Seneca Falls	Lv	9 09	9 36
6 58	7 01	44.9	Lv Waterloo	Lv	8 54	9 26
7 10	7 10	51.5	Ar **Geneva**	Lv	8 41	9 17
7 25	7 16	51.5	Lv **Geneva**	Ar	8 25	9 07
7 33	7 24	56.3	Lv Oaks Corners	Lv	f 8 19	f 9 00
7 43	7 29	59.4	Lv Phelps	Lv	8 14	8 54
7 53	7 41	63.7	Lv Clifton Springs	Lv	8 01	8 45
8 03	7 49	68.2	Lv Shortsville	Lv	7 51	8 36
f 8 07	f 7 53	70.9	Lv Chapin	Lv	f 7 41	f 8 28
8 13	7 59	74.0	Ar **Canandaigua**	Lv	7 35	8 22
8 28	8 09	74.0	Lv **Canandaigua**	Ar	7 20	8 12
8 40	f 8 24	84.0	Lv Victor	Lv	7 05	7 55
9 10	f 8 40	94.5	Lv Pittsford	Lv	6 43	7 38
9 18	f 8 46	99.5	Lv Brighton	Lv	6 33	7 28
9 40	9 05	102.3	Ar **Rochester**	Lv	6 25	7 20
AM	AM				PM	PM

6

This is the local page from the above timetable. It shows the passenger train that ran from Niagara Falls in the morning going east (No. 42) and returned from Rochester in the evening going west (No. 49). The train usually had three cars: a freight car, mail car, and a passenger car. All of the mail reaching the towns listed arrived by rail in those days. This rail service continued until 1955. After that, the New York Central's Falls road line only serviced freight. The switch engine would come from Niagara Falls heading west in the morning and travel as far as Medina, and then it would return to Niagara Falls with its load and prepare for the next day. In those years, Niagara Falls had a tremendous switchyard. The trucking industry eventually eroded the need for major rail shipments while at the same time industry diminished. (Author's collection.)

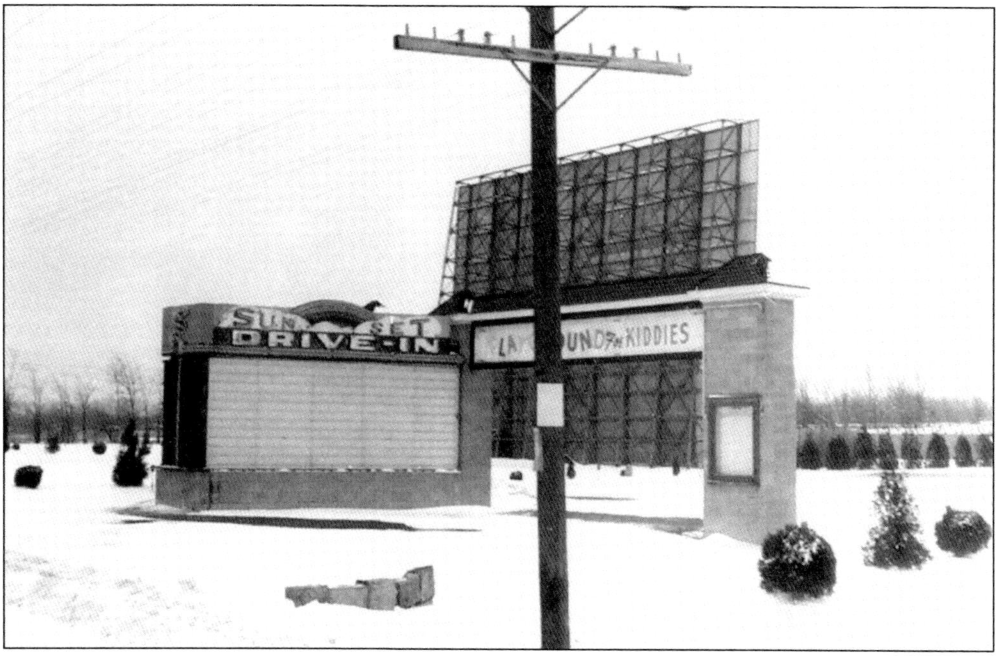

The Sunset Drive-In has been in operation since August 31, 1950, and has become an institution. Currently, it is one of only two that are still in operation in western New York. It began with just one screen, a snack bar, and a small playground, and it now boasts three screens and a year-round restaurant. In the beginning, the price of admission was 50¢. (RTH.)

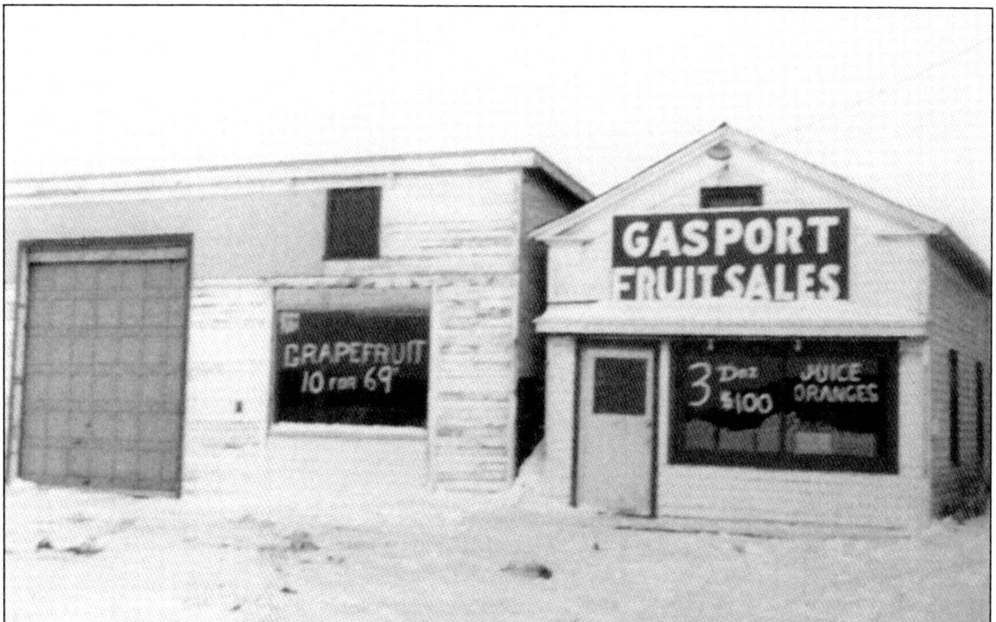

Moving on to Gasport, this fruit stand operated at the western terminus of West Avenue where it met Route 31. The man who ran the store only sold fresh fruit and was affiliated with the Locust Fruit Company of Lockport. The store remained in operation for a number of years, and later the building housed an antique dealer. The building remains today. (RTH.)

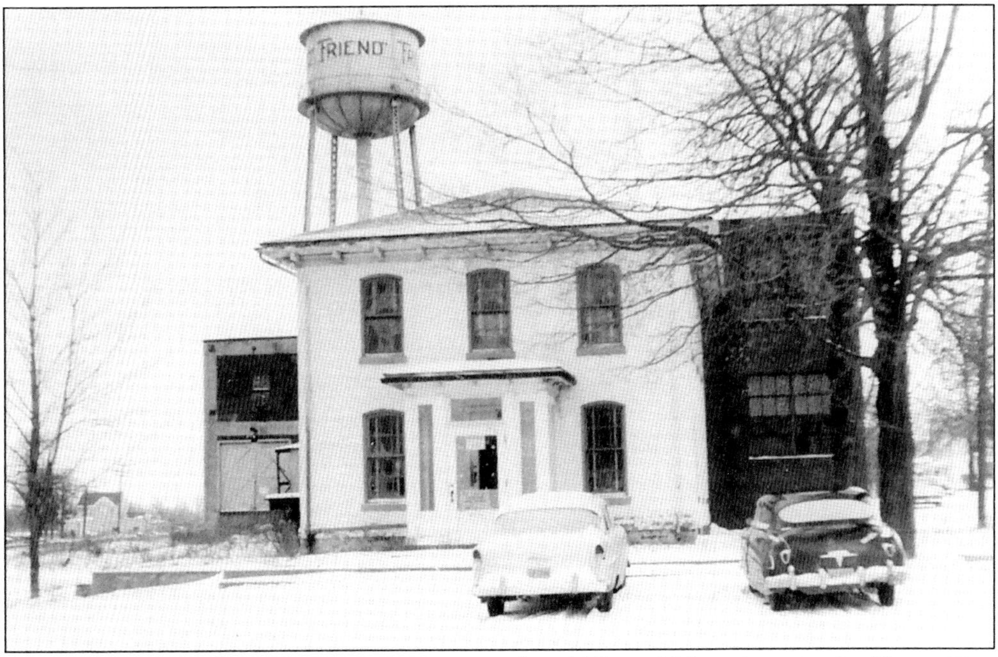

Across from Standish and Jones in Gasport are the old Friend Manufacturing buildings. One section was used by Duracraft Homes in the late 1950s and 1960s as a production facility for prefabricated houses. Jim Coppolla of Middleport owned the business. The site was well suited to this industry, as it offered a rail siding for the shipment of lumber. (RTH.)

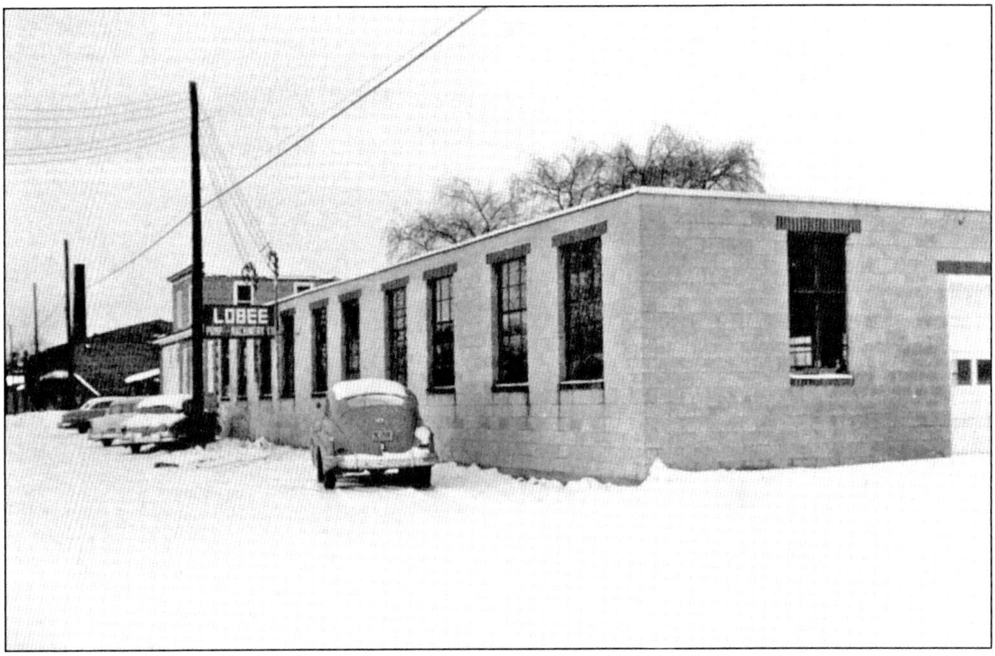

On State Street in Gasport, heading east out of town, stood the Lobee Pump Company. The first patent granted to this company was in the early 1900s for a rotary pump. Lobee was one of the Gasport industries that helped the locals work close to home. Lobee was later sold, and its name is still prominent in industrial circles.

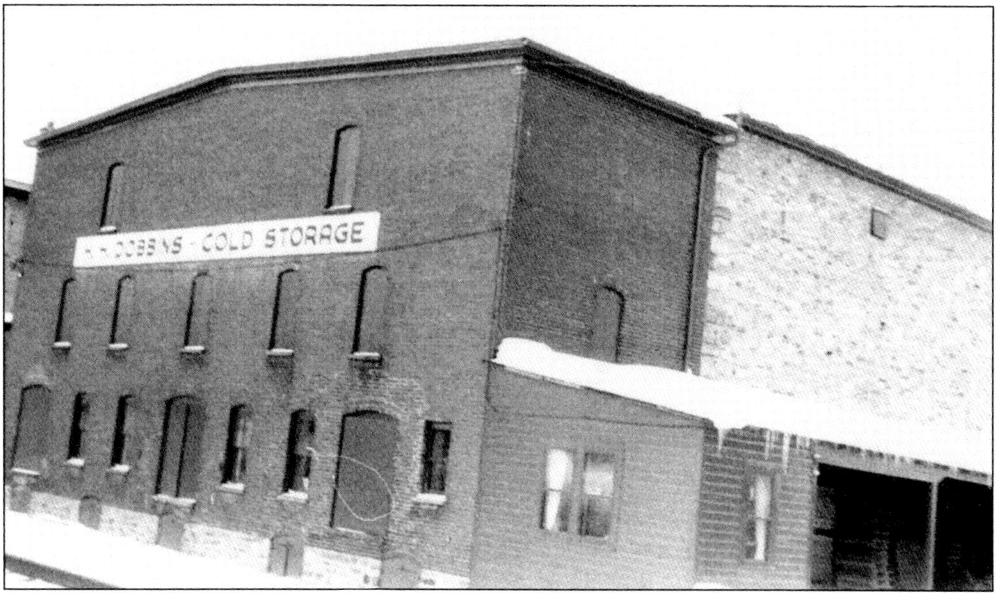

As Gasport was heavily involved in the fruit-processing industry, one of the many local cold storages that appeared during the 1920s was the Dobbins Cold Storage. This building was located along both the railroad and the canal and was an excellent site for transshipment of product. (RTH.)

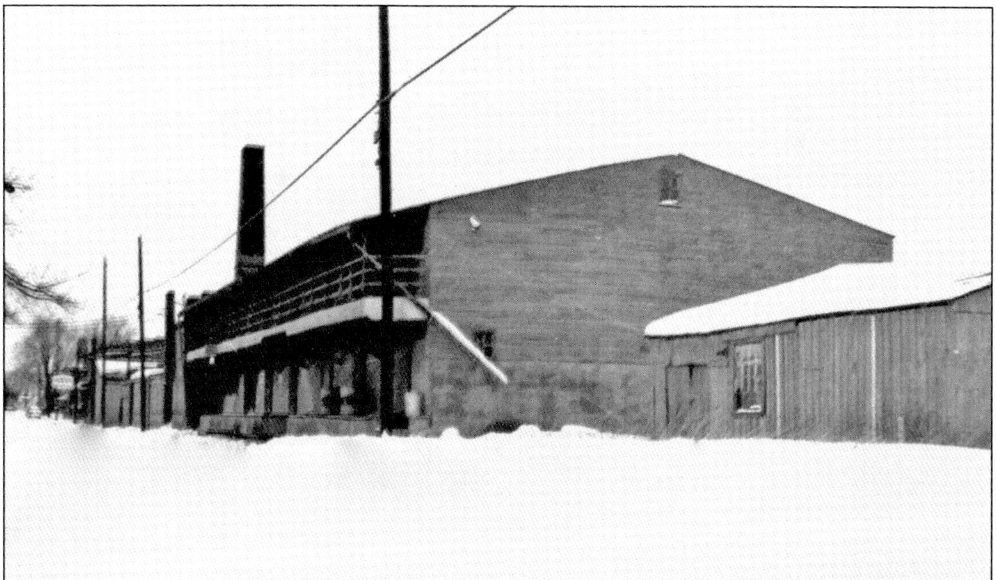

State Street in Gasport, located along the canal and near the New York Central Railroad, was a varied industrial and agricultural corridor. Another one of the local businesses was the John Bacon Company. This site engaged in wood products and similar to most of the other local businesses survived into the 1960s. (RTH.)

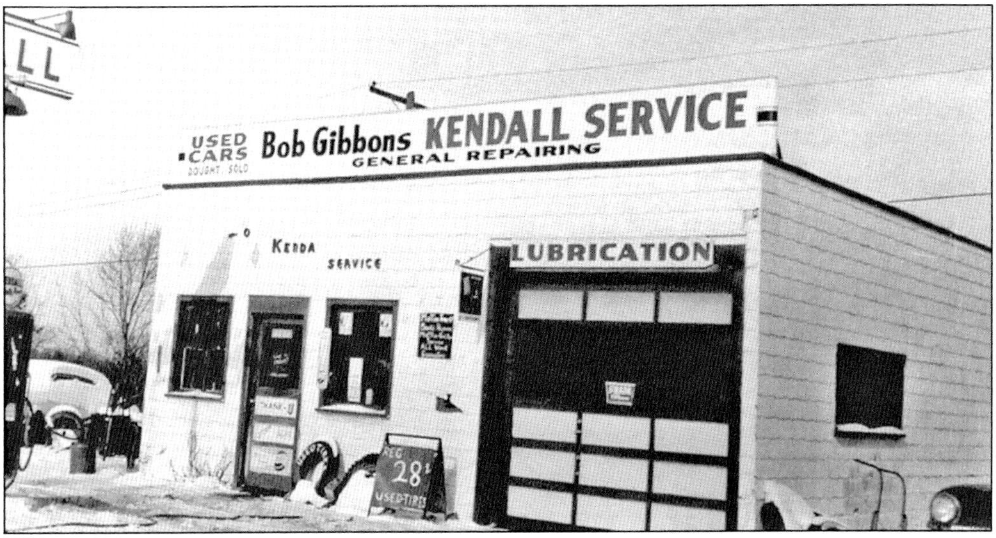

On the east end of East Avenue in Gasport, where the road meets Route 31, there was a gasoline station operated by Bob Gibbons. This was a very active place for many "hot-rodders" who used the station as a base of operations. It remained associated with automobiles through the end of the century but has since been converted into a diner. (RTH.)

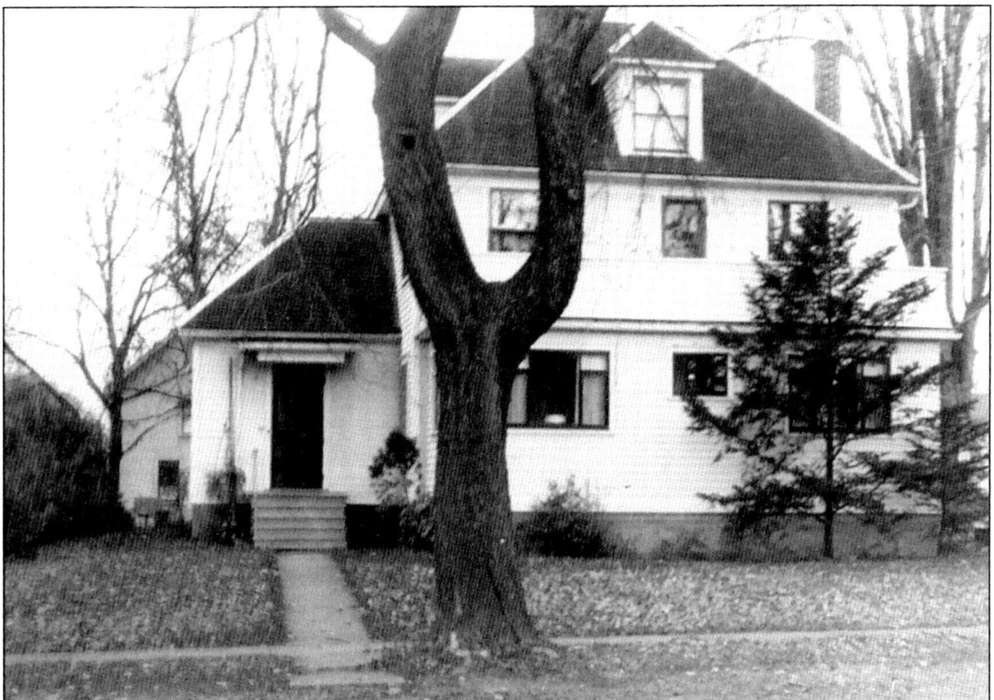

If a family lived in Middleport or Gasport during the 1950s, their family doctor was more than likely Dr. James Cole in Gasport or Dr. Kent Williams in Middleport. Pictured here is Dr. Cole's office located on Main Street in Gasport. Either of these two medical professionals would make house calls. (RTH.)

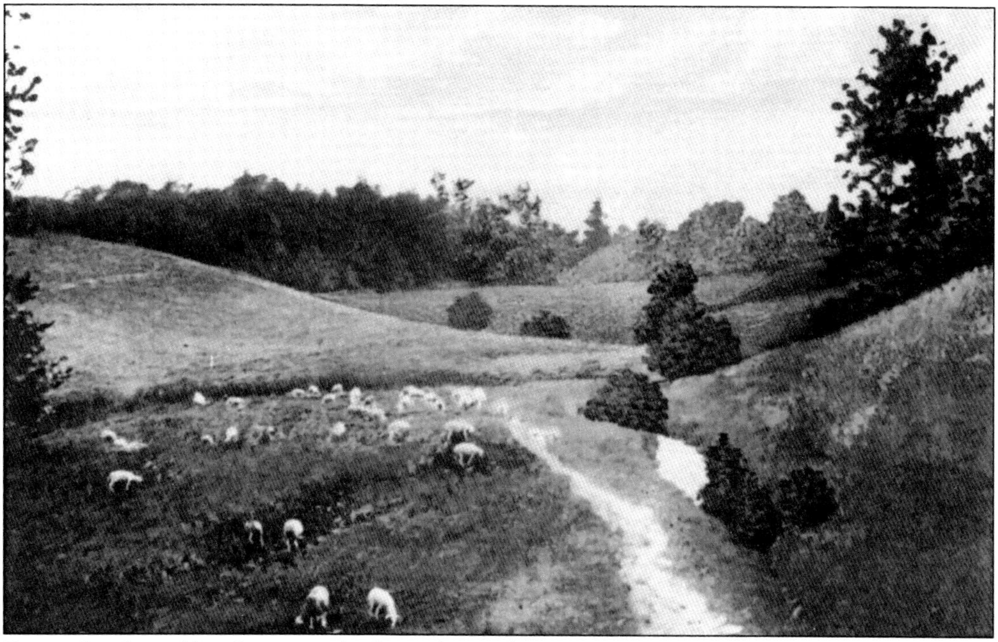

Pictured is the gulf in Gasport, which was located on Gasport Road just south of Route 31. Today it is part of the Gasport Ravine, a town of Royalton park. The water is caused in part by the quarrying, which took place further to the east on Mountain Road. There are many hiking trails, and the area has become a favorite for picnics and parties. (Niagara County Historian's Office.)

The Friend's Meeting House in Gasport is located on Maplewood Drive and appeared this way in 1962. It was the first church in Gasport and remained active through the years. It is currently used as a day care, classroom, and for meetings. It is truly one of the historical jewels of the community. (Niagara County Historian's Office.)

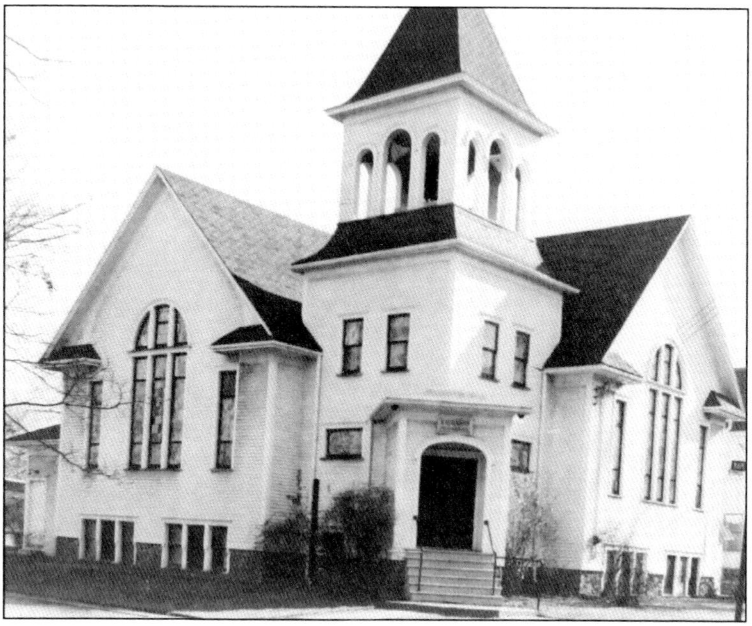

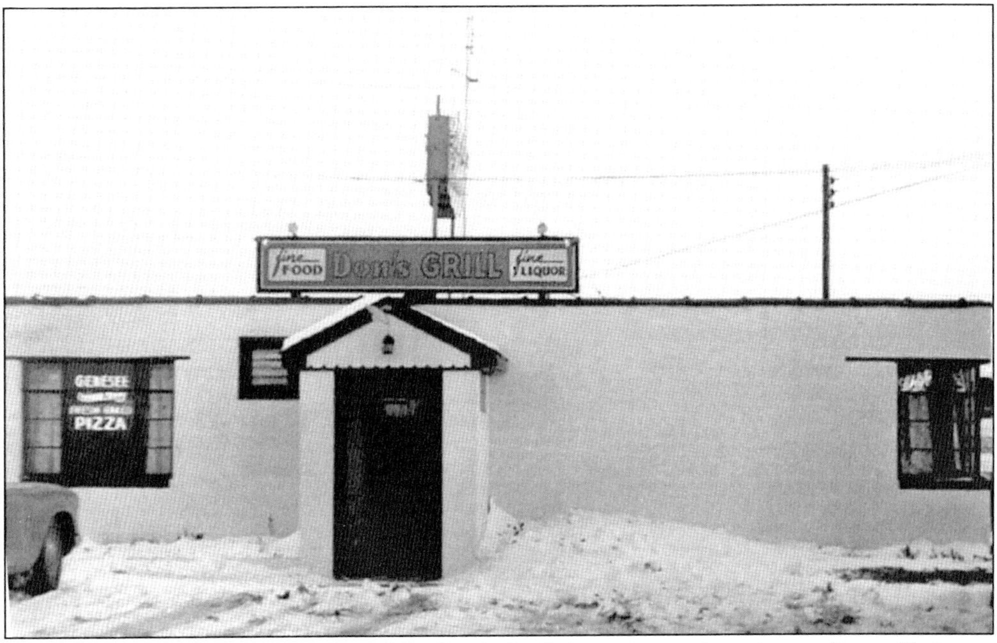

One of Gasport's three bars in the 1950s, Don's Grill thrived in its location on Route 31. It was a favorite with the Harrison workers on their way home as well as with the high schoolers that jammed the place at night (the drinking age was 18 then). This bar was owned by the Clack family, who had five bars in Niagara County. The place is still a bar today. (RTH.)

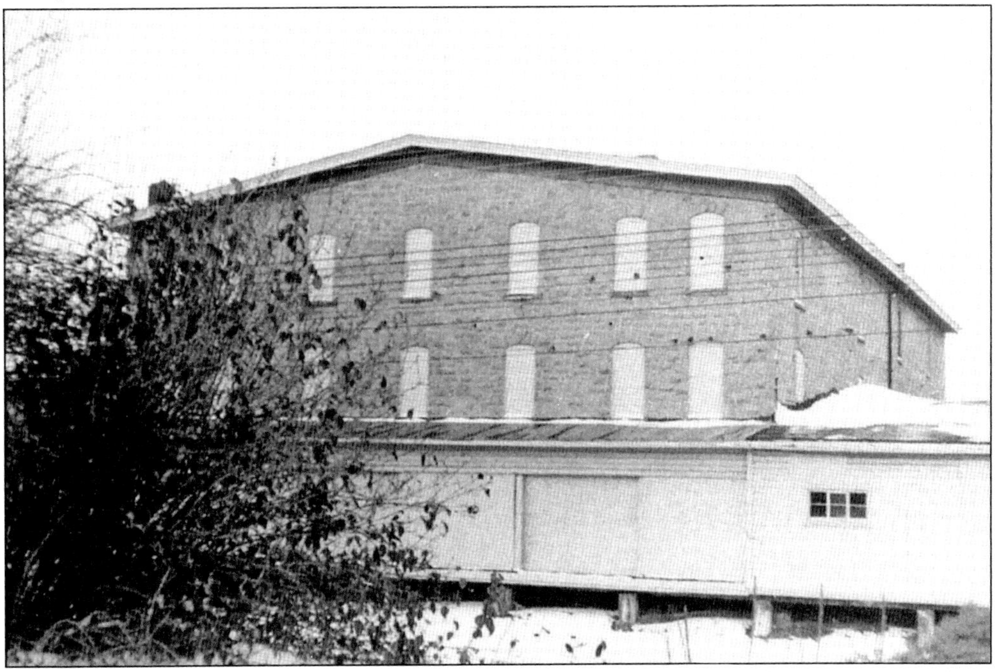

In Gasport, there were numerous cold storage facilities built during the early 1900s. One of them was Sweeney's, which was located on West Avenue, along the New York Central Railroad tracks. This building stored produce and made ice for the local citizens. Many of these buildings still exist in Gasport, but none of them are currently active. (RTH.)

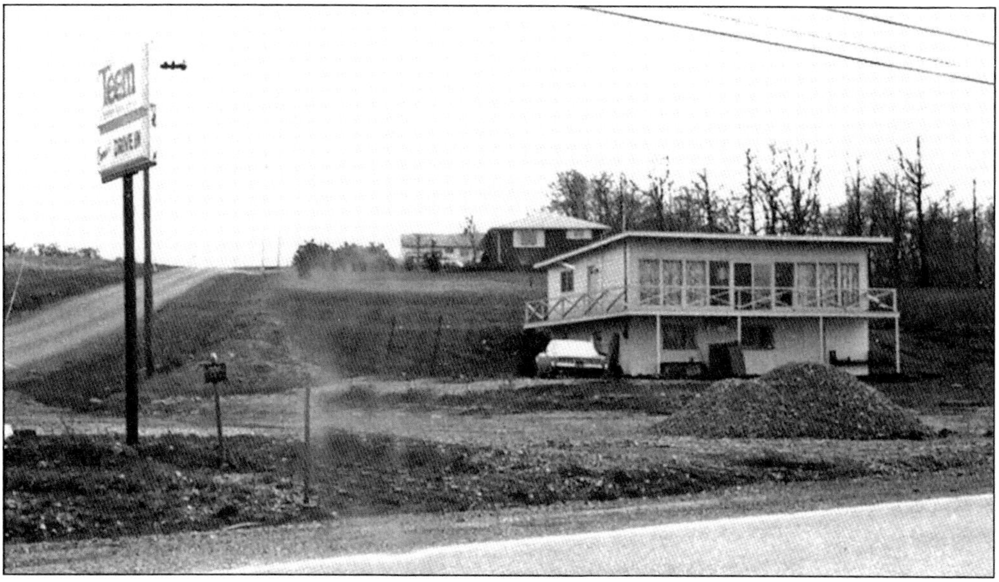

On the corner of Cottage Road and Route 31 stood Ernie's Drive-In Restaurant. This was a favorite for people who enjoyed a drive in the country, usually from Lockport. The specialty of the house was beef on weck, and they also sold ice cream. The Cottage Road to the east is unpaved in this photograph, and the housing development up the hill had not been started. (RTH.)

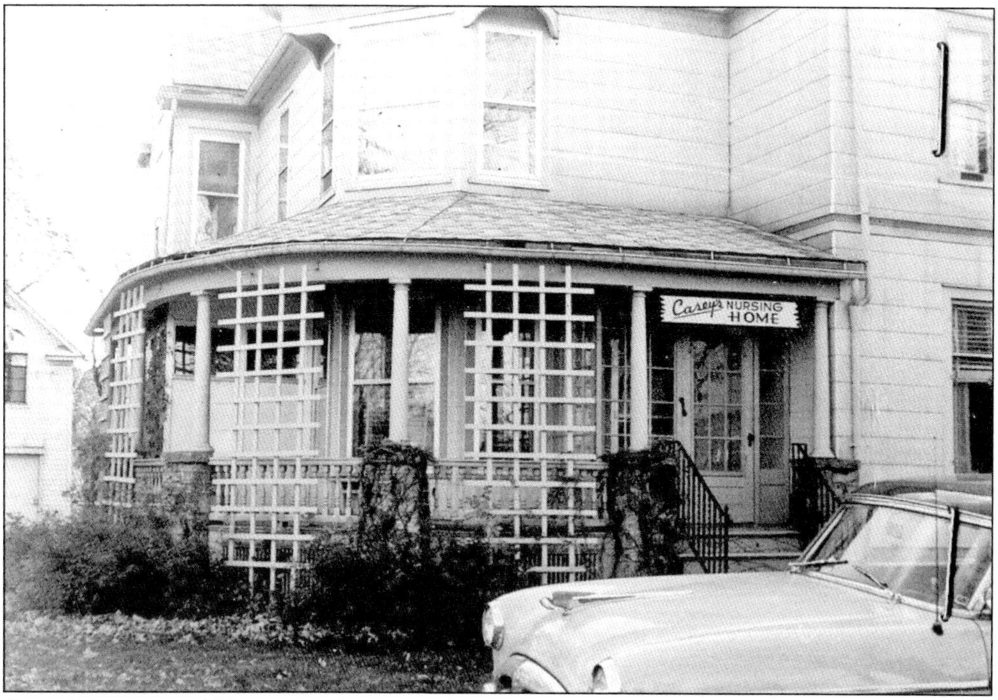

One of the nicest old houses in Gasport is located on West Avenue. In the 1950s, as pictured, it was Casey's Nursing Home. Many local residents recall the various patients who resided at Casey's. The home returned to a private residence and is still a very nice building. (RTH.)

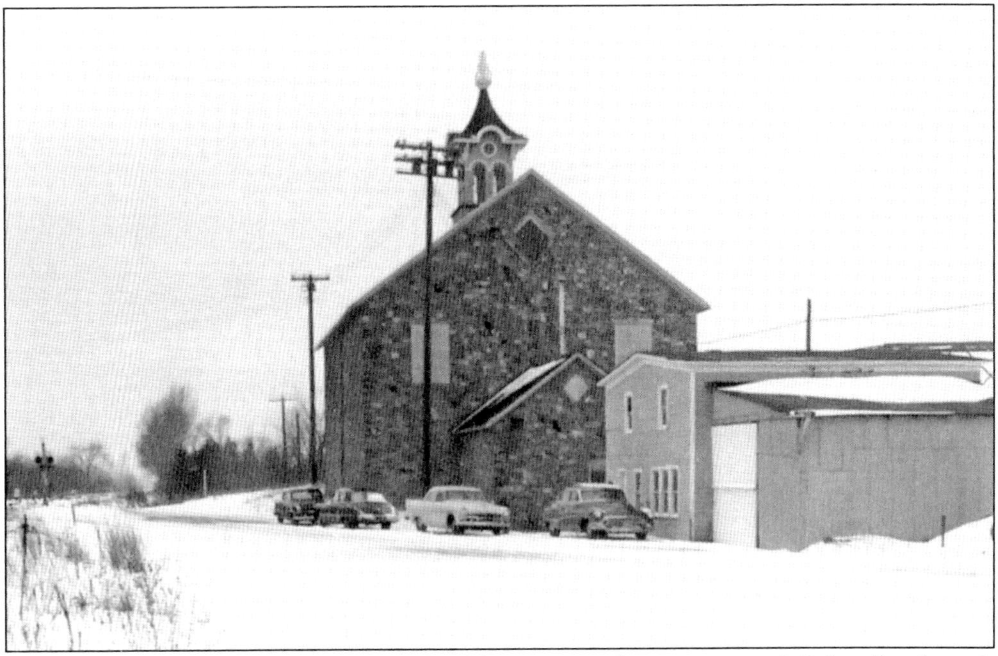

Between Reynales Basin and Gasport on the old Route 31 and its junction with Bolton Road stands a large stone building, which was the Shafer Cold Storage. This facility served the farmers in the Slayton Settlement and Mabee areas. No production was done at this site, merely transshipment to the canal on the one side or to the railroad tracks on the other side. (RTH.)

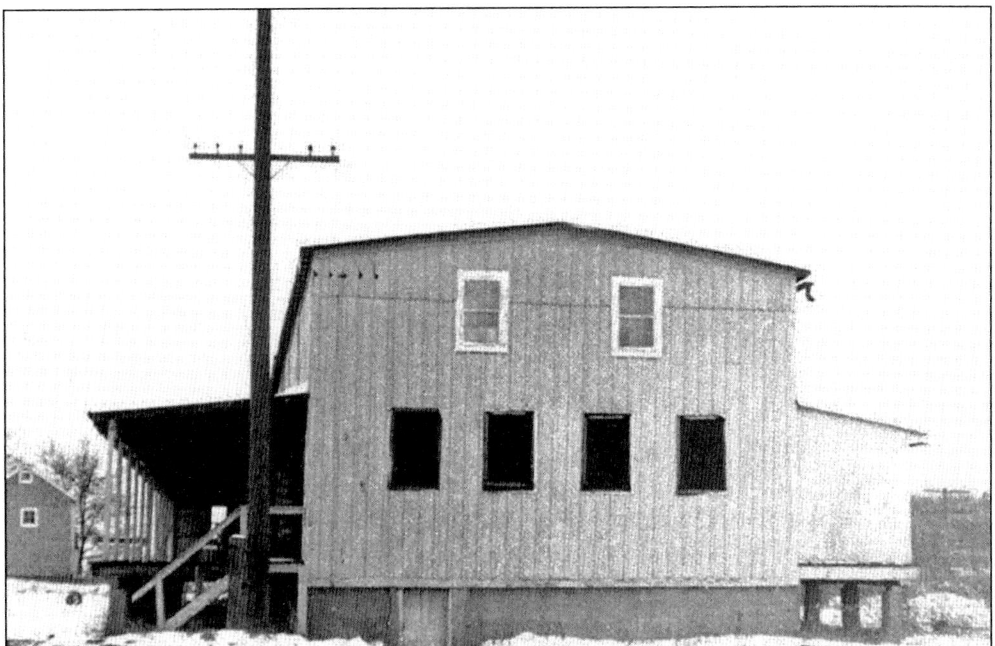

Directly across the road from Shafer Cold Storage stands a warehouse building last used as the Randolph Seed Company. It sits on the main New York Central Railroad link through the town of Royalton and served the agricultural industry. It has been abandoned for years. (RTH.)

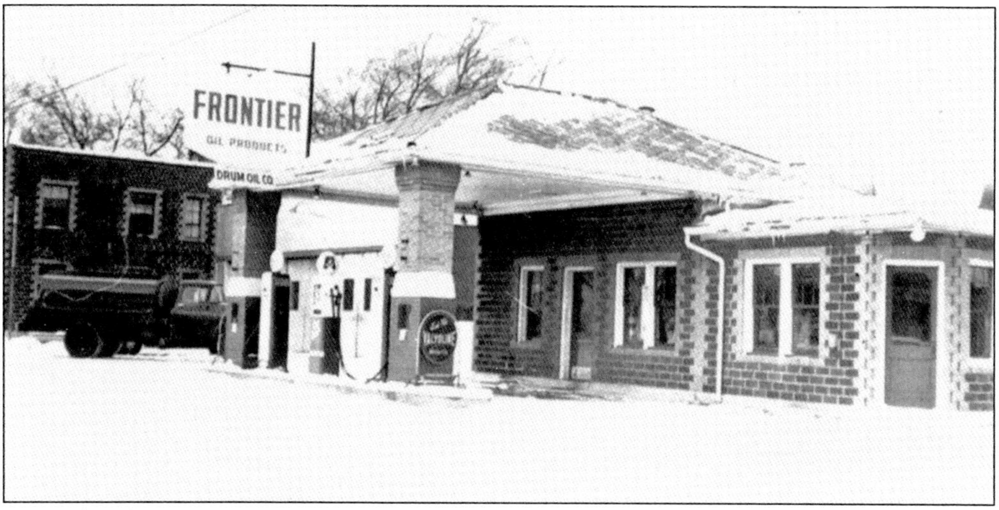

Located on State Street in Gasport, the original home of the Drum Oil Company was located on the south bank of the canal. Not only did the site serve as a gasoline station, it was the headquarters for the emerging home heating company, which would eventually dominate the industry in eastern Niagara County. It has since relocated to Route 31 near Royalton Center Road. (RTH.)

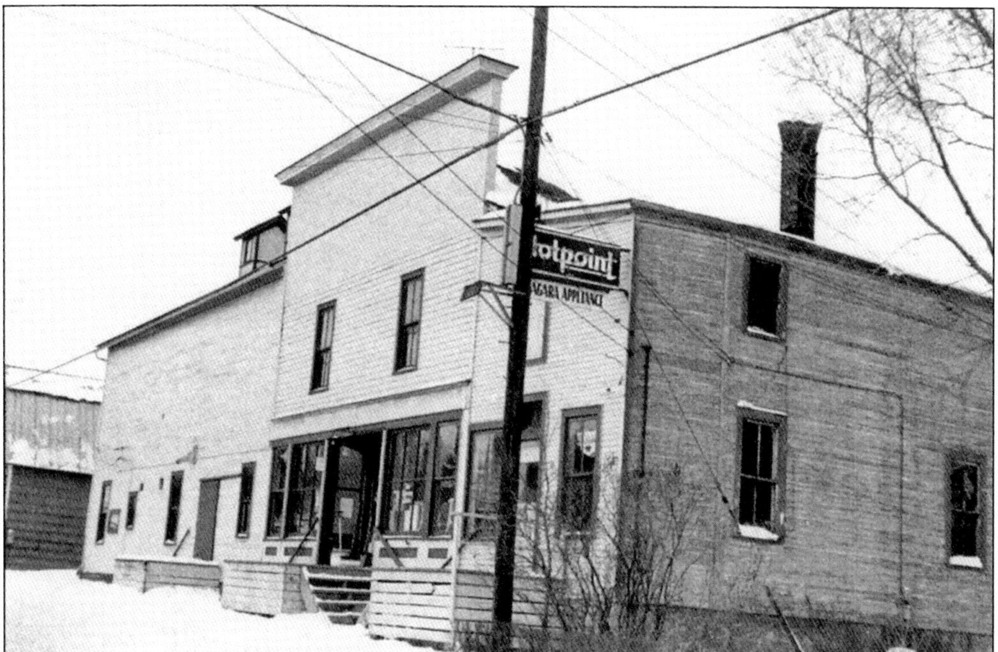

Also located on State Street in Gasport was the Drum Hardware store, close to the oil office. This was a general hardware outlet, which competed with the Standish Jones lumberyard around the corner. Drum Hardware faded from the business scene as the family focused on the oil business. (RTH.)

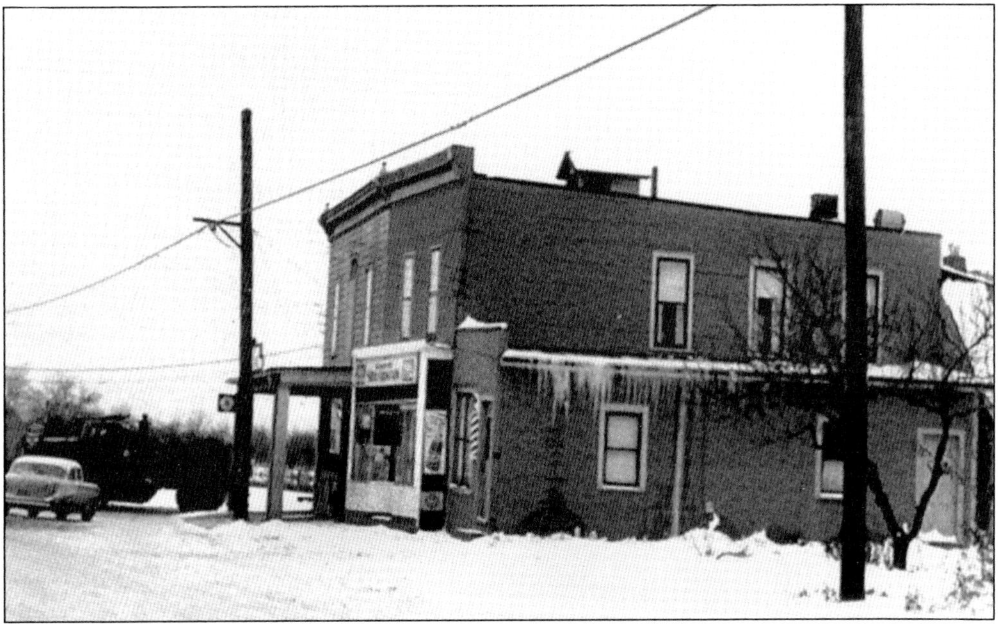

Near the corner of State and Main Streets on the canal side, stood one of the two grocery stores located in downtown Gasport. The Smalley family operated this typical village grocery for many years. It outlasted its competitor and only closed because there was no one available to continue the business. (RTH.)

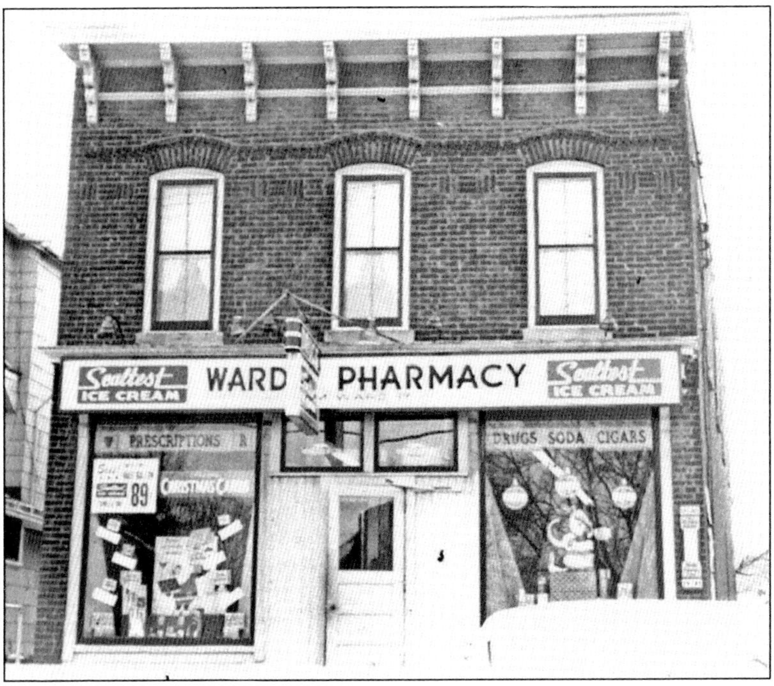

The main business venture in Gasport in 1959 and the 1960s was Ward's Pharmacy, located on the south side of State Street in the same building occupied by numerous enterprises over the years. Ward's sold everything and it had an ice cream counter. It was also the Greyhound bus terminal for Gasport. (RTH.)

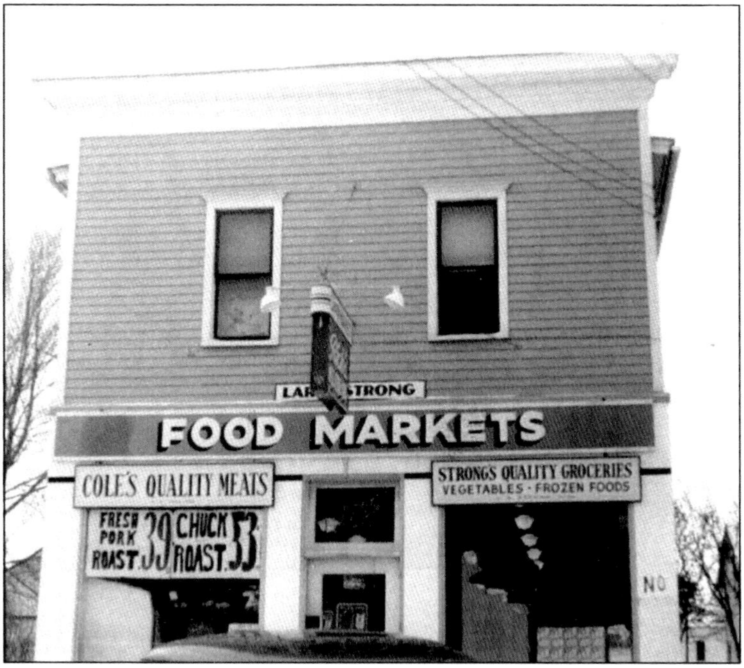

The other grocery business in Gasport was a joint venture between Strong's (who owned several rural stores) and Charlie Cole's meat market. Cole was a Gasport native. This joint venture did not last long and the grocery business belongs entirely to the Smalley's. Strong's Market continued in other areas. (RTH.)

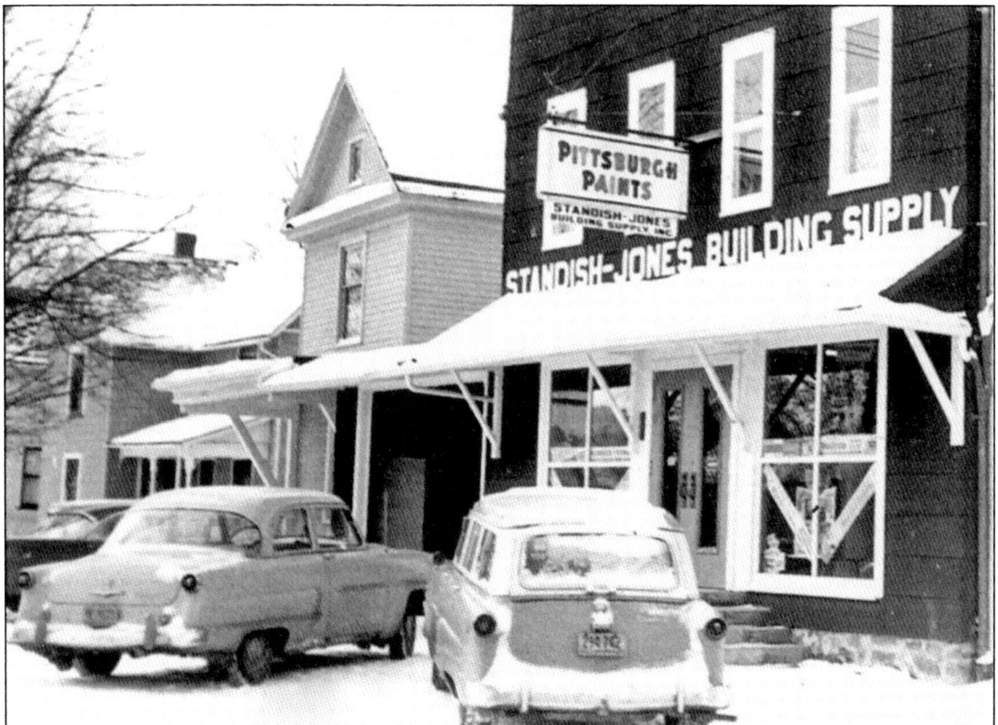

The Standish Jones Lumber Company has been in Gasport for decades. It was once owned by Mr. Standish and Mr. Jones, but has been in the same family—the Ulrichs—for many years now. The store has always offered an incredible amount of stock and a large variety of items. It is still going strong today. (RTH.)

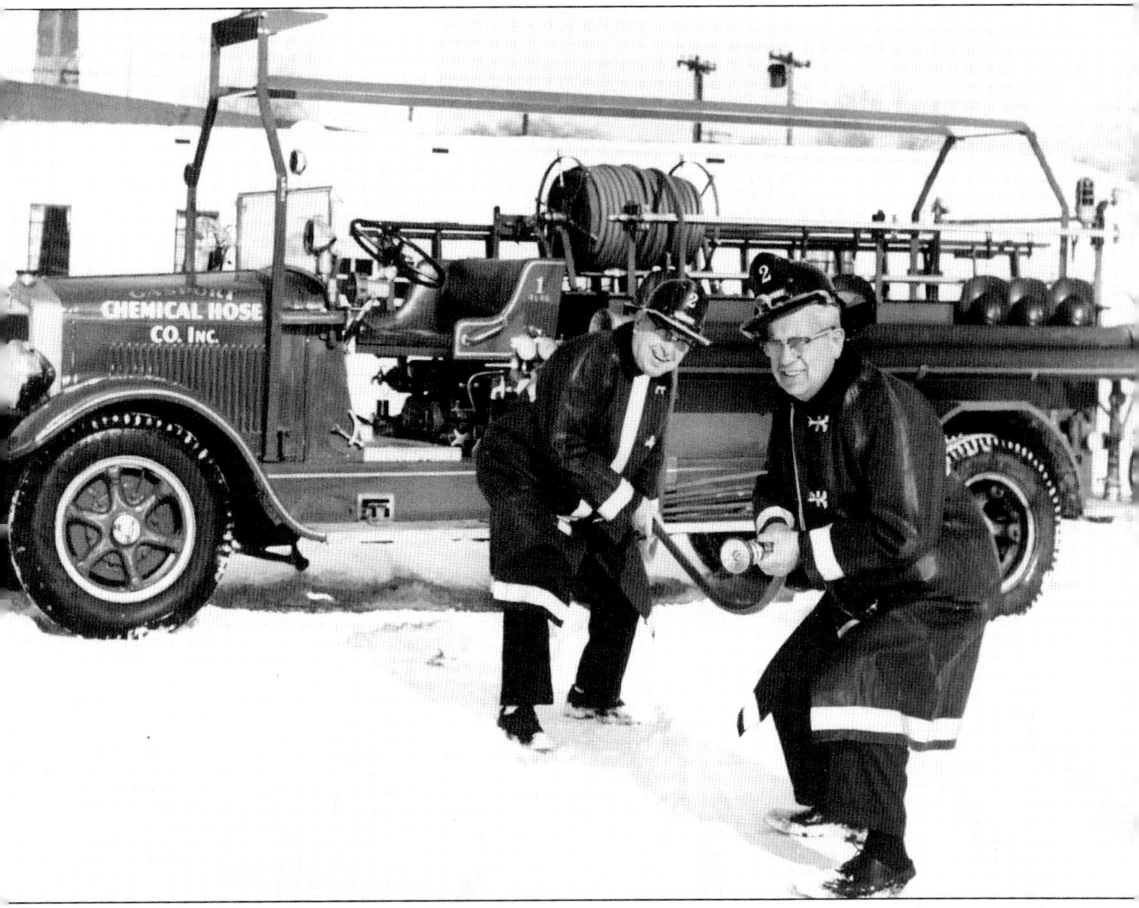

The Gasport Fire Department began in a very small building on State Street as shown in earlier photographs. It moved to its present location in the 1950s and became known as the Gasport Chemical Hose Company. As with many volunteer fire companies in the rural areas (and Middleport is no different), the Gasport unit quickly became the central social component of the hamlet. It would host parties, weddings, sponsor training, and raise funds through bingo. Throughout the 1940s and through the 1970s, most of the volunteers also hosted field days, which were highlighted by a huge parade. Those who remember the parades will recall that the music was usually provided by the Wolcottsville band, the Shawnee band, and, if one was fortunate, by the Bergholz German Marching Band, a traditional German band clad in lederhosen. (NCH.)

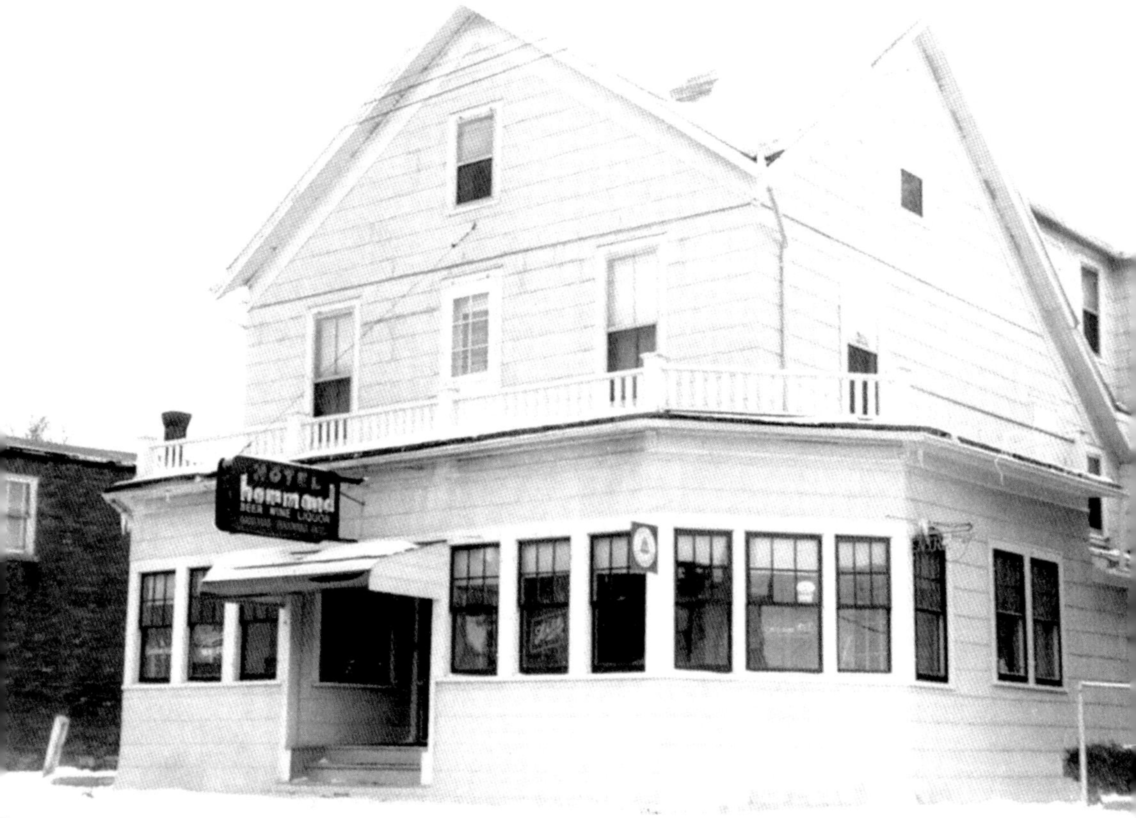

The hotel in the hamlet of Gasport was once known as the Knights Hotel, but during the last century, it was primarily known as the Hotel Hammond. It was always a cozy place with its small taproom and small dining room. The place offered a quiet surrounding as opposed to the other two local watering holes. There were many card games that secretly took place at the Hammond. It was the type of place that one would not readily notice, but it was greatly appreciated. It ceased operation as a hotel in the 1980s and sadly the handsome building is gone. It was razed to make room for another structure that was never built. Today all that remains of the Hammond Hotel is a vacant field. For those who remember, however, that vacant lot represents much more. (RTH.)

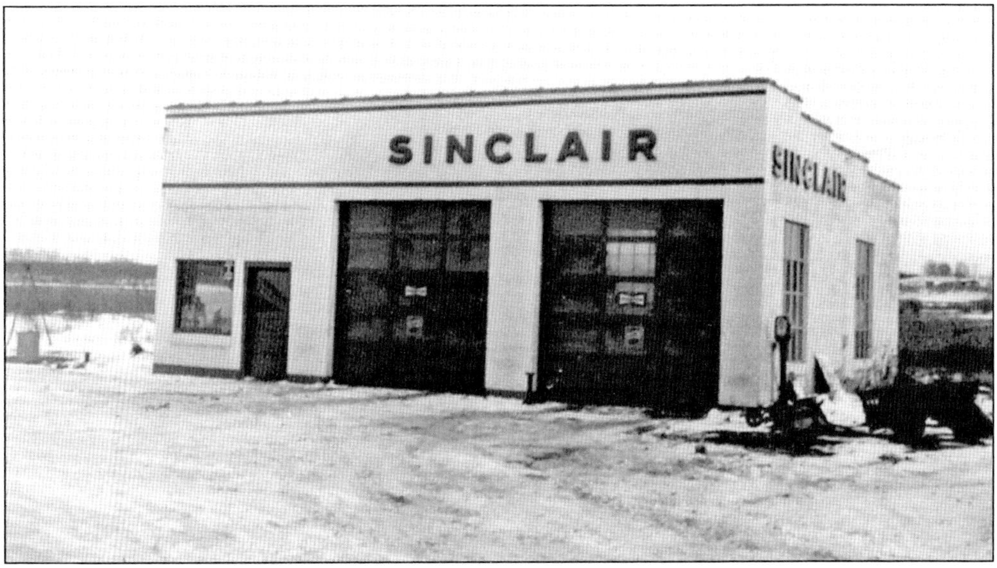

On Route 31 west of Gasport stood this Sinclair service station. It operated from the 1940s through the 1960s. Later it would not retail gasoline but remain a repair shop. It remained dormant for some years before becoming a used car lot. The building was expanded to more than twice its original size. (RTH.)

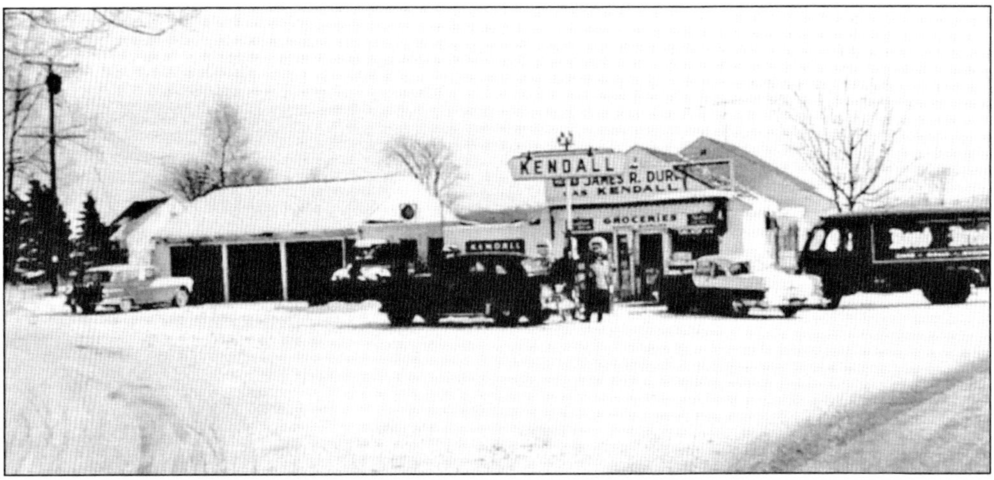

One could not complete a survey of the town of Royalton and not mention Durfy's at Terry's Corners. This is a small community located on Route 77 (Chestnut Ridge Road) at the intersection with Mill Road. The Durfy's location had always been the local store, although not always under that name. Later the only retail enterprise to survive would be O'lear's on Route 77 to the west. (RTH.)

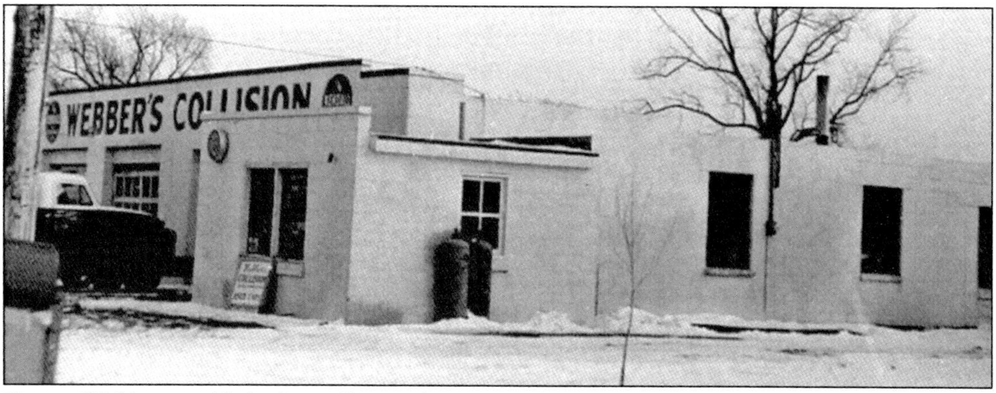

Kermit Webber established a collision shop west of Middleport on Route 31. One would often see his tow truck around town picking up vehicles for repair or getting cars started in the winter. He retired and sold his shop to Bitterman Automotive who combined it with a massive building and a used car lot. (RTH.)

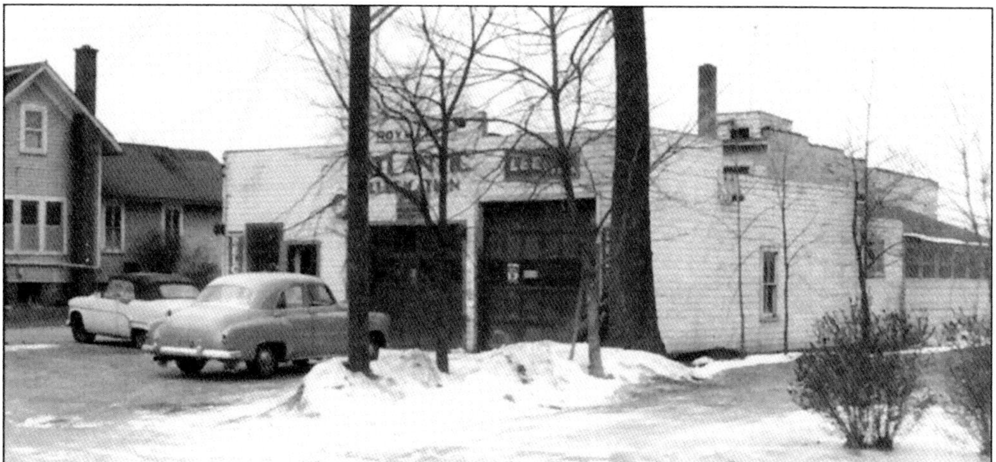

Frey's Atlantic gasoline station and garage was located on the west side of the main street running through Wolcottsville. It was one of the primary locations for local news and male interaction. The business thrived during the 1960s through the 1970s, but like most small town retail enterprises, fell victim to the larger shops in the larger markets. (RTH.)

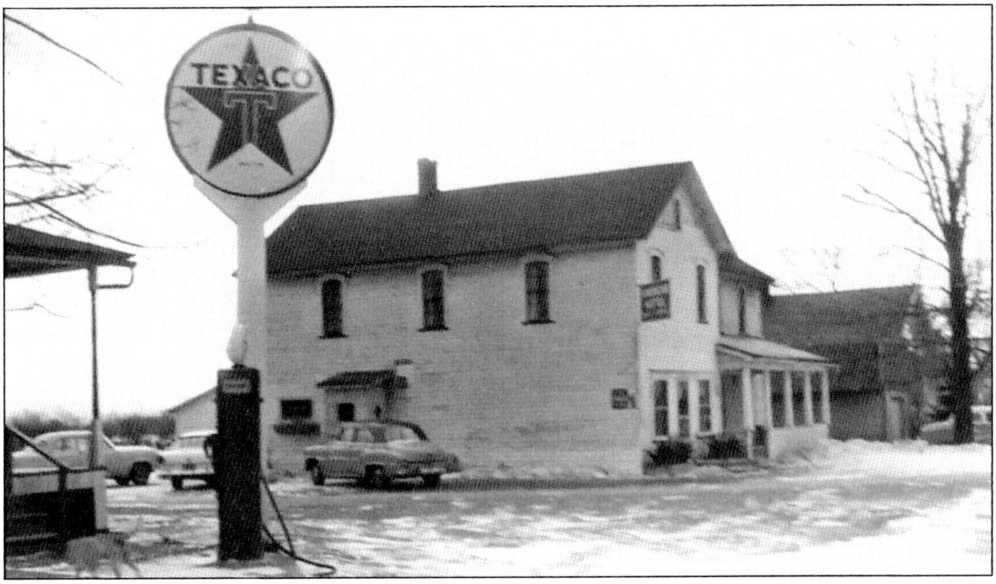

The main social gathering place in Wolcottsville was the American Hotel. During the 1960s, Bob Pechuman and his mother operated the American Hotel. They also had another bar in Akron. The establishment served meals but in the early days offered enjoyment to the local farmers and the residents of the town. It changed hands numerous times through the years and is currently vacant. (RTH.)

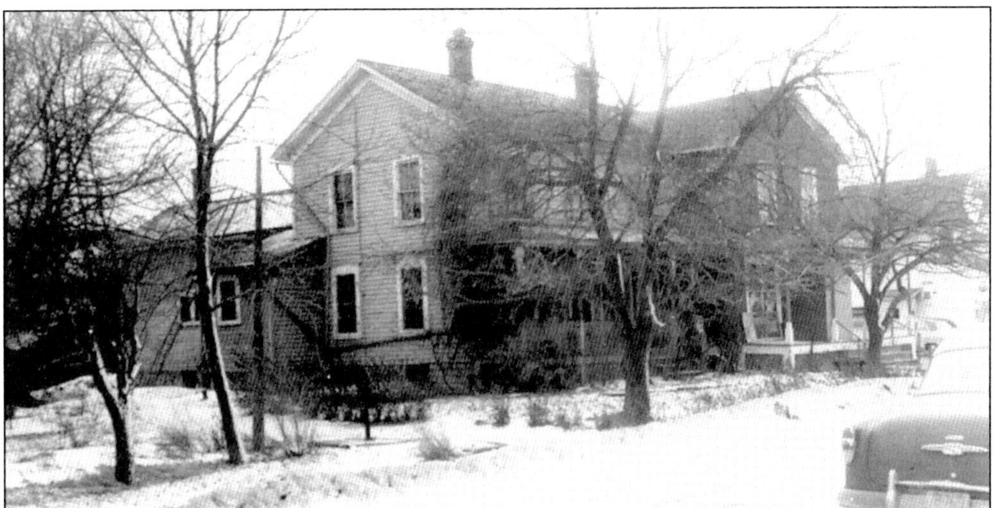

Shleef's store stood on the opposite corner from the American Hotel in Wolcottsville. This was the original Fink's store from a bygone era but served the community well through the 1980s. Like the hotel, it had numerous owners during the last two decades of the 20th century and is also vacant. (RTH.)

Five

Hartland

The town of Hartland comprises an area of 31,145 acres and is the middle township of the eastern three in Niagara County. It was originally much larger as both Royalton and Somerset were once part of the town, but those towns were broken off in 1823 and 1817 respectively.

The town of Hartland's main highway (and only east-west road that traverses the township) has always been known as Ridge Road. For obvious reasons, it followed the contour of the land as it made its way through Niagara County, ending at Fort Niagara to the west. Jeptha Dunn opened an inn on Ridge Road about 2 miles east of Johnson Creek in 1809. Later it became a tavern.

At the point where Johnson Creek meets Ridge Road, a hamlet was established in the early 1810s. The creek was named for a family who resided on its banks. The first tavern opened in 1812, and Daniel VanHorn opened a general store in 1815. The first gristmill opened on Johnson Creek around 1820.

North Hartland was a post office and small hamlet in the northwest corner of the town. A small store was located there, as well as a Methodist Church.

The first school was built in the town early on, and by 1816, Hartland had six school districts. Eventually, there would be 18 district schools.

The First Baptist Church of Hartland was organized in December 1817. Services were originally held in the school at Johnson Creek, but in 1833, a church building was erected.

A Methodist Church was organized on Quaker Road, about 2 miles north of Ridge Road. A wooden church was built in 1843, but burned in 1872. The burned church was replaced by a brick church on the same site. In 1856, St. Patrick's Roman Catholic Church was also built on Quaker Road.

The movement of goods and people through the town of Hartland diminished significantly after the opening of the Erie Canal. Also, as Niagara Falls and Buffalo became thriving business communities, Ridge Road to Fort Niagara was no longer a major east-west thoroughfare, as it was not the shortest route west.

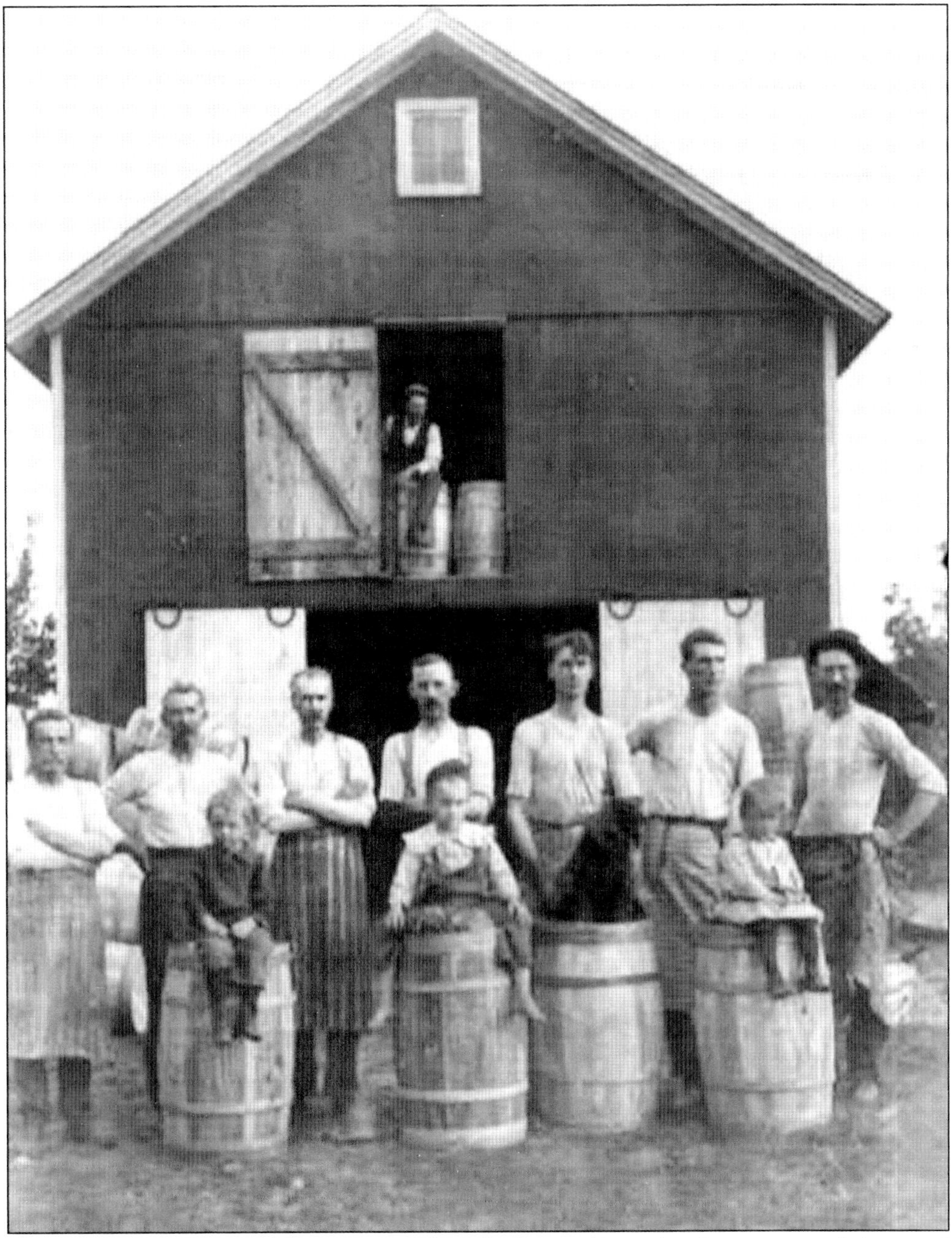

Johnson Creek had many of the necessities that all other small-populated areas required. A general store, hotel, blacksmith shops, and a cooperage were all part of the landscape on this part of Ridge Road. This photograph from 1902 shows the workers of the Metcalf Cooper Shop and their wares. Barrels were very necessary at the beginning of the 20th century and had a multitude of uses. Not only were they used for alcohol, but they also contained all types of liquid, including water. They were also used for nails and other forms of hardware, and they held grain and other edible commodities. Coopers, or the manufacturers of barrels, were highly skilled, and good coopers were in high demand. Every community in the area needed good coopers, and a cooperage was commonplace regardless of the size of the community. (HTH.)

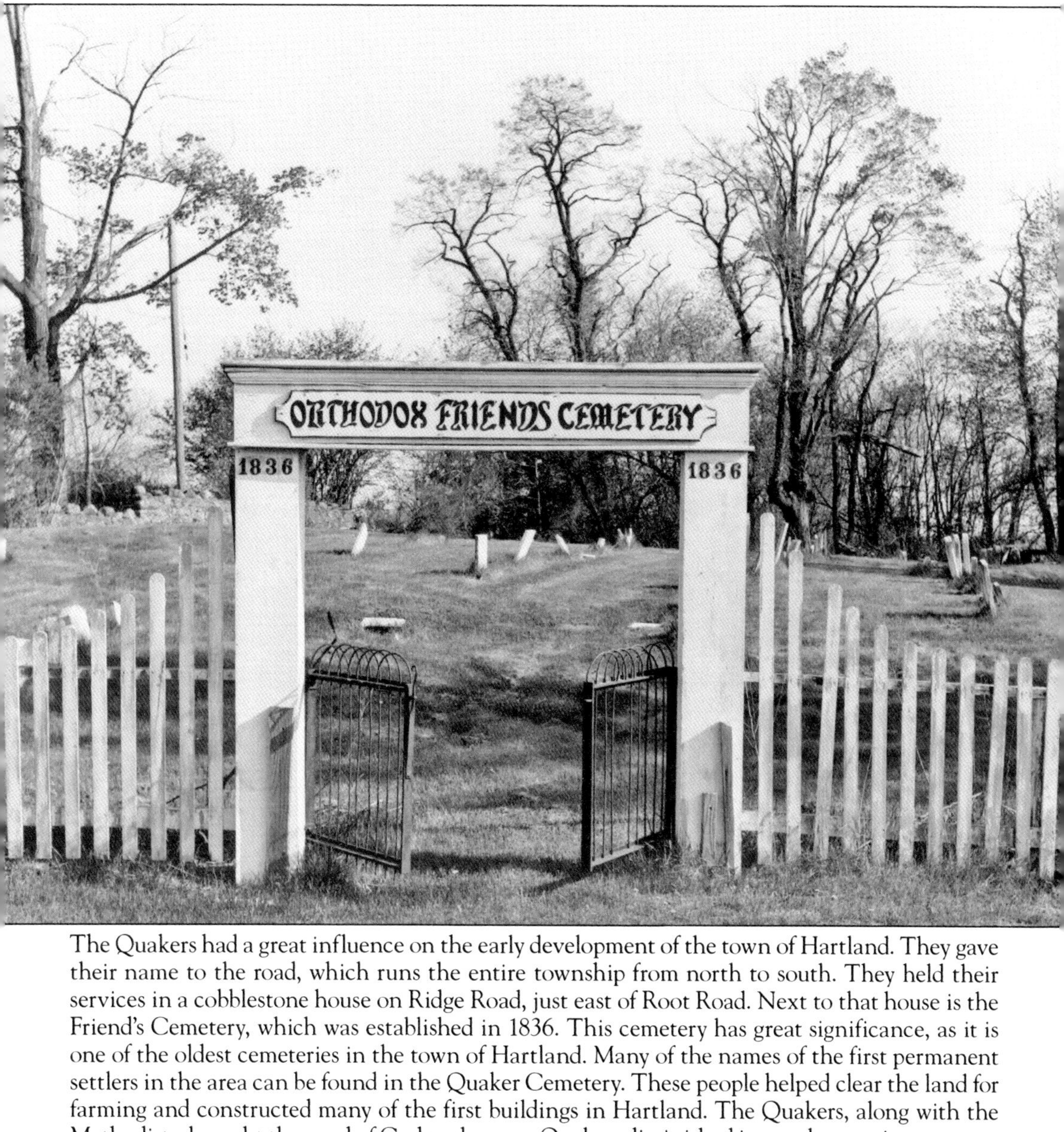

The Quakers had a great influence on the early development of the town of Hartland. They gave their name to the road, which runs the entire township from north to south. They held their services in a cobblestone house on Ridge Road, just east of Root Road. Next to that house is the Friend's Cemetery, which was established in 1836. This cemetery has great significance, as it is one of the oldest cemeteries in the town of Hartland. Many of the names of the first permanent settlers in the area can be found in the Quaker Cemetery. These people helped clear the land for farming and constructed many of the first buildings in Hartland. The Quakers, along with the Methodists, brought the word of God to the area. Quakers diminished in numbers as time went on and other religions grew. These people seemed to prefer moving onward rather than face possible assimilation into the general community. (Niagara County Historian's Office.)

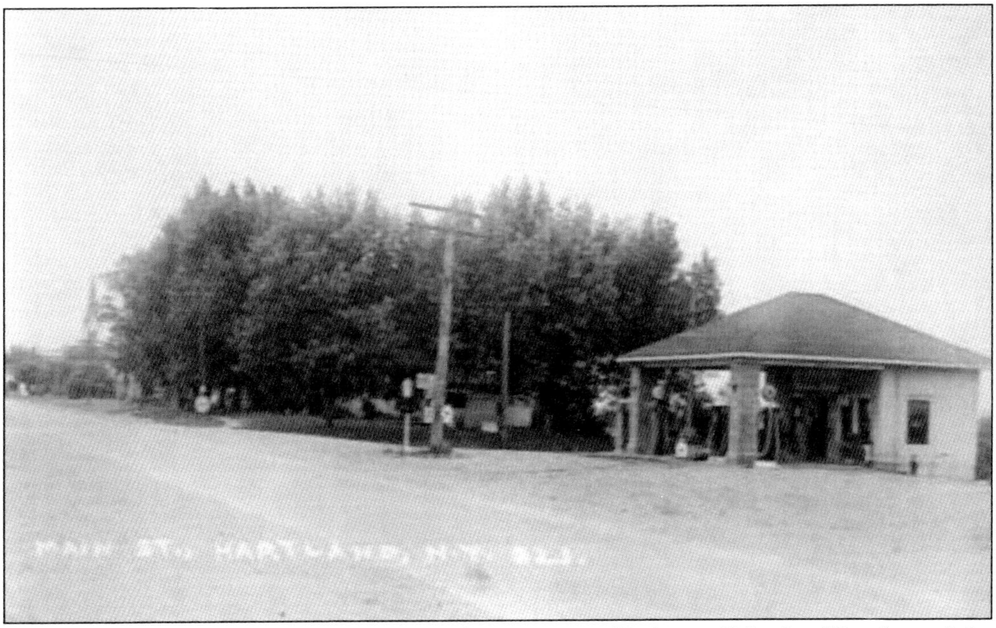

Bill Smith owned this gas station on the northeast corner of Ridge and Hartland Roads until the 1970s. It was not much more than a filling station, serving the recreational driving public, which had become the mainstay of the Route 104 traffic. Later the building would be expanded, and today it is one of the few surviving businesses of Hartland Corners. (HTH.)

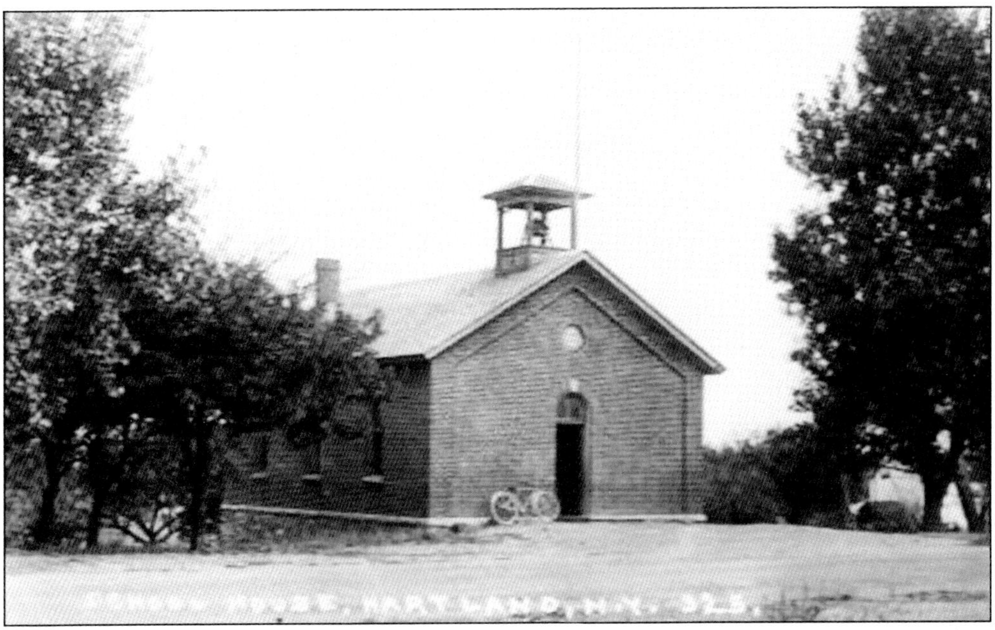

Hartland never had a high school, but rather had district schools located throughout the township. One such school was District School No. 6 located in the Hartland center. As the basis of education in the first part of the 20th century was the three R's, education in the rural areas did not encompass the broad-spectrum curriculum that is taught today. (HTH.)

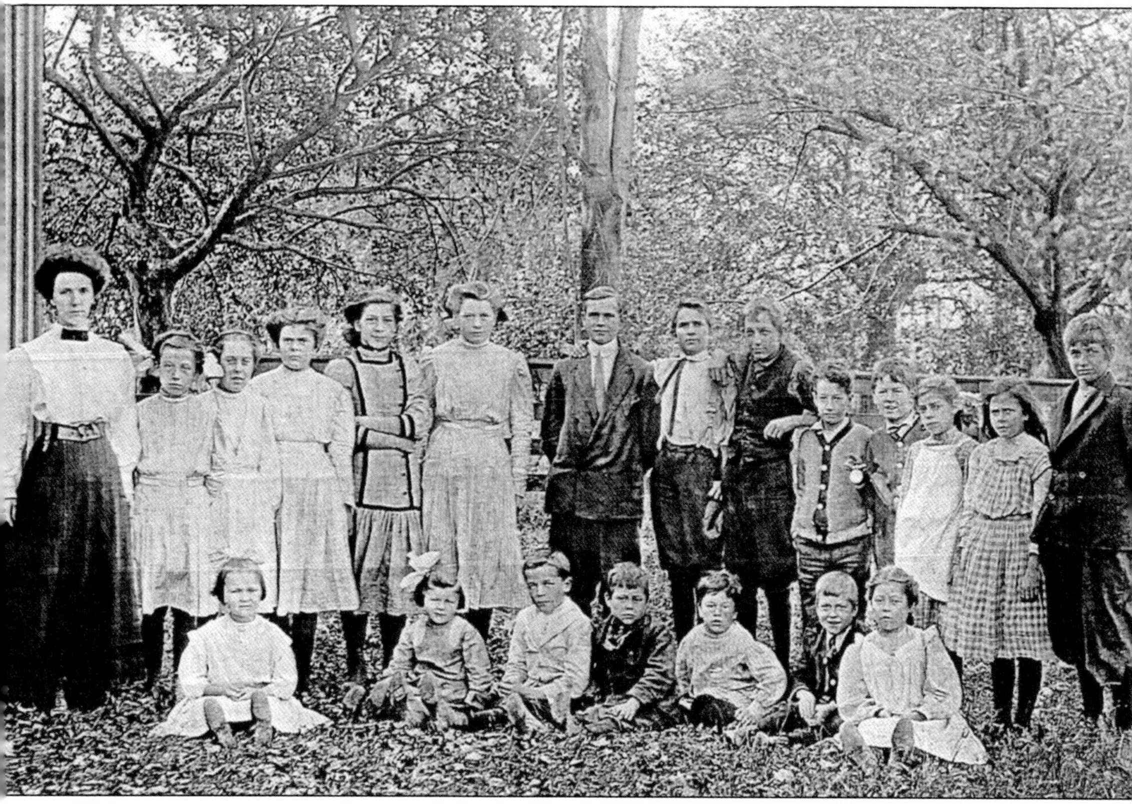

This is a very important photograph for the Hartland residents of the Middleport area. A corner of the Hartland School District No. 1 building, also known as the Torryville School, which was located on North Hartland Street in the village, is just visible to the left. It burned in 1937 and was not rebuilt. A couple of today's Middleport residents attended this school, while others from the north side of the village remember the building. The significance of its existence is that it was just about the only Hartland entity located in Middleport. People from the town line northward in Middleport, or those living generally north of Sleeper Street are Hartland residents. Instead of walking across the canal to attend the Middleport School, they would have attended this school. This is hard to imagine today, as people currently do not see or feel the township separation as much as those who lived here earlier. Pictured above with the school is one of the classes that attended Hartland School District No. 1 in the early 1900s. (HTH.)

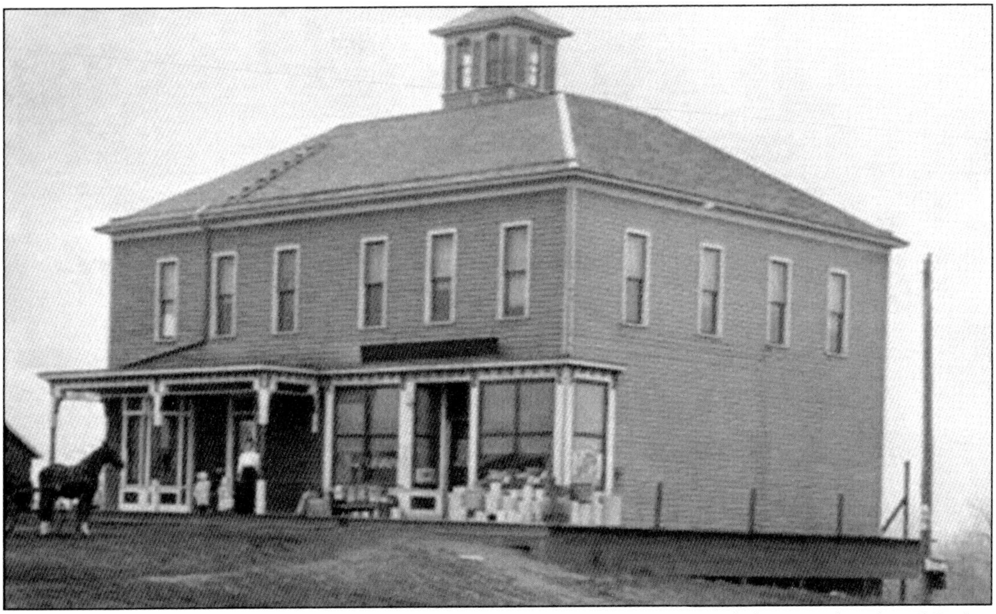

Brown's store was located in Hartland Corners at the southwest part of the Hartland and Ridge Road intersection. In this 1900 photograph, a woman and children are visible on the porch as well as some stock. Notice that the rear of the building is supported in the air due to the elevation of the ridge. (HTH.)

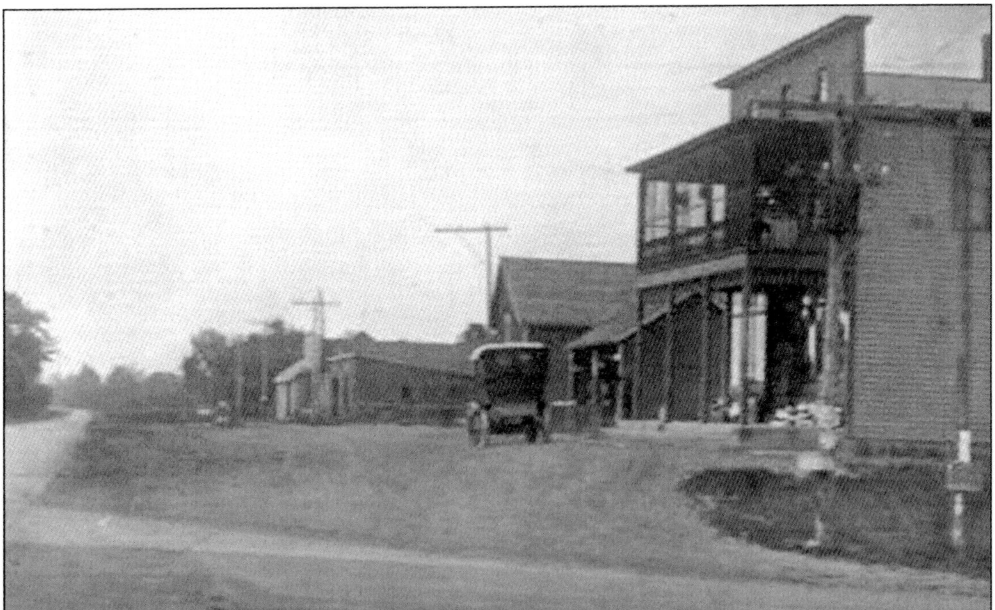

The main grocery store in Hartland throughout the 20th century was the Red and White, which was owned by several people at different times. In this 1918 photograph, Herman Dean operated the store. This was a full-scale grocery store and served the surrounding community as well. Like many spaces in small towns, it is no longer a retail outlet. (HTH.)

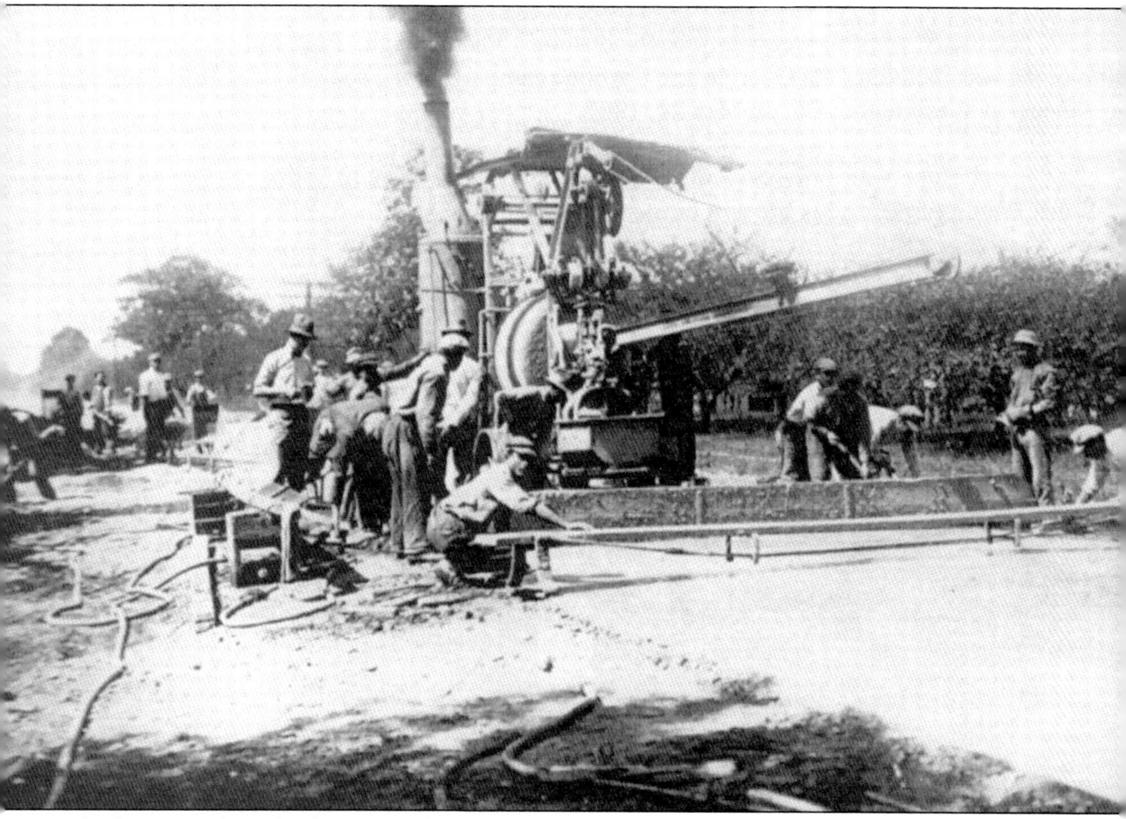

As the town of Hartland was entirely an agricultural area, a critical need arose for a major highway to transport the produce of the area. This photograph, taken in 1913, shows the Ridge Road or Route 104 being paved for the very first time. The importance of this thoroughfare had existed since the initial settlements in the area. As can be noted from its name, it does in fact follow the contour of a ridge all the way through the area to its terminus at Lewiston. Paving in the early days was a labor-intensive endeavor. The importance of the event to the development of the area cannot be overstated as the other east-west road, Route 31 through Royalton, was not completed in its present form until the early 1950s. That made Ridge Road the primary east-west highway for nearly half a century. (HTH.)

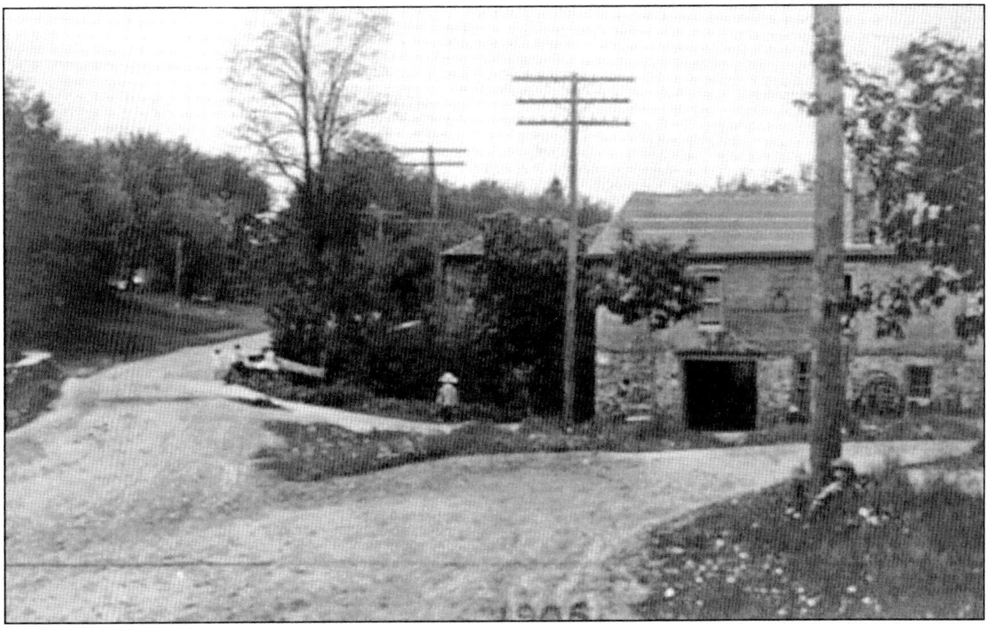

This 1905 picture shows the bend in Johnson Creek just past the Arch Bridge. Veering off to the right is Johnson Creek Road. The stone building was the blacksmith shop of Uri Andrus. As Ridge Road was essentially a commuter route, a blacksmith was as important at the time as a filling station or auto repair shop would be in later years. (HTH.)

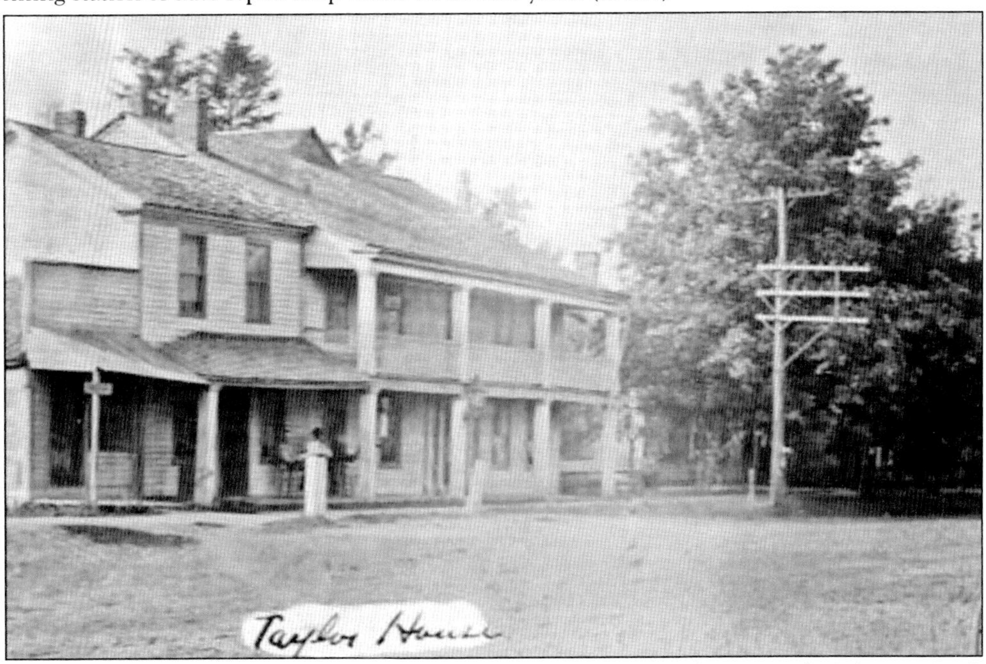

Taylor House, located on Ridge Road in Johnson Creek, was officially known as the Johnson Creek Hotel. It was built in 1835 and served as a hotel until 1917. During its time, Ridge Road was the major east-west artery serving the area and was used for passenger traffic as well as commerce. These hotels were located along the route every 20 miles or so, and the building can still be found in some places today. (HTH.)

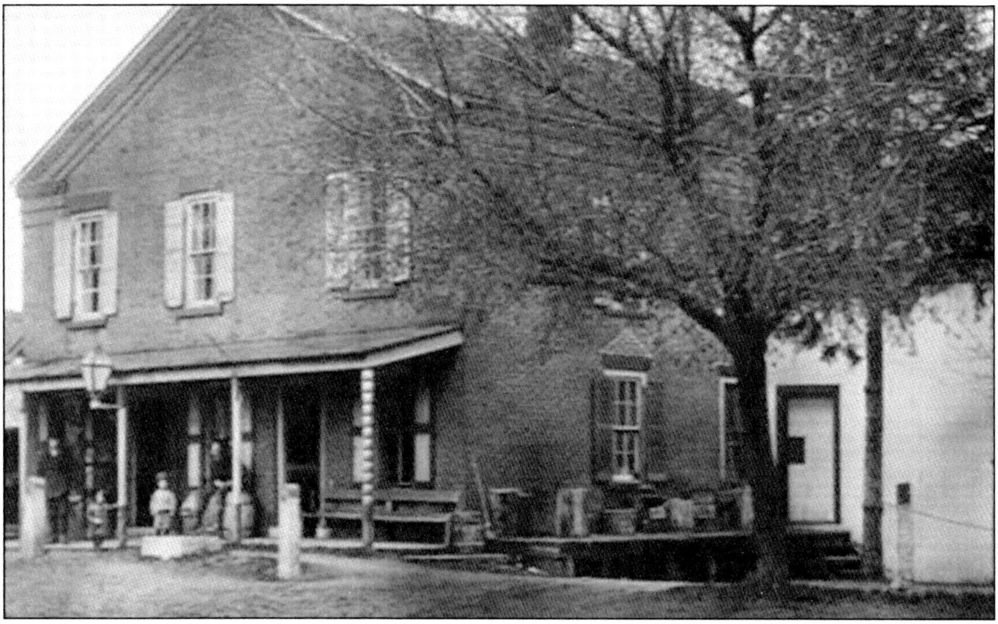

Johnson Creek had its store in the 1920s and it is pictured here when it belonged to J. Rowe. It was a general store, which served the needs of the town. It was located on the north side of Ridge Road, across from Chapman's store today. The building looks much the same as it did 100 years ago. (HTH.)

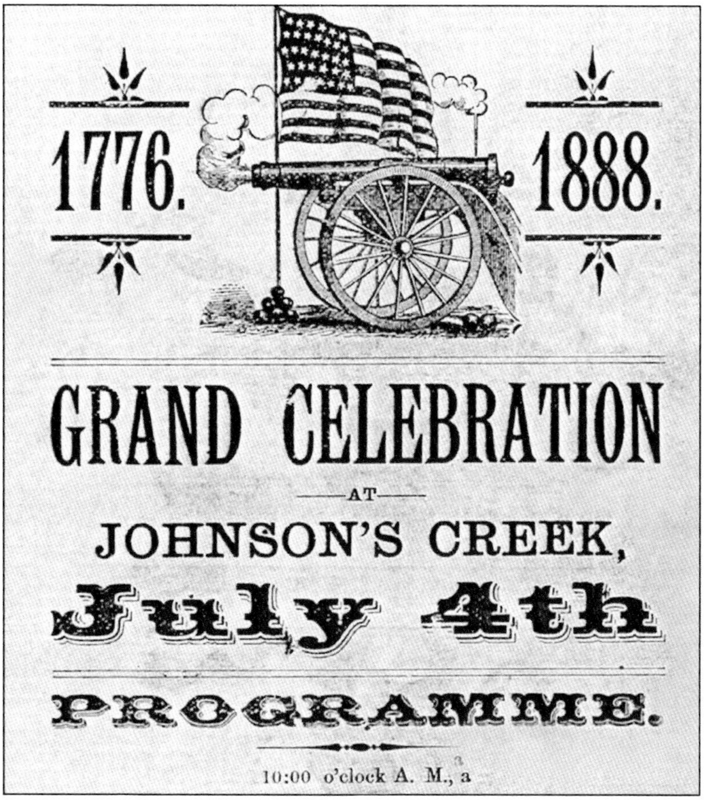

1776. 1888.

GRAND CELEBRATION

AT

JOHNSON'S CREEK,

July 4th

PROGRAMME.

10:00 o'clock A. M., a

The Fourth of July holiday was the major secular celebration of the year. This 1888 poster gives a few details for the Johnson Creek program that year. Baseball must have been popular, as a game was scheduled for 10:00 a.m. (HTH.)

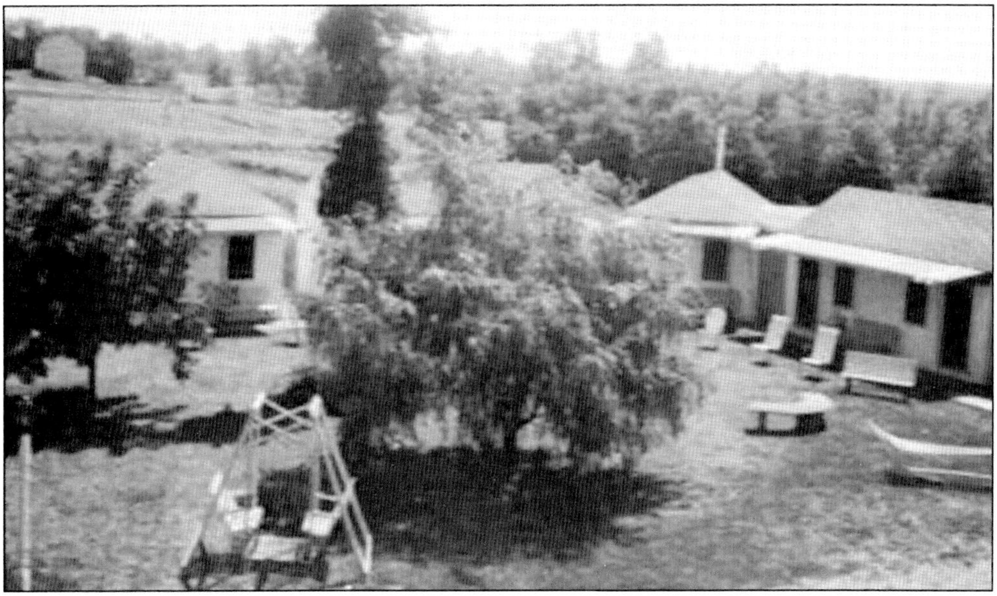

This 1950s photograph shows the Hartland Motel, which was located on the south side of Route 104 a short distance east of Hartland Corners. The establishment still exists and was the type of business that grew with the development and widespread use of the automobile along the main thoroughfares in the state. (HTH.)

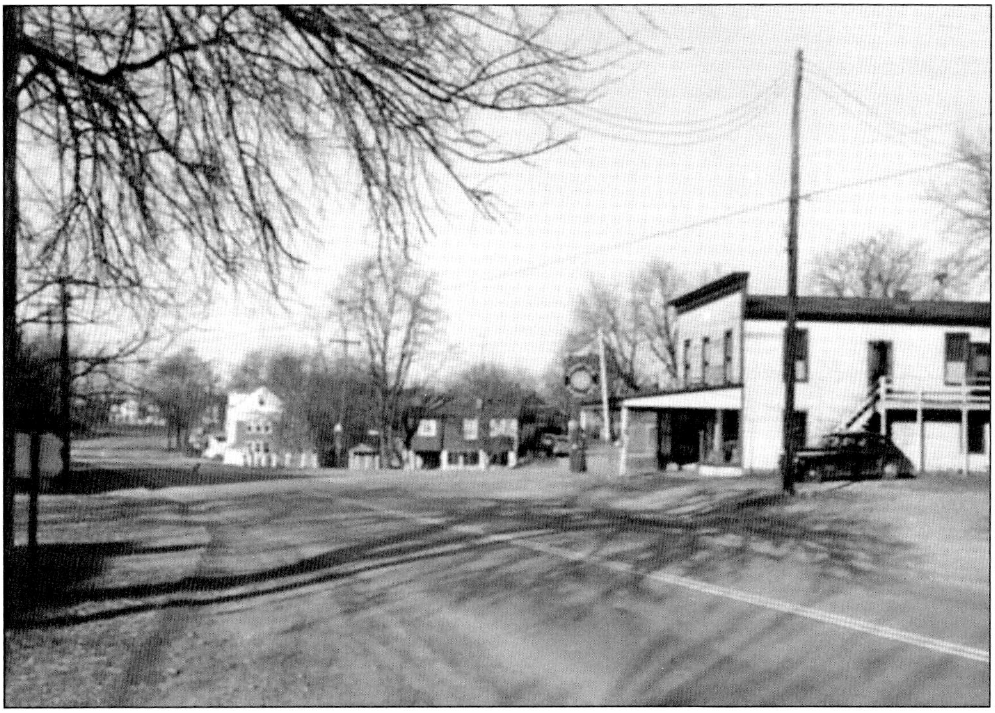

As the main roads carried more and more motor vehicle traffic through the town of Hartland, motels were not the only businesses that began to thrive. Gasoline filling stations were also very necessary. Glen Mower operated this gas station in Johnson Creek during the 1950s. It has ceased to be in operation for many decades. (HTH.)

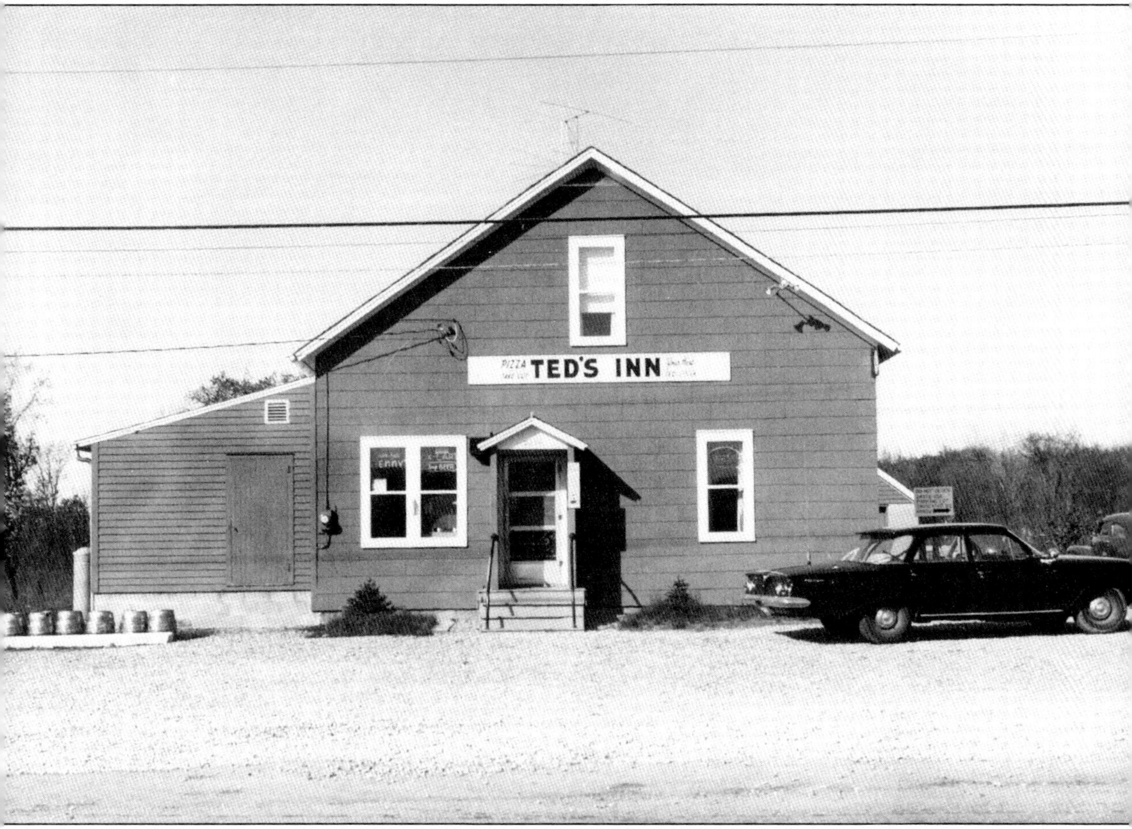

Located on Quaker Road in the town of Hartland, Ted's bar provided a very important service. The town of Somerset, which began about a half-mile north, was a "dry" township. Ted's was the nearest bar for those people in Somerset wishing to have a beverage. It essentially served as Barker's bar for decades until the town of Somerset adopted the use of liquor licenses and on-premise use. Eventually it would become Todd's, and the bar had its own baseball field across the street to serve its sponsored teams. It remained an institution in the area and still serves the residents of both Hartland and Somerset. It is still a bar today, but citizens of the area have many fond memories of Ted's. For several years, it was part of a traveling euchre card-playing league. (Niagara County Historian's Office.)